Social Chemistry

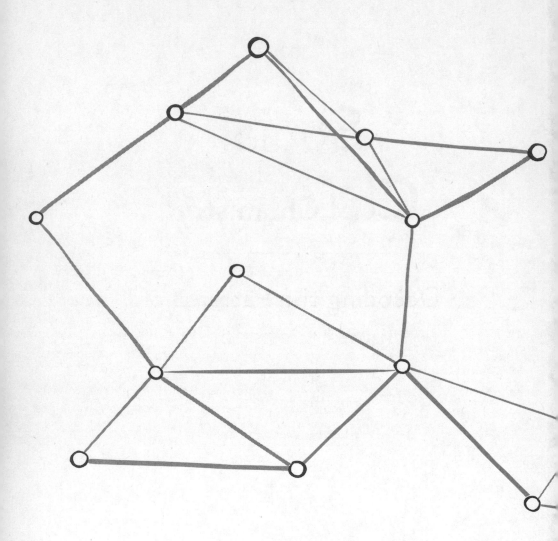

Social Chemistry

Decoding the Patterns of Human Connection

MARISSA KING

DUTTON

DUTTON

An imprint of Penguin Random House LLC
penguinrandomhouse.com

Illustrations by Tanja Russita.

LIBRARY OF CONGRESS CATALOGING-IN-PUBLICATION DATA

Names: King, Marissa, author.
Title: Social chemistry : decoding the patterns of human connection / Marissa King.
Description: New York, NY : Dutton, [2021] | Includes bibliographical references and index. |
Identifiers: LCCN 2019040363 (print) | LCCN 2019040364 (ebook) |
ISBN 9781524743802 (hardcover) | ISBN 9781524743819 (ebook)
Subjects: LCSH: Interpersonal relations. | Social networks. | Social psychology.
Classification: LCC HM1106 .K565 2020 (print) | LCC HM1106 (ebook) | DDC 302—dc23
LC record available at https://lccn.loc.gov/2019040363
LC ebook record available at https://lccn.loc.gov/2019040364

Printed in the United States of America
1   3   5   7   9   10   8   6   4   2

To Sydney, Grace, Julian, and Nick.

In the end, it is all about love.

Contents

Social Chemistry

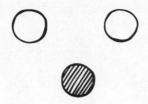

1. Making Connections

Not long before Rosa Parks refused to give up her bus seat in Montgomery, Alabama, a young Vernon Jordan interviewed for a sales internship at the Continental Insurance Company. The recruiter made Jordan, a sophomore at DePauw University, an offer. He was told to report to his new job in the firm's Atlanta office at the beginning of the summer. When he showed up—dressed in his best suit—and announced to the receptionist that he was ready to start his summer internship, there was a problem. The receptionist made a quick telephone call to the person in charge of interns, and asked him to step in.

Here's how Jordan describes what happened next:

The supervisor, a tall fellow who looked to be in his midthirties, came out. I introduced myself. "I'm Vernon Jordan. I was hired to be a summer intern in your office."

His reaction was not unlike the receptionist's. But he quickly composed himself and took me inside his office. An awkward moment passed before he said, "They didn't tell us."

"They didn't tell you what?" I asked, even though I suspected where he was heading.

"They didn't tell us you were colored," he replied. At that time we had not yet become "black." "You know," he went on, "you can't work here. It's just impossible. You just can't."

And he didn't. Jobless, Jordan was determined to find a summer position despite the fast-disappearing prospects as his college break wore on. Finally he landed a job as a chauffeur to a former mayor of Atlanta, Robert Maddox, who was in his eighties.

Jordan's own eightieth birthday party was on Martha's Vineyard, an island dotted with gingerbread cottages that has long been favored by aristocrats. During the party, Bill and Hillary Clinton boogied to soul music. President Barack Obama, the actor Morgan Freeman, Harvard University professor Henry Louis Gates Jr., and American Express CEO Ken Chenault all showed up to fete the renowned civil rights leader and power broker.

Over the ensuing decades, Vernon Jordan had become a close confidant to presidents and was christened the First Friend by *The New York Times*. He had also built an enviable network of contacts in the business world—sitting on nine corporate boards including Dow Jones, Xerox, and Callaway Golf. As John Bryan, the former CEO of Sara Lee, said, "Vernon probably knows more corporate executives than anyone in America." To jaded detractors, Jordan is emblematic of the problems created by the coziness of Wall Street and the White House. His rebuttal is that it is "not a crime to be close to Wall Street . . . If you are a politician, you have to have relationships with every kind of entity."

Jordan lies at the center of the *inner circle,* a name given by Wharton professor Michael Useem to describe the connections between corporations created by the business elite. The shortest route between any two companies on the S&P 500 was Vernon Jordan. According to Johan Chu, at the University of Chicago's Booth School of Business, "This network remained highly connected throughout the twentieth century, serving as a mechanism for the rapid diffusion of information and practices and promoting elite cohesion."

Jordan represents both the power and the perceived problems of networks. His unparalleled ability to network allowed the grandson of a sharecropper to become "one of the most connected men in America." Jordan was the civil rights movement's ambassador to boardrooms. Henry Louis Gates predicted that "historians will remember Vernon Jordan as the Rosa Parks of Wall Street." But many find the backroom handshakes that his career has been built on morally dubious.

How exactly did Vernon Jordan land at the epicenter of the professional and political elite? He gives a hint in a 2012 commencement address in which he quotes Melville:

> *We cannot live for ourselves alone*
> *Our lives are connected by a thousand invisible threads*
> *And along these sympathetic fibers*
> *Our actions run as causes and return to us as results.*

To understand Vernon Jordan's transformation, we need to be able to trace the thousands of invisible threads he spun together.

Invisible Threads

The Melville quote is more than an inspiration, it's a new lens that we can apply to the idea of networks. The structure of someone's network is a map that tells what their life has been like up to this point and where they are going. As a network analyst, sociologist, and professor of organizational behavior at the Yale School of Management, I've spent the last fifteen years studying how people's social networks evolve, what they look like, and what that means for their ability to succeed in the workplace, be happy and healthy, and find personal fulfillment. Vernon Jordan has a rare and special kind of network. To grasp its features, we have to first understand some more common building blocks.

The lowest common denominator of social connection is a *dyad*—the one-on-one relationships we form with a single individual. Over time, these relationships naturally organize themselves into networks. We've all heard that term, but what are networks, really? *Networks* are groups of interconnected people, some overlapping one another and others that have no members in common. Through networks, it is possible to leverage our relationships to manifest something much stronger than a bunch of dyads—an outcome where 1 + 1 really does equal 3. Renowned sociologist James S. Coleman explained that *social capital* makes "possible the achievement of certain ends that would not be attainable in its absence."

There is what's possible, and then there is what's plausible. Three simple topographies characterize most people's networks.

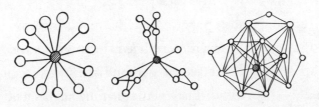

EXPANSIONISTS   BROKERS   CONVENERS

In the network maps of expansionists, brokers, and conveners, each circle represents a person. The network belongs to the person represented by the dark circle in the middle, and the lines denote relationships between them and their friends, as well as the connections between their friends. You may not immediately realize it, but in all of these pictures, there are the same number of people. What you *will* recognize is that the amount of energy, the effort, that goes into forming and maintaining these ties varies. Brokers are directly tied to only seven people but have indirect access to twelve different viewpoints, experiences, and information sources. Because conveners' friends are more likely than brokers' friends to be friends with one another, conveners maintain nine relationships to get the same information.

My colleague Nicholas Christakis frequently invokes a metaphor to illustrate how different network structures give rise to different properties. Both graphite and diamonds are made out of the exact same thing: carbon. Graphite is soft, dark, and so commonplace that we are likely to find it in the backpack of a six-year-old. Diamonds, on the other hand, are hard, clear, and rare, and are arguably one of the most expensive status signals on the planet.

What distinguishes graphite from diamonds is the manner in which the carbon atoms are arranged. In graphite, the carbon atoms are arranged in sheets. In diamonds, they are arranged tetrahedrally. These different structural arrangements give rise to different properties.

In much the same way as with carbon, the same set of social relationships—composed of the same people, but in different configurations—give rise to vastly different ends. Imagine two teams composed of the same people. In one example, everyone works together and collaborates with everyone else. In the other instance, the people remain the same but the team usually works in specialized sub-teams with a liaison going between them. Despite having the same members, the teams would have radically different strengths. The same is true with personal networks.

In a network context, expansionists, brokers, and conveners each have distinct social and professional benefits and drawbacks.

- *Expansionists* have extraordinarily large networks, are well-known, and have an uncanny ability to work a room. However, they often have trouble maintaining social ties and leveraging them to create value for themselves or others.
- *Brokers* generate value by bringing together typically disconnected parties from different social worlds. Their networks

have huge information benefits and are highly innovative, since the majority of new ideas come from recombination.

- *Conveners* build dense networks in which their friends are also friends. This type of network has outsize trust and reputational benefits.

So which type is Vernon Jordan? In fact, he strikes an exemplary balance between the deep trust of convening, creating information benefits for everyone in his network through brokerage, while maintaining a mind-boggling number of contacts.

Yet in an interview with Jordan for the National Portrait Gallery, former director Marc Pachter highlighted a seeming contradiction: "You describe yourself on occasion, and have written it as well, that you are a loner . . . You are somebody very much engaged in the world, you have many friends, you have social connections, you understand friendship, you understand all of this. That's been the core of your being, and yet you are a loner."

To which Jordan responded, "Well, most things in life you gotta figure out for yourself. And there is a small group of friends with whom you can share. And that is based on trust and confidence and friendship. I have never been one to bare my soul. And so I think *loner* maybe taking it too far. I just respect your privacy and I harbor my own."

As much as Jordan has gained through convening and trust, his ascent can be traced to the key role he has played brokering between the worlds of business and politics, as well as across racial lines. Vernon described his brokering role, stating: "When you're on the outside and as connected as I am, there's an opportunity to interpret."

Like Vernon Jordan, the characteristics and structure of our own network are partially determined by the context in which we live our day-to-day life—what type of job we have; if our office is located next to the elevator; if our house is at the end of a cul-de-sac; whether or not we go to church, join clubs, or volunteer for the PTA; and much more. The choices we make—such as whether or not to have children, whether or not to change industries, whether or not to attend the Friday meeting—all have a strong effect on our network.

We also enact and reenact our network on a second-by-second basis. Using wearable sensors that track individuals' social interactions, Ingrid Nembhard and I discovered that the amount of time you spend listening in a conversation, how frequently you interrupt, and how much your voice changes in a conversation are all strongly associated with what type of network you have. Conveners are great listeners. Expansionists tend to be louder and to talk more frequently than their peers, and are less likely to interrupt.

Given their behavior, expansionists would seem to be more likely to be extroverts. Surprisingly, according to a meta-analysis of 138 studies examining the personality and networks of thousands of individuals, extroversion has very little effect on what someone's network looks like.

Of personality characteristics, something psychologists call *self-monitoring*, which is chameleonlike behavior, has been found in study after study to be the strongest predictor of what style of network you are likely to develop. Brokers tend to be chameleons. They easily adapt to new social situations. They intuitively know when it's time to keep quiet to match the formality of a meeting or laugh a little louder.

Social scientists have spent the last four decades studying the antecedents and consequences of social network structure. How your network is shaped (consciously or unconsciously) has enormous implications for a wide variety of personal and professional outcomes. The strength and quality of your social connections and their arrangement profoundly affect your experience of the world, your emotions, and your personal and professional success.

This book is primarily about networks: how the basic elements of social structure and the psychological tendencies that accompany them shape our lives.

It's Networks, Not Networking

How did you first hear about your job? If you are like most people, it was through a friend, colleague, acquaintance, neighbor, or someone with whom you had a personal connection.

Vernon Jordan is an extreme case of this. As he said, "I am going to tell you something that you won't believe. I've not applied for a job since I applied to be a bus driver with the Chicago Transit Authority." Jordan's network had enough reach and trust to carry him from the Chicago Transit Authority to the presidency of the National Urban League to a managing directorship at an investment bank and the board of American Express.

More than forty years ago, sociologist Mark Granovetter, a professor at Stanford University, first examined how professionals working in the city of Newton, Massachusetts, found their jobs. Of the hundreds of professionals that Granovetter interviewed and surveyed who had recently changed jobs, more than half (56 percent) reported they found their job through personal contacts. Among individuals in the highest income categories, who had the highest paying and most prestigious jobs, three out of four people found their job through their social network.

To Granovetter's surprise, however, interviewees kept reiterating during their discussions: "No, no, no, not a friend, just an *acquaintance*." Respondents were twice as likely to have heard about their job from someone they rarely saw than from a close friend or family member. Granovetter's resulting paper, "The Strength of Weak Ties," was the first to challenge conventional notions about how social networks function.

And his results have withstood the test of time. Despite dramatic changes in the professional landscape since he penned his article—the advent of LinkedIn, Glassdoor, and other online job networking sites—more than half of job seekers still find out about their job through their network. People who use their personal contacts to find their next job spend less time searching and end up in higher paying and more prestigious occupations.

To understand why we are more likely to hear about jobs through acquaintances or weak ties and why social networks remain more effective for a job search than their online alternatives requires an understanding of how networks work. The same principles that explain the strength of weak ties also explain why conveners are more likely to get buy-in, brokers have better ideas, and expansionists are more likely to burn out.

In the popular press, we are repeatedly told that it is the size of your network that matters: How many people do you know? And this assumption underlies most social media platforms. We're told to mix and mingle, urged to expand our connections on LinkedIn, and encouraged to go to networking events (usually with people who are just like us). Each year, more than 200 million people in the United States attend conferences and large meetings. They spend over $280 billion in doing so.

Why do most people go to conferences? To meet new people. There is a belief that simply knowing more people will somehow magically translate into value. But knowing more people—particularly when those people are very similar to you—doesn't create more value; it simply creates more work.

Decades of research has shown that the myopic focus on network size is misguided. The *quality* (not *quantity*) of your social connections is a strong predictor of your cognitive functioning, work resilience, and work engagement. In addition, the *structure* of your contacts—whether you are an expansionist, broker, or convener—helps explain everything from your pay to the quality of your ideas.

Beyond the workplace, your social connections have a profound effect on your health and happiness. The compiled findings from seventy studies found that loneliness increases the chance of premature death by 26 percent. Loneliness is as deadly as obesity or smoking fifteen cigarettes a day. The surgeon general of the United States has warned that the biggest threat to middle-aged men's health isn't heart disease or obesity, but an "epidemic of loneliness."

According to John Cacioppo, who was a professor at the University of Chicago and an expert in the field of social neuroscience, up to 80 percent of youth and 40 percent of older adults experience loneliness. In addition to deteriorating physical health, loneliness can lead to depression, personality disorders, psychoses, even suicide. Sixty million Americans—one out of five people—are deeply affected because they are lonely.

There's a paradox here. This profound sense of isolation comes at a time when we are more connected than ever. Facebook has 2 billion users per month and a market capitalization larger than the GDP of Norway. In 2017, people spent about four hours a day on mobile devices but around twenty minutes on actual calls.

Last night my husband and I went out for a rare dinner without our kids. As I waited for him, I quickly scanned the room and noticed that most people had a phone sitting next to them on the table. More than one in three were actively fiddling with it. Even at a meal, they couldn't step away.

For teens who grew up with an iPhone, this phenomenon is worse. Athena, a high school senior, describes her summer to Jean M. Twenge, writing in *The Atlantic*: "I've been on my phone more than I've been with actual people . . . My bed has, like, an imprint of my body." Over the past fifteen years, there has been a more than 40 percent decline in the number of teens who see their friends each day. When we meet face-to-face with friends, we get a higher fidelity version of who they really are, not just the image they project on social media. Positive social interactions—making eye contact, listening to one another, placing a hand on another's shoulder—can activate physical responses in our body that lower stress. The plastic projected images on social media, on the other hand, invite social comparison. It's no coincidence that rates of depression, anxiety, and suicide among teens have precipitously increased.

So what is the network fix? In a series of studies, Joseph Stokes, a psychologist at the University of Illinois at Chicago, examined several factors that one would think predict loneliness: how big someone's network is, how many close friends they have, how they get along with their relatives, and how connected their contacts were to one another. Among all of the predictors he examined, the extent to which people's networks looked like those of conveners was the strongest protector against loneliness. Conveners are also happier and more satisfied with life. But that same network structure doesn't make us happier at work. At work, the relationship is more complicated. Brokers are more satisfied with the instrumental aspects of their jobs, while conveners are more satisfied with the social aspects of their professional lives. And it is brokers who have more work/life balance.

Mixing network styles by changing your network over time or picking a network partner can maximize the benefits of these different configurations while minimizing the downsides. But mixing styles comes with its own set of challenges.

While not the same as the type of networking people often think about—working a room or trying to collect business cards—thinking purposefully about relationships can be off-putting for some. Why? It is easy to confuse networks and networking.

Feeling Dirty

When Adam Ruben's second son was born, his wife posted an obligatory photo of the snuggly newborn in a white hospital hat on Facebook. Among the congratulatory comments, one stuck out: "Ha ha looks smurf." Despite the beauty of the moment, this comment from a complete stranger detracted from the purity and joy of his son's arrival. It led Adam to ask himself, "Why on Earth had I accepted the friend request of someone I've never met, someone creepy enough to comment on photos posted by my wife?

"The answer is one word, and it's a word that makes me sound callous and careerist, though it's something we've all been told we need to do: networking.

"I hate the concept of networking. It just feels icky. You schmooze with strangers, subtly selling yourself while not selling yourself. 'I'm pretty great,' you tell them, 'though I'm not, you know, the sort of person who claims to be pretty great.'" He continues, "You 'connect' with people you have no interest in as people. You 'build relationships,' when in fact you're not interested in having relationships. You practice an effective handshake like some sort of Jack Russell terrier."

Adam isn't alone. In a study of dozens of newly promoted service professionals, management professor Ben Bensaou and his collaborators found that two-thirds of the professionals were either ambivalent about or completely resistant to strategically thinking about social relationships. They divided the professionals into three categories based on their responses to surveys—devoted players (35 percent), selective players (46 percent), and purists who are skeptical (at best) about networking (19 percent). Expressing his resistance and consequential loss of a relationship, one purist said, "He's an associate partner. He should be important for me, but since I see a network as something which happens naturally and not artificially, I didn't really try to keep him."

Time after time, in MBA and executive classes, I see a subset of students close off when we begin to talk about networks. Around a third of the class becomes noticeably physically uncomfortable. Students cross their arms, avert their eyes, shuffle papers. People just don't want to think about the people in their lives in a purposeful manner.

Consider for a moment the following questions: How important do you think your relationships are for your own personal well-being? For your career success? Now reflect about how much time you spend intentionally developing and maintaining your relationships. For the majority of people, there is a disconnect.

Not feeling like they have enough time is one reason. Relationships usually don't have an immediate payoff. They are long-term investments, which makes them easy to neglect in the short term. When trying to corral kids while making dinner, tackling a big work proposal, or finally ticking off the item on your to-do list that has been there for months, you might find it hard to pick up the phone and reach out to that old friend you've been meaning to call. I'll get to it this weekend.

Another reason is that people often confuse purposefully cultivating and maintaining relationships with the type of "networking" Adam spoke about. And they feel like they don't have either the skills, disposition, or charisma to network. For some, even the word *networking* makes their stomachs turn.

This of course makes sense. Relationships—with our family, our dear friends, mentors, and colleagues—are intimately personal. They are invaluable. They shouldn't be strategized or commoditized. Thinking intentionally about relationships can be morally disconcerting.

The purposeful pursuit of all relationships, though, doesn't always make us uncomfortable. The quest for romantic love has been one of humanity's favorite plot lines. Chance encounters don't seem to bother us much, either. It is the idea of networking in particular that generates feelings of smarminess.

Take a look at the following words and fill in the blank: W _ SH, SH _ _ ER, and S _ _ P. If you are in a giving mood and haven't been assaulted by LinkedIn requests, you are likely to see *wish, sharer,* and *step.* A clever study by Tiziana Casciaro, Francesca Gino, and Maryam Kouchaki found that one particular type of interaction—instrumental professional networking—may make you see differently.

In a controlled lab experiment, researchers asked participants to recall and write about an instance in which they had either engaged in spontaneous professional networking (you happen to run into someone at a wedding who provides you with a job lead) or instrumental professional networking (you went to a party with the specific intention of trying to get career help). Instead of seeing neutral words like *wish, sharer,* and *step,* participants exposed to the instrumental networking condition were roughly twice as likely as their spontaneous counterparts to see cleansing words such as *wash, shower,* and *soap.*

In a second experiment, the authors asked participants to think of the same types of scenarios (spontaneous versus instrumental networking) and then to rate the desirability of a set of cleaning products (e.g., soap and toothpaste) and neutral objects (e.g., Post-it Notes and juice). You guessed it—participants exposed to the instrumental networking condition found the cleaning products more valuable than participants asked to think about forming a personal tie by happenstance.

We feel compelled to literally wash away our sins when we experience feelings of moral impurity. Our relationships with others are sacred. Subconsciously, the idea of intentionally profiting from relationships brings them into the realm of money, the realm of taboo. As a consequence, feelings of disgust can lead to disengagement for those who experience it. Even if you don't have any personal qualms about networking, chances are many of the people you are talking to do.

Connecting Is Hard

Anxiety, inauthenticity, and feeling self-conscious are common when talking to strangers. Francesca Gino, a professor at Harvard Business School, and her colleagues ran an analogous study exploring feelings of dirtiness, but made a key change. Instead of asking people to recall a networking experience, they asked participants to reflect on a time that they expressed attitudes, emotions, or opinions that either matched or did not match their internal feelings. Just as with the case of networking, participants that were assigned to recall an *authentic* experience were significantly less likely to recall cleansing words and rated cleaning products as less desirable than participants reflecting on an inauthentic experience. Perhaps authenticity is an antidote to networking?

If someone feels disingenuous, chances are that they are going to avoid opportunities to form new relationships and are certainly not going to seek them out. Even if they don't completely disengage, impression management can lead to increased anxiety, emotional depletion, and self-consciousness, which in turn can lead to more awkward and less effective social interactions.

I had to learn this the hard way. Teaching is in many ways an evaluation of how well you connect with students in the classroom. The first time I stepped into an MBA classroom to teach, I was terrified. I had also been given what in retrospect was bad advice—to try to emulate someone else's teaching style. That's what I tried to do and the results were disastrous. Our teaching evaluations are publicly posted at the end of the year, and mine were the worst. Not second or third from the bottom, but dead last. In the classroom, I was visibly uncomfortable and clearly inauthentic. My students said as much. Much of the time I adopted a pose that can best be described as "leaning pretzel": legs crossed and arms wrapped tightly across my chest, with a slight bend backward away from the class. This led to a quick downward spiral in which I continued to try on different personalities—the serious mathematician, the laid-back "cool" professor—with increasingly negative consequences. My teaching evaluations suffered, my confidence dropped, and I became more and more anxious. A communication course convinced me that punchier openings, more eye contact, and a clear call to action would make things better. Things didn't get better. The problem was deeper than a lack of presentation skills. I went from fear of my students to something closer to self-protective hostility. By my third year, I needed beta blockers in order to get in front of the classroom. Then I pretty much cracked. I ran out of personalities, started asking for help from my colleagues, and began to teach things I believed in rather than what I thought my students wanted to hear. In talking with others, I began to find my own voice. Once I began to open up, the fear left. I wasn't terrified of getting found out anymore.

Self-awareness, self-acceptance, consistency in behaviors and beliefs, and being open and truthful in your relationships with others are at the heart of authenticity, according to a summary of research in the field of authentic leadership led by Bruce Avolio at the University of Washington.

To be more authentic, we first need to become more self-aware. Start by noticing how you feel in different social interactions. When and with whom do you feel comfortable? When does your heart race and your skin crawl? When do you feel the need to force laughter or stifle comments? When do you simply want to make a run for the door? From self-awareness you can begin to move toward acceptance and challenge yourself. What is there really to fear?

People aren't either authentic or inauthentic. We all (thankfully) engage in self-presentation some of the time. I honestly don't want my colleagues to bring their whole authentic selves to work. In many social situations, we have to adapt to circumstances. As a boss, it is my job to put my own bad mood aside and help people who need it. They don't need to know or see that I'm in a bad mood. It's about them, not about me.

Misunderstanding authenticity can create complacency. "When we view authenticity as an unwavering sense of self, we struggle to take on new challenges and bigger roles," argued Herminia Ibarra, a professor at the London Business School. "The reality is that people learn—and change—who they are through experience." But how easy is it to change?

Even if it doesn't evoke moral repulsion, meeting new people can be anxiety provoking. Imagine you are having one of those awkward social moments—drink in hand, clinging to the safety of a high top, pretending to check your phone for the tenth time, with no one you know visible on the horizon. To distract yourself, you try to guess whether or not a woman in a blue dress across the room is going to strike up a conversation with a stranger.

Simply knowing if she was shy would give you a decent idea about how likely she is to engage the stranger. But knowing if she was shy—and whether or not she perceived her shyness to be a fixed or flexible trait—would make you much more accurate.

People with a fixed mindset tend to agree with statements like "I have a certain personality, and it is something that I can't do much about." They believe we are gregarious or we aren't. We are sociable or we are not. This point of view is consistent with the fixed mindset defined by Stanford psychology professor Carol Dweck. People who have a more flexible sense of themselves think their personality changes over time and in given situations. They believe they can overcome their shyness.

Shy people are unsurprisingly always more likely than outgoing people to avoid social interaction. But a series of studies by University of Texas psychology professor Jennifer Beer found that shy people with a flexible mindset were substantially more likely than those with a fixed mindset to chat up a stranger.

As part of the study, trained observers who were blind to how shy participants perceived themselves to be, as well as whether they had a fixed or flexible mindset, watched videos of social interactions and rated the study participants' social skills and likability, as well as how much they seemed to be enjoying a series of five-minute get-to-know-yous. A fixed mindset combined with shyness made people less likable and less socially adept. Over time, however, the behaviors of shy people with flexible mindsets were indistinguishable from the behaviors of those who weren't shy.

The same applies to social intelligence. Broadly defined, *social intelligence* is a set of interpersonal competencies that influence your ability to get along with others and successfully navigate social interactions. As Daniel Goleman, the author of a book by that name, wrote: "The ingredients of social intelligence I propose here can be organized into two broad categories: social awareness, what we sense about others—and social facility, what we then do with that awareness." Social intelligence, like shyness and cognitive intelligence, can be viewed as either fixed or flexible.

Holding a fixed mindset about social intelligence makes people less likely to socially engage because they feel like it will yield limited returns and creates unfair advantages for the people they perceive to be preternaturally socially gifted. But social intelligence, like shyness, is not fixed.

Now, suppose the woman in the blue dress came up to you. You talk for a couple of minutes about the weather and then you stumble across the fact that she knows someone you've been trying to meet for months. She says she'd be happy to make an introduction. After the conversation it would be quite common to second-guess how things went. "Did I talk too much?" "Ugh, I wish I hadn't said that." Or perhaps, "Well, that was awkward. We had nothing to talk about."

Take heart—the conversation probably went far better than you thought it did. A series of five studies that involved groups ranging from Yale students to British attendees of a "How to Talk to Strangers" workshop found in the words of the researchers that "others like us more than we know." The study, led by Erica Boothby and Gus Cooney, once again paired strangers for get-to-know-you conversations. Rather than seeing how things appeared to go, in this study, the researchers asked both participants to rate their conversational partners. They also asked each member of the small talk duo to guess how their partners rated them.

Consistently, people underestimated how much their conversational partner enjoyed the conversation. The researchers dubbed this phenomenon the *liking gap*.

Whether the conversation was two minutes or forty-five minutes, the liking gap persisted. Even though participants whose conversations were longer felt more positive about one another, the misperception continued. And skewed perceptions continued well on into relationships. The researchers found that differences in how much people thought someone liked them, as opposed to how much they really did, continued for five months.

"Conversation appears to be a domain in which people display uncharacteristic pessimism about their performance," the team concluded. In most arenas of life, people see themselves in the most positive light. They tend to think they are more intelligent, more creative, more trustworthy, happier, and healthier than others. But this tendency, known as *the better-than-average effect* by psychologists, doesn't extend to conversations with strangers.

The researchers hypothesize that it is because we are so absorbed in worrying about how we are coming across that we often miss the smiles, laughing, and leaning in that signal our conversational partners are enjoying themselves.

But it isn't just in initial conversations that people frequently invoke a self-deprecating and defeatist attitude about their social life. People also consistently think their social lives pale in comparison to others'. In a series of eleven studies by Sebastian Deri, Shai Davidai, and Thomas Gilovich, the researchers asked 3,293 participants ranging from shoppers at a mall to students to an income-representative sample of Americans how their social lives stacked up to the social lives of others. Respondents thought other people were likely to go to more parties, have more friends, eat out more often, operate in more social circles, and see their extended family more often. This was true for people of varying ages, educational backgrounds, income, and political views.

The reason, according to the trio, is that people naturally compare themselves to their most social friends—to expansionists. As they wrote: "It appears that because extroverts and socialites spring to mind more readily than introverts and recluses, people compare themselves to a tough benchmark and conclude that their social lives are subpar." Setting up the comparison in this way doesn't just make them feel socially less than, it also makes people less satisfied with their life in general. When prompted to compare themselves to people in their social circles who were less social, the effects disappear.

Comparing oneself to the Vernon Jordans of your local social circle makes networking seem futile. So does a fixed mindset. Both can be a threat to one's sense of competency, efficacy, and self-reliance. Feelings of futility prevent people from purposefully reflecting on their networks. In turn, research led by Ko Kuwabara, a professor at INSEAD, suggests that these feelings lead to smaller, less diverse networks.

The truth is that people like us more than we think they do.

But the feelings of awkwardness that interacting with strangers can evoke can make it difficult to be authentic. Inauthenticity—like networking—makes people feel morally impure, leading to disengagement.

Think of What You Can Give

In the study of why networking makes us feel dirty, one group was protected from experiencing networking as gross—people with power. Of course, a simple explanation of this is that powerful people are better at networking, which is precisely why they became more powerful. They may also be more confident so don't have to struggle as much with feelings of futility or authenticity.

However, the researchers found that the effect persisted when they made people feel more powerful through experimental manipulation, rather than solely relying on where someone sat in the organizational hierarchy. This led the authors to conclude: "This makes sense. When people believe they have a lot to offer others, such as wise advice, mentorship, access, and resources, networking feels easier and less selfish."

The fundamental building block of social relationships is reciprocity. It is the currency of social exchange. This led renowned sociologist Howard Becker to argue that our species should be renamed *Homo reciprocus*. If we walk into a social exchange thinking about what we can get out of the exchange, rather than what we can give, we have the equation backward.

This is the crux of Adam Grant's book *Give and Take*. As

Grant, a professor at Wharton, writes with respect to networks, "givers are able to develop and leverage extraordinarily rich networks. By virtue of the way they interact with other people in their networks, givers create norms that favor adding rather than claiming or trading value, expanding the pie for all involved." Giving is a good strategy in the long term because it leads to a network imbued with greater value and reciprocity.

In the short term, giving can also be an effective way of overcoming resistance to building a network, because it invokes positive moral sentiment. Giving creates a warm glow or a helper's high. Functional MRI scans show that when we give, the same reward-processing areas of your brain that are activated when you eat ice cream or receive money light up. These positive emotions can override the negative sentiments that make networking feel dirty. Plus, it is just a nicer way to interact.

What can you give? Heidi Roizen, a venture capitalist and one of the most well-connected women in Silicon Valley, frequently gets this question. Her response: "You always have something to give, everyone has something to give. Good lord, you can come and talk to me and babysit my children while you're talking to me. I had one guy who traded me: I would talk to him about his business and he was a personal trainer, so he would train me while I was talking to him about his business."

When you are just starting out, are switching careers, or are new to a community, it can often be hard to figure out what you can give. In their book *Influence Without Authority*, Allan Cohen and David Bradford offer different types of resources that may broaden your view about what you can give. One category is task related, like information, technical support, or money. These are often the things people default to when thinking about what they have to offer. Another realm of resources are those related to visibility, reputation, or introductions. Gratitude, ownership, or comfort are often overlooked as potential things one has to offer, as is the ability to provide others with a sense of meaning or a feeling of morality or mastery. Asking for help is in many ways a gift. It allows others to be of service. And as the Melville quote Vernon Jordan invoked highlights, "we cannot live for ourselves alone."

Looking Closer

Focusing on ourselves can often get in the way of developing more beneficial relations. Worrying about how we are coming across in a conversation leads us to underestimate the value of encounters. Focusing on what we can get out of relationships generates feelings of immorality. Directing attention toward others is a way out.

Psychological biases can prevent us from understanding social reality. Take this example. Imagine you are walking into a social event by yourself. You walk into the room and see nothing but a sea of people. An expansionist would feel right at home. Early in my career, I would have simply left. The braver among us would head to the safe harbor of the bar. Your heart beats a little faster. Where to go?

A certain cognitive framework transforms this experience:

People almost always interact in dyads—those quintessential pairs of two. We are biologically and socially wired to do so. We have two eyes that point in a single direction. Our auditory processing system leads us to hone in on a single voice, a phenomenon known as the *cocktail party effect*.

The next time you walk in that room, instead of seeing a wall of people, look for small clusters, islands of people. They always exist and are often near a piece of furniture. Now look for an island with an odd number—one, three, five. You've just found your conversational partner. Your addition will create numerical balance. The woman in the blue dress was probably looking for someone to talk to. When I give this very simple guidance based on one of the most fundamental principles of social interaction—dyads—it helps reduce the amount of anxiety people experience and appears to improve social intelligence as a result.

If we take time to better understand the nature of our own relationships and connections, we have the power to change them—in ways that are potentially beneficial to us, to the people with whom we're connected, and to the people they're connected to as well.

Here are three simple tests to help you figure out the extent to which you are an expansionist, broker, or convener. To get a more complete picture of your network, you can visit www.assessyour network.com.

Expansionist

First, let's estimate the size of your active network to see how likely it is that you are an expansionist. Take a look at the following four names:

Alan
Adam

Rachel

Emily

How many people do you know with each name? In this context, we are going to consider that you "know" someone if: (1) you recognize them by sight or name, (2) you could contact them without googling their email address or connecting through social media, and (3) you've been in contact with them by phone, snail mail, or face-to-face in the past two years. Don't think too hard about this (it goes against the spirit of the exercise). Next to each name write how many Alans, Adams, Rachels, and Emilys you know.

Looking down the list, if you knew one Adam, one Alan, one Rachel, *and* one Emily, the size of your acquaintance network hovers around 900. Using this method with many more names, Tian Zheng, Andrew Gelman, and Matthew Salganik, professors at Columbia and Princeton, found that the average person had 610 people in their network. As a point of reference, around 90 percent of the population have acquaintance networks somewhere between 250 and 1,700 individuals. If you saw a number greater than one next to several of those four names, you are likely an expansionist—on the upper end of the spectrum. Most of us would expect to see at least one or two zeros down the column.

Convener

Beyond network size, we really care about network structure. Drawing your network will allow you to start to assess whether you are more like a broker or a convener.

Thinking back over the last six months, who are the people you have discussed important matters with? Write the names of the five people with whom you have most frequently discussed important matters or from whom you have received emotional support in the circles below. For instance, Nick has discussed important matters with Dave, Guy, Sean, Grace, and Sydney.

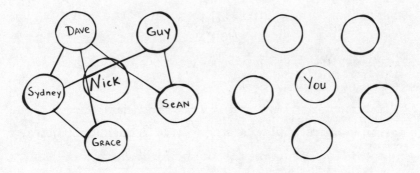

Now we want to start to understand the relationships that exist among our confidants. Draw a line between any individuals in your network who are close. Guy and Sydney work together. Sean and Guy are old friends from high school who regularly get together for beers. If your contacts have simply met each other but don't have any real relationship outside both being your friends, don't draw a line between them. To keep things simple, do not draw a line between yourself and everyone in your network.

How many lines exist in your network? The average person has five lines. If everyone has a close relationship with everyone else, there would be ten total lines. The closer you are to ten, the more likely you are to be a convener.

Broker

Now that we've considered expansion and convening, let's take a look at brokerage using a scale developed by David Obstfeld.

For each of the questions below, mark the response that best characterizes how you feel about the statement, where 1 = strongly disagree, 2 = disagree, 3 = somewhat disagree, 4 = neither agree or disagree, 5 = somewhat agree, 6 = agree, and 7 = strongly agree.

	Strongly Disagree						Strongly Agree
1. I introduce people to each other who might have a common strategic work interest.	1	2	3	4	5	6	7
2. I will try to describe an issue in a way that will appeal to a diverse set of interests.	1	2	3	4	5	6	7
3. I see opportunities for collaboration between people.	1	2	3	4	5	6	7
4. I point out the common ground shared by people who have different perspectives on an issue.	1	2	3	4	5	6	7

Source: David Obstfeld, "Social Networks, the *Tertius Iungens* Orientation, and Involvement in Innovation." *Administrative Science Quarterly* 50, no. 1 (March 2005): 100–30.

People score around a 4.5 on average for the full six-question survey. If you're seeing 6s and 7s, you may be a broker. However, identifying as a broker doesn't necessarily make you a structural broker. On the whole, people are not great at evaluating their network type and there are different types of brokers as we will see.

If you are still not sure what type you are, not to worry. As humans we don't always fit into a neat typology. We may have a tendency to be a broker but act like a convener in some areas of our life.

Our networks are also constantly evolving. The network that would be supportive for someone looking for an early stage investor wouldn't be helpful to a recent empty nester. As we advance in our professional lives and as we form families and our friendships shift, our networks transform. Each different network style has different strengths at different moments. As you move forward, there is often a tendency to want to focus on your current type. But arguably more important than understanding your current network is gaining a deeper insight into what might be gained from other types, as well as the mental models of others around you.

The goal of this book is to help you see the "invisible threads" of connection that Vernon Jordan found so inspiring. These threads form the basic elements of social structure that play a large role in determining who gets a coveted job, how happy you are, and whether children feel supported.

While the term *networking* may evoke moral sentiments— Vernon Jordan is an archetypal example—networks themselves are simply structures. They are traces of social lives lived and foretell what is likely to come. What happens within them and how we see them, though, are certainly not neutral. As Melville wrote, "Our actions run as causes and return to us as results."

The truth is, your network affects your life in ways that cannot be understood by looking at your behavior alone. Whether your friends are friends with one another, for instance, has an enormous effect on whether you are seen as trustworthy. Beyond your own life, these same structures also explain which teams will be successful, if organizations are inclusive and diverse, and whether social movements like the civil rights movement are able to take off.

More than eight decades ago, Jacob Moreno, a Romanian-born psychotherapist, first devised sociometry, the way of drawing social networks that we still use today. He wanted to understand the relationship between social structures and psychological well-being. At that time he told *The New York Times*: "If we ever get to the point of charting a whole city or a whole nation, we would have . . . a picture of a vast solar system of intangible structures, powerfully influencing conduct, as gravitation does bodies in space. Such an invisible structure underlies society and has its influence in determining the conduct of society as a whole." Recent advances in network analytics, physics, engineering, sociology, and computer science have made this possible. What Moreno didn't realize at the time was that the elemental structures he had already drawn based on patterns of interactions in a girls' reform school in Upstate New York held the key to understanding how the social world works. These structures—brokerage, convening, and expansion—are a way of seeing the invisible forces playing out every day—at work, at home, and on vacation. They are at the center of what this book has to offer.

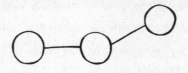

2. THE NATURE OF NETWORKS

Stacked end to end, the cards in David Rockefeller's Rolodex would stretch for nearly sixteen miles. The breadth of his Rolodex, which contained more than 100,000 contacts, is legendary, as were the people included in it, ranging from Nelson Mandela and Pablo Picasso to Sigmund Freud and Bill Gates.

While his contacts included heads of state, intellectuals, celebrities, presidents, and business scions, he recorded interactions with "most people I have met since the 1940s." But he didn't just jot down names and dates of fleeting encounters. Instead he kept detailed notes on everyone from virtual strangers to his closest friends and even former dates.

The hotly controversial secretary of state under Richard Nixon, Henry Kissinger was one of Rockefeller's oldest and closest friends. Kissinger's Jewish family had fled Nazi persecution in 1938, but an immigrant's story of assimilation is reflected in the thirty-five cards containing details of his and David Rockefeller's hundreds of meetings going back to 1955. During a lunch at his sprawling manor in the Hudson Valley a few years before his death, Rockefeller gave a copy of the cards to Kissinger, who remembered telling David that he was "astonished that we have seen each other so much."

One less public figure from Rockefeller's Rolodex described the use of this social tool. "If you were so fortunate to be a 'fly on the wall' for any of his countless meetings and interactions, you would hear him inquire about the smallest details of his guest's life, from a child's ballet recital to a parent's recent health concern. This was not done for show or effect, though it never failed to delight and disarm his visitors. To be in the company of David was to have an audience with greatness, but his interactions were always transformational, never transactional."

Some found the documentation calculating and his approach off-putting. Rockefeller recognized this and defended his practice, arguing that "some may feel this technique is cynical and manipulative. I disagree. Such an approach enabled me to meet people who were useful in achieving goals and gave me opportunities to form lasting friendships."

Regardless of how you feel about the Rolodex, Rockefeller's social acumen was potent. Those cards represent a keen awareness of a human limitation. We cannot build a vast network of contacts while still maintaining old and strong ties.

Or can we? Rockefeller grasped the cognitive constraints that limit the size of human networks and sought to overcome them.

While he was arguably one of the most connected people in the world, as a child he was shy and insecure. Even upon entering

Harvard, he "initially felt like a misfit with few social skills." This was in stark contrast to his brother Nelson, who was "sociable and outgoing and loved to be the center of attention." David preferred to spend his time collecting beetles rather than fraternizing. His penchant for beetles persisted until his death—he left a collection of 150,000 different specimens to Harvard.

It was his experience as an intelligence officer in World War II that showed him the importance of human connections. As he wrote, it made him recognize the need to "develop a network of people with reliable information and influence" despite his natural tendency toward shyness.

Even when faced with accusations that the time he spent building relationships was a distraction from his duties as CEO of Chase, he continued expanding his personal ties internationally. And while there were periods during his tenure when the bank underperformed rivals domestically, it would be difficult to deny his claim that these efforts benefited the bank's international profits and prestige. It helped bring the practice of calculated investment and Western banking into Egypt, the Soviet Union, and China. These feats drew directly on Rockefeller's extensive personal connections.

Homo Sapiens Scale

While a few extraordinary individuals have hundreds of thousands of connections, most of us have networks on a more human scale. In fact, the size of our networks—from how many close friends we have to the length of our holiday card list—largely conforms to a relatively predictable pattern.

The most famous of the numbers on this scale, known as Dunbar's number, is 150. The magic number 150 is the number of stable contacts we can maintain. Or as Dunbar put it, it's "the number of people you would not feel embarrassed about joining uninvited for a drink if you happened to bump into them in a bar."

The anthropologist Robin Dunbar discovered his eponymous number somewhat inadvertently. During the 1980s there was widespread interest among primatologists in the social brain hypothesis. The idea behind this hypothesis was that the brains of primates may have evolved in order to meet social needs, rather than environmental demands such as an expansion in territory. Supporting the theory was a strong coupling between the size of primates' social groups and the size of their brain—more specifically, the size of the neocortex relative to the size of the rest of the brain.

The ratio for gibbons is around 2:1, and their social groups are estimated to have around fifteen members. The ratio is substantially larger for chimpanzees, 3:1. Dunbar put their group size at sixty-five members. This line of work led the researchers to conclude that primates' brains may have evolved in order to help manage social complexity. While studying primate grooming, Dunbar realized that his team also had data on humans. With this data, he should be able to predict the average group size for humans by knowing their neocortex ratio. For humans, the ratio was 4:1. Dunbar did the math and predicted that 150 should be the average size of our social group.

Dunbar has spent much of his career exploring the boundaries of this number—what it actually means and whether social media has changed it. Dunbar's "number" is really a range between 100 and 200. And that numerical range has historical and contemporary significance. Villages in modern hunter-gatherer societies, ranging from the Kung San in Botswana to the Ruhua Nualu in Indonesia, have an average group size of 148.4. Neolithic villages in Mesopotamia were roughly the same size, ranging from 150 to 200 people. Army companies from sixteenth-century Spain to the twentieth century in the United States all had around 150 soldiers.

Surprisingly, technology and social media have done little to change this fundamental number. While the average user has several hundred Facebook friends, a massive study of Facebook found that less than 5 percent of users had contacted more than a hundred people through the platform. Similarly, a study of 1.7 million Twitter users found that users maintain between a hundred and two hundred stable relationships. People who spend more time on social media have larger social media networks but do not have larger offline networks; they also do not feel emotionally closer to the people in their network. Social media hasn't expanded the number of friends we have or made us feel closer to them. It has simply changed our ability to keep track of the outermost layer of former acquaintances. It has become our equivalent of Rockefeller's Rolodex.

Your social network can be conceptualized as a series of concentric circles that decrease in emotional intensity as you move outward. Decades of research by Dunbar and his colleagues have unveiled a pattern: the size of our social circles expands in roughly multiples of three.

Our innermost circle, the people we turn to in times of severe emotional and financial distress, typically consists of two to five people. The next layer, which Dunbar refers to as our sympathy group, are the fifteen or so individuals we feel emotionally close to. We are usually in touch with them monthly. If we move another band out, we find your close friends. This is the fifty people you would feel comfortable inviting to a barbecue but wouldn't necessarily disclose your innermost secrets to. Beyond that is Dunbar's most famous number—150—our set of casual friends or stable contacts. It is at this boundary that a sense of reciprocity and obligation ends.

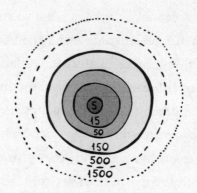

Multiplying that by three, we typically have between 450 and 600 acquaintances. These are people we have seen in the past couple of years but do not regularly keep in touch with. At the outermost edge are the roughly 1,500 people we recognize by sight.

It is precisely at these far edges of our networks that social media plays a role. It allows you to see what your college roommate's best friend from high school did over the weekend. It offers a way of contacting the chatty pharmacist you met at a party. But it is highly unlikely you will ever reach out to either of them.

While everyone has roughly the same capacity to form and maintain relationships, people tend to allocate their energy differently across the different layers of social relationships. Thinking of our social relationships as a form of capital—social capital— can be helpful in this regard because it highlights that our relationships require investments and trade-offs. As Dunbar says, "The amount of social capital you have is pretty fixed . . . It involves time investment. If you garner connections with more people, you end up distributing your fixed amount of social capital more thinly."

Part of the reason the size of our networks is limited is our cognitive and emotional capacity. The other is time. There is a limit on how much time we can devote to relationships. If you are deeply invested in your innermost circle, you have less time for casual friends. If you spend a significant amount of time catching up with and seeing acquaintances, you may find it difficult to develop a strong sympathy group.

Many of us live in what feels like a time-starved era. Most adults spend less than forty minutes a day socializing—and that figure has declined by 10 percent over the past decade. The additional eighteen minutes a day (including travel time) the average person devotes to volunteering, religious, and civic engagements don't offer much more in terms of time for community. Today we have less time for relationships than it seems our parents had.

Of course, it is possible to increase the size of your network to the upper limits of Dunbar's number or beyond by investing more time and effort. This is precisely what David Rockefeller did. But is that how we want to spend our time?

In order to help understand whether a brokerage, convening, or expansionist network—or some combination thereof—is right for you, it is worth exploring the key trade-offs that time and cognitive constraints create. Expansionists, brokers, and conveners all deal with the constraints imposed by time and our inherent human and emotional limitations differently. In some cases, these may be conscious choices. In other instances, they may not seem like choices at all. By examining these trade-offs and their consequences in detail, we can understand how one became or can become a broker, convener, expansionist, or a mixture thereof.

What Is a Friend?

How do friends differ from acquaintances? Tie strength lies at the heart of this distinction. You can think of strong ties as your closest friends and weak ties as acquaintances. Which of Dunbar's circles do you devote the most of your time and attention to? We can have many weak ties as expansionists do or a smaller number of strong ties, which is a signature of conveners. But the amount of time and emotional energy that goes into strong ties means most people can't maintain many deep relationships.

The strength of a tie is partially—but by no means completely—determined by the amount of time you've invested in the relationship. A recent study by Jeffrey Hall at the University of Kansas found that it takes around fifty hours altogether to go from acquaintances to casual friends. An additional forty hours is necessary to become "real" friends. To become close friends likely takes more than two hundred hours.

Yet simply investing more time in a relationship won't necessarily transform an acquaintance into a friend, supporter, or ally. Think of a particularly prickly boss. You've probably spent more than two hundred hours with them, but they aren't necessarily a close friend. The amount of time you've known someone and how frequently you see them aren't great predictors of the strength of your tie. Mark Granovetter, the Stanford sociologist who first discovered that you are more likely to get a job through weak ties, intuitively argued that tie strength was likely a combination of the amount of time, emotional intensity, intimacy, and reciprocity invested in a relationship.

The poet Maya Angelou eloquently made this point: "There's a marked difference between acquaintances and friends. Most people really don't become friends. They become deep and serious acquaintances." What Maya Angelou instinctively understood—and decades of research has confirmed—is that closeness and intimacy underlie tie strength.

Intimacy can be frightening because what we have to lose from betrayal becomes all the greater the closer we are to someone. Yet we need deep ties. This is true even in seemingly unlikely places such as the workplace. This can be seen in the evolution of the relationship between a bank employee and her manager as they navigated the diagnosis of the manager's father's cancer: "At her hardest times I cried and she cried. She opened herself up to me and I opened myself . . . Here you spend more time with people than with people at home. So you feel for them."

A lack of intimacy is why the coworkers you've seen every day for the past two years are probably more acquaintances than friends—you really don't know that much about them and you haven't disclosed that much about yourself to them. It is also why most of your Facebook "friends" aren't really your friends. The images we present on social media and the thinness of the medium make it nearly impossible to transform repeated interactions into stronger ties.

The Character of Strong and Weak Ties

Strong ties, which are imbued with intimacy and affection, provide emotional support, help guard against depression, and increase feelings of well-being. Your strong ties are also your most likely source of companionship and small favors. However, we rarely receive financial support from even the closest of our friends—only from our family.

Our strong ties are the people we turn to in times of crisis and the friends we call on to get us through losing a job or a divorce. They sit with us through chemo and show up at the hospital to help welcome our babies to the world.

Yet strong ties can become straitjackets. Part of their strength comes from norms of reciprocity: if I do something for you, you will in turn do something for me. While this is an important source of relationship strength, the expectation that you will be available for someone and willing to help them out in the indefinite future can be emotionally and financially taxing. With close friends, a long shared history can often make it difficult or impossible to turn down a request for help or support—even when these asks are so large or frequent that you desperately want to say no.

The difficulty of saying no to our closest friends can also reinforce behaviors—both negatively and positively. If you want to quit smoking, you will find it harder if your best friend smokes. Even if he doesn't offer you a cigarette, you're going to feel awkward when he steps outside for a smoke and you're sitting alone on the couch. The same is true for drinking, changes in diet, or even shopping. On the flip side, our strong ties can also provide reinforcement and make it more likely we will be able to make and sustain positive behavioral changes.

While our casual acquaintances are unlikely to play a key role in helping us make major behavioral changes, our weak ties are likely to give us our next great idea or business opportunity and to get our community on board with a new initiative.

We also turn to acquaintances with surprising frequency to discuss issues important in our lives. A study by Mario Small, a professor of sociology at Harvard, asked 2,000 adults which people they frequently consulted in considering matters important to them, like careers, money, health, and happiness. More than 45 percent of discussion partners were considered unimportant by the respondents. In part, this is because we will often seek out advice from people with experience or expertise, rather than someone we feel emotionally close to. If I find out I have high blood pressure, I might ask advice from a colleague who has also been dealing with it for years or from an acquaintance who is a doctor. Often we also simply turn to people for advice "because they were there." In a child care center Professor Small studied, for instance, mothers frequently asked other parents for advice about their children, not because they felt close to them, but simply because they crossed paths during pickups and drop-offs. Similarly, college students reported that roughly a fifth of the time they needed help with a paper or advice about an issue with a roommate, they turned to someone primarily because they were available.

When a weak tie will generate value is somewhat unpredictable. It is hard for an acquaintance to know if they have information that would be valuable to you and similarly difficult for you to know who might have information that could help you. The randomness of weak ties is where their value lies but is also exactly what makes them difficult to purposefully mobilize.

To see how strong and weak ties operate differently in our lives, let's step inside Dan's world. Dan is a middle-aged insurance salesman and sailing enthusiast who recently had a milestone birthday. While he is reasonably healthy, that birthday and nudging from his wife have prompted him to try to hit the gym. The first days at the gym are brutal. It turned out that he was far more out of shape than he realized, and squeezing in the gym meant he had to rely on his wife to bear more of the burden at home. Luckily, she was more than willing to help, both because she wanted Dan to exercise more and he can drive her nuts sometimes, so having him out of the house was a bit of a bonus. At the office, Dan commiserated with his close friend, the gym rat Tim, and in so doing found a gym buddy who was willing to help support his effort. Even on days when he dreaded the thought of lifting weights after work, he wasn't willing to bail on Tim. So he continued to show up. Over the weeks, a consistent routine of exercise started to pay off. Dan lost seven pounds, could walk the five flights of stairs to his office without losing his breath, and even generated a sales lead on the elliptical. It turns out that the gym is a good place to sell life insurance.

Dan's case is fairly typical. His strong ties provide emotional support and positive behavioral reinforcement. But a change in his typical routine resulted in a new weak tie with information and resources.

The number of people in our innermost circle is a strong indicator of how much our network skews toward strong attachments. The average American has two confidants. More than 40 percent of phone calls people make are to the same three friends. And evidence suggests that we are limited to around five close friends—very few people have more. If you do, it likely says something about you.

Strengthening Attachments

Why do some of us prefer intense intimate relationships while others derive satisfaction from more fleeting encounters? Although many models—from Freudian accounts to evolutionary theories—have been proposed to explain this puzzle, attachment theory is arguably the most extensively studied and supported.

The British psychologist John Bowlby, who was raised primarily by nannies and nursemaids, conceptualized attachment theory over fifty years ago. He developed his model to explain how

45

the nature of a child's relationship with their primary caregiver influenced their subsequent social, emotional, and cognitive development. According to the theory, if infants receive responsive and consistent care, they will expect others to continue to behave toward them in this way. These expectations determine how we behave toward others in close relationships. Researchers believe that your attachment style, which can be assessed as early as age one, is more important for personal development than IQ, social class, temperament, and parenting.

The vast majority of people can be characterized by one of three attachment styles: secure, anxious, or avoidant.

The securely attached are comfortable with intimacy and interdependence, believe that others will respond to their needs, and are confident in their own sense of self-worth. They tend to agree with statements like "I feel like I have someone to rely on," "I feel like others care about me," and "I feel I can trust the people who are close to me."

People who experience attachment anxiety doubt their own sense of self-worth, have a deep need for interpersonal closeness, and worry frequently about abandonment and rejection. Statements like "I want to share my feelings with someone," "I wish someone close could see me now," and "I really need to feel loved right now" resonate with the anxiously attached. Elizabeth is a classic example. Her friend described her to a mutual acquaintance as being "crazy about love" and "a hopeless romantic." In response she recalled, "I felt my face get hot and swallowed back a rush of hurt feelings, pretending I didn't care. I knew she hadn't meant it in an unkind way—she thought she was simply stating the obvious—but somehow it still stung . . . I guess I've always been afraid that I have a little bit of a 'Crazy Ex-Girlfriend' streak in me. Anyone who knows me will tell you I require absolute loyalty from my friends and lovers, and I can be jealous and vindictive." The clingy ex is a textbook example of someone who is anxiously attached.

Finally, the avoidant are hyperalert to ensure no one gets too close to them. At the first sign of too much intimacy, they freeze or disappear. Avoidants are reluctant to trust, tend to be self-reliant, are intolerant of intimacy, and stuff their emotions. Or to put this more generously, they are "fiercely independent." Though in truth they are actually just as needy as the anxiously attached.

Unsurprisingly, avoidance is associated with fewer strong ties. But so is attachment anxiety. A recent series of studies by Omri Gillath and colleagues examined the relationship between attachment style and an individual's network tendencies. Across three studies, the authors consistently found that attachment anxiety and avoidance were associated with weaker ties.

An increased tendency to *dissolve* existing ties accounted for the lack of strong ties within the networks of the insecurely attached. For the avoidants, it isn't that they don't initiate relationships with people who could become a part of their inner circle, but that they back away from those relationships before others become too close. Avoidants tend to focus on their partner's flaws—"she wasn't good enough for me"; "he's a wreck"—to create distance.

For the anxiously attached, a desire and need for closeness paradoxically lead to a network full of weak ties. The underlying anxiety about potential loss can lead them to preemptively end relationships or emotionally engulf their friends to the point that their friends back away.

Take Brittany Wright as an example. The attractive, funny, outgoing South Carolinian lamented:

> If you were to look at my Instagram, Facebook, or Twitter, it would seem that I have lots of close friends—but the truth is, I'm one of the loneliest people I know.
>
> I don't have a significant other, I don't have many friends, and my weekends usually consist of solo Netflix binges and gossiping with my grandma.
>
> It isn't that I hate people or that I'm an awful person—at least I *hope* not; I just have a difficult time making deep, long-lasting friendships.

Brittany's mother instilled in her the importance of self-reliance and independence, which she has admittedly taken too far. As she described, "I refuse to let anyone be there for me, but I end up getting mad at the other person when it's actually my own fault." Her inability to be vulnerable and lack of trust eventually led to the dissolution of her closest friendship. She started to think the relationship was superficial, so she stopped returning calls and texts. The friendship ended. She eventually realized it was her fault.

> In the end, I've got to allow myself to be vulnerable. I need to just trust that someone will have my back in a bad situation. I'll need to let them see all the things that make me me—that I'm indeci-

sive, talk too much, and sometimes a bit selfish—and I'll hope that they choose to love me and stick around, regardless.

Brittany is far from alone. Many people are insecurely attached, "around 20 percent are anxious, 25 percent are avoidant, and . . . 3 to 5 percent" are both, according to the book *Attached* by Amir Levine and Rachel Heller.

Men and women are equally likely to be securely and insecurely attached. But when they aren't securely attached, limited and controversial evidence suggests that men tend to be avoidant while women are more likely to be ambivalent. Unlike sex, poverty during childhood substantially increases the risk of insecure attachment.

While historically attachment styles were thought to be relatively fixed, recent research has found that purposeful interventions, awareness about self-sabotaging tendencies, positive experiences in relationships, and simply reminding people of times when they felt secure can change people's attachment style. After recalling a time in which "a close personal relationship . . . provided love, comfort, and support," anxiously attached individuals reported being significantly less likely to dissolve ties than their counterparts in a control group. The same effect occurred among the avoidant. Essentially, the idea is to try to overwrite early negative experiences with more recent positive ones. In turn, this can lead to an increased propensity to develop strong ties.

One defining feature of brokerage, expansion, and convening networks are their distinct arrays of strong and weak ties. Conveners tend to favor strong ties, while expansionists trade the strength of ties for a larger volume of weak ties. Given the emotional and cognitive investments that strong ties require, it is simply impossible to have a large network full of strong ties.

But not every relationship can or should be an intimate one. Acquaintances and casual friends play an important role in most people's social worlds. Which begs the question of how we meet acquaintances in the first place. Oftentimes it feels like chance. Other times it seems fated.

Getting Close

Humans are about as predictable as plants. If I know what you've been doing over the past couple of weeks, it is possible to predict where you will be tomorrow at four P.M. with a high level of certainty—with a greater than 90 percent predictability.

Describing the results of a study of 50,000 cellphone users' mobility patterns, physics professor Albert-László Barabási wrote: "Spontaneous individuals are largely absent from the population. Despite the significant differences in travel patterns, we found that most people are equally predictable." If everyone is predictable, then the set of individuals you could possibly interact with is quite constrained—which makes who is likely to end up in even the outer reaches of your network foreseeable. Unless you purposefully create spontaneity, your network will likely suffer the same fate as a garden that never experiences crop rotation—productivity will decrease.

Space has such a strong effect on our patterns of interactions it has been given an unnecessarily complicated name, the *law of propinquity.* This law—that the probability of two people communicating is inversely proportional to the physical distance between them—was first formulated by James Bossard after examining 5,000 marriage licenses in Philadelphia issued during the 1930s. More than one in three couples who were about to marry lived within five blocks of each other. This led Bossard to quip, "Cupid may have wings, but apparently they are not adapted for long flights."

Leon Festinger and his colleagues added further evidence to this idea while studying patterns of friendship formation in the Westgate housing developments at MIT in Boston, where families were randomly assigned to apartments. People who were assigned to live next door to each other were most likely to be friends. In fact, 41 percent of friendships occurred among next-door neighbors, 22 percent lived two doors down, and 10 percent of friends lived on opposite ends of the hallway.

Seating assignments produce a similar effect. When studying friendship formation among trainees in the Maryland State Police Academy, Professor Mady Segal realized that friendships were more likely to form among cadets whose last names started with the same letter. This was entirely due to the alphabetic seating chart at the academy. Seating proximity was a stronger predictor of friendships than religion, age, hobbies, and marital status.

Despite technological advances that have dramatically lowered the cost of communication since Bossard's and Festinger's time, geography is still a major force defining the contours of our social networks. A study that used wearable sensors to investigate patterns of interaction among employees at two firms confirmed just how strong the effect of propinquity remains—close to half of all interactions occurred among employees sitting next to each other, an additional 30 percent were among employees in the same row, while the majority of the remainder were among colleagues on the same floor. This was true for email communication as well as face-to-face interaction. Although the world has become increasingly global, our social lives remain extremely local.

Both at home and in the workplace, space has a strong effect on our relationships. Careless assignments of offices, desks, teams, and task forces can substantially disadvantage our friendships, productivity, and happiness.

Part of this effect is simply probabilistic—where we are determines whom we have the opportunity to get to know. But it is also partially due to the psychological phenomenon known as the *mere exposure effect*. Merely being exposed to people, objects, and ideas leads us to have more favorable evaluations of them. The psychologist Robert Zajonc documented the effect in the 1960s by showing that the more frequently people saw faces, words, and made-up "Chinese" characters, the more they liked them.

In Zajonc's study, subjects were presented with a variety of pictures of white men taken from a yearbook. Some photographs were shown a single time, while other photographs were presented up to twenty-five times. Each person was then asked to rate how much they thought they would like the person in the photograph if they met them. Seeing a photograph ten times led to a roughly 30 percent increase in perceptions of likability compared with seeing someone only once. In the decades since Zajonc's original study, this finding has been replicated across more than two hundred studies.

Where Do You Go?

Take a moment to think about your own network. Recall once again your five or six most important relationships. Now consider where you met them. For most people, two or three different institutions (e.g., work and college) account for the vast majority of relationships. But when we are considering which job to take, where to live, or what desk to sit at, we rarely consider how our network is shaped by where we go.

Take the case of Robert Solow and Paul Samuelson, who independently won Nobel Prizes. As Professor Solow recalled of their chance co-location, "Paul and I were close enough together so that either of us could holler and the other would hear . . . We would go back and forth all day long: 'I've got a problem.' So we'd talk about the problem." He continued, "The truth is, it may have changed my whole life in a respect . . . In a way the location of that office and the fact that we liked each other so much had a major influence on the direction my career took."

Companies have built cathedrals based on the belief that more social interaction will lead to more innovation. This has led close to 70 percent of offices to adopt an open layout. At Facebook's headquarters, 2,800 employees work in the world's largest open-office space. Zappos CEO Tony Hsieh tried to redesign the downtown of Las Vegas with the idea of increasing the number of probable interactions per acre per hour. But by many accounts these efforts have not yet had the effect that engineers and designers may have hoped for.

Walk into open offices around the world, and you will see

people with headphones on and others holed up in structures that are reminiscent of telephone booths of the days of old. While open offices can create a sense of unity and shared purpose, a review article on office design by organizational psychologist Matthew Davis and his colleagues found that employees in open offices were less productive, less creative, and less motivated than workers in offices with a more traditional layout. Working in an open office was also associated with greater stress and unhappiness.

Simply increasing the quantity of interactions through spatial proximity doesn't lead to innovation or higher rates of job satisfaction. You need repeated interactions, trust, and diversity to improve job satisfaction and creativity.

Where Should You Go?

If you are trying to cultivate relationships at work, the best place to sit is in an office across from the bathroom or the break room. Everyone usually goes there at least once a day. Unlike an open-office space, there is concentrated and repeat traffic in these areas—and you can shut your door.

While dead-end hallways are social death at the office, cul-de-sacs are social gold in neighborhoods. In a study comparing social cohesion among residents living on either cul-de-sacs that end in a circular turnaround, dead-end streets, or linear through streets in a relatively homogenous area of Connecticut, Thomas Hochschild Jr. found that families living on cul-de-sacs were more likely to see their neighbors as friends and interact with them more frequently than residents of dead ends or through streets. Living "around the circle" had a surprising power.

As Karen described her idyllic cul-de-sac life, "Every year, the ladies on this street get together and organize a street party. We get the men to put picnic tables in the middle of the road . . . After we're done eating, we move the picnic tables away and play kickball or volleyball. We've been doing it for almost twenty years now—wow, I can't believe it's been that long." Residents of dead-end streets are not as sociable as those around the circle, but their kids were still more likely to get together and there was a stronger sense of belonging than among families on through streets.

We may be wondering, as the Beatles famously did in "Eleanor Rigby," where do all the lonely people best belong? Without the circle for kickball, neighborhood barbecues, and gossip over white picket fences, one might think city dwellers have stunted social lives. Eloquent descriptions of the urban alienation abound. Describing New York City, Mark Twain wrote, "I have at last, after several months' experience, made up my mind that it is a splendid desert—a domed and steepled solitude, where the stranger is lonely in the midst of a million of his race."

And then there is the story of Joyce Carol Vincent, the thirty-eight-year-old whose body wasn't discovered in her London apartment for more than two years after her death.

Despite the grim portraits that frequently emerge of urban life, city dwellers are more socially connected to their neighbors than their rural counterparts. Within cities, people who live in large apartment buildings are the most likely of all to be sociable with their neighbors. There is no truth to the myth of urban loneliness.

If you want to get to know someone, you need to get physically close. Where we spend our days has an enormous effect on what our networks can look like. Yet it is the rare individual—the expansionist—who has a network that shows traces of spatial spontaneity. Much of the time a convener's network results from keeping the same job, staying in the same home, and being a lifetime member at the same social club.

When people are considering how to develop a network, far too often the focus is on whom you know. Popular culture advises us to seek out connections with key individuals, to try to get to know the magical person who will launch our careers or become our life partner. That is a mistake. A much more productive perspective to take is to think about where you go. Being thoughtful about how you allocate your time in social space—do you sit at a long table or take the two-seater in the corner? choose the cul-de-sac or the high-rise?—paves the way to the strongest network. It's not so much whom you know that matters, it is where you go.

While we have considerable control over the spaces we drift in and out of (whether that be physical space or institutions), whom we will form relationships with in those spaces is far more uncertain. This idea led the legendary social scientist George Homans to describe social behavior as "familiar chaos." As he wrote, "Nothing is more familiar to men than their ordinary, everyday social behavior." But despite the ordinariness, predictability, and familiarity of our social life, there remains an unpredictable chaos to our social relationships. This chaos makes seeking out a relationship with one specific person an uncertain endeavor. Instead, if you put yourself in the right spaces, chances are you will meet someone who can be of help.

Meeting, Maintaining, and Terminating

For most of us, our networks are largest when we are twenty-five. High schools and colleges create ready-made friends, they organize clubs and parties we simply have to show up to, and create a common shared identity. In short, they have all of the necessary ingredients for making close friends: social proximity, repeated interactions, and an environment in which people naturally feel a sense of belonging. And at twenty-five, you have a lot of free time. Family and work obligations have not usually reached their peak.

At our quarter-life social pinnacle, we are in regular contact with nearly twenty other people during a month. From this peak of sociability, our core network tends to get smaller and smaller. We are down to less than fifteen people by the time we turn forty and closer to ten by the time we turn sixty-five. The composition of our networks also changes over time, with increasing attention devoted to family.

Our networks tend to not simply shrink, they churn. Take a moment and think about the colleagues with whom you have frequent and substantial business. How many of them do you think will still be central to your work life a year from now? Half? A third?

Typically, only around one out of four will still be central in your work world a year from now. In two years, it will be one in ten colleagues.

Social relations tend to evolve more slowly than work relationships, though the adage "once a friend, always a friend" is far from true. Half of our social relationships beyond family will cease to exist in roughly two years. Adolescents experience even greater turnover in their network—a third of adolescents have an entirely new set of friends every six months. Less than 15 percent of teen and tween friendships continue for multiple years.

To some extent these network changes reflect changes in our interaction spaces—moving, changing jobs, joining clubs. But they also reflect life transitions—getting married, getting divorced, having children, and retiring. Beyond our station in life, different personalities, gender, and approaches to relationships also shape the extent to which we focus on meeting, maintaining, or terminating. And collectively these have consequences for our success and well-being.

Consider the following statements: (a) I frequently catch up with colleagues from different departments, and (b) I use company events to make new contacts. A study that followed 279 employees over the course of two years to understand what predicted career success found that agreement with either of these statements significantly predicted employees' current salary, their salary growth trajectory over the next two years, and their career satisfaction. Agreeing with the first statement, however, which focuses on network maintenance, predicted close to half of the variance in salary growth and career satisfaction. Focusing on meeting new people, which is reflected in the second statement, was much less important.

Outside of work, it is new friends—not the old—who make us happier and create a greater sense of well-being. Despite the benefits of meeting new people, few people make it a habit. Instead, we let history and a desire for self-similarity and familiarity drive our networks. At the same time, we hold on to relationships far longer than we should, even though deteriorating relationships can induce emotional stress and result in poor health.

We constantly make choices about whether to expand our inner circle, to continue to invest in relationships, and whether it is time to let a friend go. Should I go to the happy hour or head home for some much-needed time with the family? Has our friendship finally become toxic enough that I'd be better off ending it? Do I walk over and introduce myself or just hang out with my regular crew? These decisions can have significant consequences, but we often make them unconsciously. And in that unconscious decision-making, what often goes unrealized is that there are necessary trade-offs between the extent to which we can focus on meeting, maintaining, and terminating.

Hi, I'm Alice

Many of us say we want to meet new people. And we may even go through the motions of trying to make it happen. But in reality, the vast majority of us—particularly people over forty—rarely expend effort expanding their network.

Columbia University professors Paul Ingram and Mike Morris studied meeting in a cleverly titled article, "Do People Mix at Mixers?" In the study, they asked close to a hundred highly successful professionals to don wearable sensors that tracked social interactions and attend an after-work cocktail event. When surveyed prior to the event, 95 percent indicated that creating new ties was a greater priority than reinforcing old connections. Despite their stated intentions, the executives were three times as likely to interact with someone whom they had a strong positive connection with prior to the mixer than someone they did not know. So the answer to the question was no, people do not mix at mixers.

Other than sheer laziness and a lack of time, fear can also be a major psychological barrier that inhibits us from meeting new people.

Fear of strangers and social anxiety are common. As social animals, we are wired to want to be accepted. The fear of not being accepted, which is heightened when interacting with strangers, is at the core of social anxiety. Over the course of a lifetime, 13 percent of people will suffer from clinically diagnosable social anxiety. This makes it the third largest mental health problem. Even if it doesn't reach clinical levels, almost all of us experience social anxiety at some point.

Anxiety and fear are not all bad. Anxiety can improve performance. It also shows you care. It's when the fear becomes so great that you start avoiding situations or isolating yourself that it becomes problematic. The good news is that it is highly treatable.

According to Stefan Hofmann, director of the Psychotherapy and Emotion Research Laboratory at Boston University, cognitive behavioral therapy in which clients identify maladaptive thinking patterns and then address them through repeated exposure to difficult social situations leads to a response rate of at least 75 percent.

Some exposure ideas that have been used by Hofmann at his clinic:

- Asking an employee at a bookstore for books on farting
- Approaching a table at a restaurant and asking them to listen to you practice your maid-of-honor speech
- Requesting condoms from a pharmacist and then following up to see if it's "the smallest size you have"

The point of these "social mishap exposures" is not to provide truth-or-dare style entertainment to the group. Instead, by having participants confront their greatest fears (which are usually along the line of "what will they think of me?"), they realize that even the worst-case scenario really isn't that bad. This significantly helps reduce fear.

If you aren't quite ready to sing on a street corner for ten minutes, studies have also found that simply being kind can help reduce social anxiety. A study by social psychologists at the University of British Columbia and Simon Fraser University split 115 socially anxious undergraduates into three groups. One group engaged in forms of exposure therapy, a second group was asked to simply do nice things for others, and a third group that just wrote about their day served as a control. All three groups tracked their levels of social anxiety before and after they were assigned to acts of kindness or exposure activities. The kindness group experienced the biggest decline in social anxiety, though exposure also reduced social fear.

A second cognitive bias rooted in fear that makes meeting difficult is a desire for perceived predictability. If we've already met someone, and especially if we know them well, we think we know how they are likely to behave. Whether or not this is true, the perception of predictability makes people we know less frightening. As a result, we cling to them. While someone with extreme social anxiety would likely avoid social interaction altogether, perceived predictability will lead people to hang on to people they already know in social situations.

It isn't just fear that keeps people from focusing on network expansion. Sometimes meeting many new people simply doesn't make sense. At the beginning of your career, knowing more people has enormous benefits. But as your career progresses, the returns diminish. Early in your career there are probably a lot of people who have more knowledge and resources than you do. However, as you progress up the corporate ladder or gain more status, a chance encounter is less likely to provide access to resources and knowledge that you don't already have at your disposal. Of course, this isn't true for everyone. If you need a huge platform—you are a marketer, are in public relations, or are a preacher, for instance—expansion is always going to be useful.

And sometimes rather than fear or strategy, it's simply a preference for devoting more energy to the people you already know and love.

Life Gets in the Way

Even when we cross the threshold and meet someone new, it can still be difficult to turn a meeting into a relationship. Alex Williams deftly described this difficulty in a *New York Times* article:

It was like one of those magical blind-date scenes out of a Hollywood rom-com, without the "rom." I met Brian, a New York screenwriter, a few years ago through work, which led to dinner with our wives and friend chemistry that was instant and obvious.

We liked the same songs off Dylan's "Blonde on Blonde," the same lines from "Chinatown." By the time the green curry shrimp had arrived, we were finishing each other's sentences . . .

That was four years ago. We've seen each other four times since. We are "friends," but not quite friends. We keep trying to get over the hump, but life gets in the way.

It's not just new friendships that can be difficult to develop and maintain. Without face-to-face contact, our emotional attachment to friends and family quickly deteriorates. After two months without an in-person gathering, feelings of closeness between family members dropped by more than 30 percent.

In the first two months of not seeing one another, rates of intimacy between friends declined at a rate similar to that of family. After that, friendships go frigid. After 150 days without seeing each other, friends' feelings of closeness dropped by 80 percent.

The investments required to maintain friendships differ for men and women. A study of call patterns among 20 million cellphone users found that men tend to maintain a greater number of ties than women. Rather than preferences, though, life events such as marriage and parenthood create the biggest differences in the extent to which men and women maintain relationships.

Parenthood—especially early parenthood—is frequently like

falling off a social cliff. Practically everyone who has brought home a newborn knows this. In the months before your baby arrives, everyone gathers, bearing teeny-tiny onesies and cuddly teddy bears. Little do you know, you probably won't see most of them again until your child is speaking in sentences. A baby shower could more aptly be called a going-away party.

A year or two after the shower, your relationship with a few attendees will be far stronger than it was before baby. But many of the others will have become much more like acquaintances than friends. Sadly, that is true even for very close friends. You don't even have time to bathe properly, much less go out for cocktails. But psychological processes also play a role. After parenthood, there tends to be an increased focus on your child and romantic partner and your interests diverge from those of your childless friends.

When we are between twenty-five and fifty, there is a precipitous decline in the size of our network. This is true for men and women, but the drop-off is greater for men. Women's networks shrink by roughly 20 percent, compared to a 35 percent shrinkage for men over the same period. This is primarily because men start off more social than women. It isn't until age forty or so that women's networks become bigger than men's.

A report that analyzed findings from 277 studies involving nearly 180,000 participants confirmed the common presumption that our networks suffer most during the transition to parenthood. Our ability to maintain personal contacts also decreases substantially when we get married and when we move, but it's during the transition to parenthood when they take the greatest hit.

Whether it is parenthood, moving, or marriage, life events and changes in our everyday interaction spaces are the moments when we are most likely to lose friends and colleagues. And we usually don't make new ones to replace the ones we have lost—at least not at the same rate. Our networks simply shrink. This is part of the reason that loneliness is so endemic among older adults. Their networks have slowly decayed.

How can you help buffer against these inevitable life events? Conveners have either knowingly or unwittingly figured it out. Examining the actions that conveners take and understanding how their networks evolve can help anyone become better at maintaining their existing ties.

Not Fade Away

We rarely break up with friends or family. Instead, most of our relationships slowly die. We ghost.

Less than 15 percent of relationships end because of a disagreement or quarrel or another fundamental change in the relationship. In a Dutch study that followed 600 adults over seven years, the primary reasons people cited for their relationships dissolving were a decrease in the frequency of contact and no longer sharing a social context, such as a book club or church. Collectively, these two reasons accounted for roughly 40 percent of relationships that disappeared. People faded away, they weren't cut off.

Yet many relationships persist even when we find them difficult. In a study of 1,100 Californians' relationships, people who were described as demanding or difficult accounted for close to 15 percent of relations. Close family members were particularly likely to be listed as difficult ties. While many found their mothers to be difficult, twentysomethings were more likely than fifty- to seventy-year-olds to find their wives, brothers, and sisters challenging. By the time people hit retirement, their kids increasingly made the list.

Hanging on to difficult and draining relationships causes stress, poor health, and psychological distress. So why is breaking up so hard to do? Of course, one could cite guilt, fear, desire to avoid conflict, potential loss of income, and dread of the painful aftermath (much of the time, anyway). But it isn't just that people try to avoid being uncomfortable in the short term.

Sometimes, as is the case with family and colleagues, we simply can't get rid of them. Frequently, though, we also waver because relationships are multidimensional. Perhaps she is clingy and annoying, but she is a really great conversationalist. He always steals others' ideas, but he can be really helpful. This was at the root of many of the difficult relationships Professors Shira Offer and Claude Fischer studied. For twenty-somethings, advice givers often proved difficult. Among older respondents, those who were common sources of emergency help and support were more likely to be demanding than those who provided other types of relational benefits.

Adding to the complexity is the fact that while we talk about friends, family, and colleagues, these aren't really distinct categories. We often are friends with our colleagues. Our family members are sometimes our closest friends. This entanglement makes ending relationships complicated and costly. How do we know when the cost of exit is worth it?

We usually don't think of sticking with a friendship or ending one as involving a set of trade-offs, but that is a reality. Except in the extreme case of breaking up with one romantic partner for another one, most of our relationships aren't simply a one-for-one trade. And even in the seemingly straightforward case of romantic relationships, people often regret their decisions, recognizing the virtues and failings of the relationship only in retrospect. However, if we don't think consciously about these decisions, our psychological predispositions, life events, and entanglements will lead us to feel like our networks weren't a choice, they were chance—thus leaving us disempowered, at the mercy of fate.

Your Social Signature

Most people end up as a broker, convener, or expansionist without even realizing it. Worse yet, they wake up lonely at seventy and wonder what happened. Whether the decisions have been made consciously or through a combination of habit, psychological tendencies, and circumstance, our networks are social signatures.

Expansionists favor weak ties, have vast interaction spaces, and expend most of their social effort meeting new people. They also have an easier time ending relationships, because their investments don't have a lot of reciprocal obligations.

Brokers have some strong ties, but the strength of their network comes from their weak ties. Their interaction spaces typically revolve around many social worlds. Brokers spend a good deal of time maintaining weak ties. Without continued investment, the weak ties they do have easily disappear.

Conveners prefer strong ties and devote most of their effort to maintenance. They don't spend a lot of time exploring multiple social worlds but tend to have deep roots in a few.

The nature of social reality—time constraints and cognitive limits—creates inescapable trade-offs about whether we invest primarily in strong or weak ties, whether we travel in a wide range of social spaces or know a few intimately, and how much effort we devote to expansion and maintenance. We simply can't make more time or be in two places at once.

Much of the time, decisions in each of these dimensions hang together in predictable ways. It is no surprise that if you invest a lot in network maintenance, you probably have strong ties. This tends to arise more from habit and character than from anything else. But brokers, expansionists, and conveners can't simply be described by their interaction spaces, propensity to maintain or terminate ties, or the extent to which they favor strong ties. The beauty of networks, including your own social signature, is that their properties are greater than the sum of their parts.

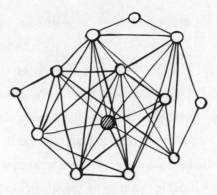

3. CONVENERS

It's the first Monday in May. Hundreds of paparazzi are gathered on the steps of the Metropolitan Museum of Art awaiting jewel-encrusted headdresses, wings, fur, veils, leather, and chain link. They soon appear adorning those fortunate enough to be invited to "the undisputed party of the year on the New York social schedule."

With her skeletal figure, signature bob, and omnipresent sunglasses, Anna Wintour has final say over who is invited to the Met Gala and who isn't. The six hundred other anointed attendees from Oscar winners to Silicon Valley wunderkinds spend months anticipating the event. In feting Anna's accomplishment as chairman of the Met's Costume Institute, First Lady Michelle Obama joked, "I know that Anna hates being the center of attention, so this all is probably killing her—but we love it . . . The truth is, I'm here today because of Anna. I'm here because I have such respect and admiration for this woman who I am proud to call my friend."

More is spent on fashion each year than is produced by the entire economy of Brazil. Anna Wintour is the queen of the industry. And as the matriarch, she is both feared and revered.

From the most illustrious seat in fashion as editor of *Vogue*, she has fielded an influential army of allies who make her one of the world's most formidable brands—a brand that extends far beyond fashion. *Forbes* named her the most powerful woman in media and entertainment, and she is an invisible power player in the world of politics.

Although Ms. Wintour is at the epicenter of culture, fashion, and art, she is notoriously private. She rarely stays at parties (other than her own) for more than twenty minutes and is seldom out past 10:15. Many people would consider calling her *private* or *guarded* an understatement. Her coldness prompted others to nickname her Nuclear Wintour. She was the purported inspiration for the tyrannical boss in the novel *The Devil Wears Prada*, written by a former assistant. Wintour once told Oprah to lose twenty pounds before appearing on the cover of *Vogue*.

Among those close to her, however, she inspires intense trust and loyalty. As her protégé Marc Jacobs observes, "Her genius is picking people very astutely, whether in politics, movies, sports or fashion." He goes on: "She gets such a bad rap. She stands by the people she believes in, and if you're not one of those people, perhaps you take a different view." Veteran Met Gala maestro and former Wintour assistant Sylvana Durrett puts it similarly: "I'm thankful to Anna. She stands behind me and her decisions and our decisions, and so it's nice to have somebody in your corner . . . And she's been such an ambassador and a champion of anything I've wanted to do. She treats all her employees that way."

Wintour keeps clearly demarcated boundaries. As she put it, "I care deeply about my friends and my family and they know it, but work is work." While occasionally friendships emerge from professional relationships (tennis player Roger Federer and *The Late Late Show* host James Corden are friends), her closest friends are largely anonymous. Describing the importance of these friendships, Wintour reflected, "I have a really close group of wonderful women who I'd rather keep to myself . . . I have one girlfriend in London that I'm thinking about . . . We've known each other since we were sixteen; you just pick up the conversation and there's nothing we're embarrassed about saying to each other and we're also very honest. And it's a great joy."

"Behind the publicly cold facade is a devoted and generous mother and friend; there is no limit to the lengths she will go to for those in that tight circle of people she trusts," confirmed one friend.

Anna's fortified social circle is also part of what gives her fame and power. To study what makes a star, University of Southern California professor Elizabeth Currid-Halkett and her colleague Gilad Ravid of Ben-Gurion University set out to understand what differentiates exclusive A-list celebrities from the ubiquitous C-listers you've never heard of. They studied a year's worth of photos from nearly 12,000 events taken by Getty Images, the world's largest photography agency with access to red carpets across the globe. Hundreds of thousands of photos were used to create a network of who frequently appears with whom. The networks of such A-listers as George Clooney, Angelina Jolie, and Matt Damon, who appear at the top of the Forbes Star Currency index, look completely different from the networks of other celebrities.

A-listers "have a tight and densely connected social network." They appear to maintain convening networks with other celebrities. As Currid-Halkett wrote: "While A-listers' friends tend to be friends with one another . . . the middle and bottom [rung of] stars have virtually no special connections with the others in their group." The density of A-lister networks helps reinforce their status, ensures their exclusivity, and makes it hard for outsiders to penetrate the celebrity elite. Anna Wintour's network is emblematic in this regard. It is a fully connected clique.

The key value that motivates her, it seems, is trust. As she explained, "I try to remain open to new people, but obviously there's a stronger element of trust with people you've known for a long time."

Who Do You Trust?

Around one in three people in the United States believe that strangers can be trusted. And the proportion of Americans who believe most people can be trusted has been steadily declining since the 1970s. Globally, the extent to which we trust one another varies widely. In Sweden, the belief strangers can be trusted is 60 percent more common than it is in the United States. But in Brazil, where distrust runs high, it is close to only one in six.

It isn't just strangers. Only half of Americans feel that they can trust their neighbors. Work isn't better, either. A global survey of 9,800 full-time employees found that less than half have a high level of trust in their employer.

It can also take a surprisingly long time for people to decide whom they trust at work. On average, according to a study that Ron Burt conducted of employees in three firms, deciding takes more than three years. Given that onboarding in many companies can take months and most hourly employees stay with an employer for only about four and a half years, conveners' ability to swiftly develop trust can be critical to getting ahead.

Trust is essential for our social relationships and ability to operate in the world. Brides and grooms take a leap of faith at the altar. When complaining about coworkers, colleagues trust that those they speak to won't share their gripes with the rest of the world. On a smaller scale, we make dozens of decisions every day that require us to trust people we do not know. We let strangers drive us around in taxicabs, invite unknown contractors into our homes, and hand over deposits in the hope that work will actually get done. As Anton Chekhov put it, "You must trust and believe in people, or life becomes impossible."

In friendship and love, trust allows for forgiveness, creates the willingness to sacrifice, and promotes relationship stability, accommodation, and collaboration. The more we trust our husbands and wives, the less stressed and depressed we are likely to be. As a consequence, we are healthier.

At school, kids learn more from teachers they trust. In teams, trust improves performance, learning, and task coordination. Paul J. Zak, a professor at Claremont Graduate University, has found that "people at high-trust companies report: 74% less stress . . . 50% higher productivity, 13% fewer sick days . . . 29% more satisfaction with their lives, [and] 40% less burnout."

But how do we know whom to trust?

Imagine that you've just sat down next to a stranger at an airport. He's medium height, wearing jeans and a button-down shirt. If you needed to, how would you decide whether to trust him? Check to see if his arms are crossed? Is he glancing to the right? No? Wait, maybe he is lowering his voice? For decades researchers have looked for signals of trustworthiness that could be picked up within a single interaction. Despite enormous effort—studying everything from eye movement to body language to vocal cues—scholars have been unable to identify any foolproof physical signals of trustworthiness.

Most people lie some of the time.

Situational factors influence people's propensity to lie. Being in a dark room, not having time to think, feeling emotionally exhausted—even what we are wearing—can all make us more likely to lie and cheat. In four separate experiments by researchers at Harvard Business School, Duke University, and UNC Kenan-Flagler Business School, participants were asked to wear either real or knock-off sunglasses under the guise that they were participating in a marketing study. People who were randomly assigned to wear the fake sunglasses cheated more on tasks and lowered their ethical expectations of others. Wearing fake sunglasses made people less honest.

Despite what the researchers told them, the fake sunglasses weren't obviously fake. The fakes were in fact sunglasses from the same designer. If we can't rely on external signals to tell us whom to trust, what are we supposed to do? Ultimately, trust requires vulnerability. Here is one definition of *trust* offered by a group of interdisciplinary researchers that is frequently cited: "a psychological state comprising the intention to accept vulnerability based upon positive expectations of the intentions or behavior of another."

It is fairly easy to imagine how vulnerability might make us less trustworthy. If someone is afraid, shouldn't he or she be more willing to lie? It seems to be just the opposite. A study led by psychologist Bernadette von Dawans found that vulnerability makes people more honest. To examine the relationship between vulnerability and honesty, the researchers had half of participants in their study give a short speech to and answer math questions in front of an audience of confederates trained to remain unresponsive. The control group didn't have to endure this social pain. Groups who had to give the stressful presentation were roughly 50 percent more likely to engage in trustworthy behavior in subsequent trust games than the control group. Vulnerability makes us feel a strong need to belong, and in turn we become more trustworthy and cooperative.

Rather than figuring out whom to trust and then allowing ourselves to be vulnerable, we first have to allow ourselves to be vulnerable. What does that look like?

Arguably, no one wants to (or should) disclose their innermost secrets to someone within five minutes of meeting them. As Jeff Polzer, a professor at the Harvard Business School, explains: "People tend to think of vulnerability in a touchy-feely way, but that's not what's happening . . . It's about sending a really clear signal that you have weaknesses, that you could use help. And if that behavior becomes a model for others, then you can set the insecurities aside and get to work, start to trust each other and help each other."

Sometimes people choose to be vulnerable, but sometimes circumstances choose for them. Jeffrey Sonnenfeld, the CEO of the Chief Executive Leadership Institute, is probably not the first person you would think of as a poster child for vulnerability. He regularly throws himself into the middle of highly visible business and political battles on CNBC and in the pages of *The Wall Street Journal*. He has famously taken on the National Rifle Association and defended Jamie Dimon, the CEO of JPMorgan Chase, during times when he thought Dimon was the unfair target of a "witch hunt."

Sonnenfeld's willingness to defend others during some of their most difficult moments can be traced to his own experience. During the late 1990s, Sonnenfeld was at the peak of an academic career. CEOs of companies ranging from Coca-Cola to the Chicago Bears were attendees at the conferences he convened.

However, after nine years as a professor at Emory University's Goizueta Business School, he accepted a deanship at crosstown rival, Georgia Tech. In the weeks before Sonnenfeld was set to leave, his reputation came under attack in what *60 Minutes* referred to as "the scuffed halls of ivy." He was accused of vandalism. A camera captured him jumping up and down in the hallway, which the school claimed damaged the walls. As Morley Safer of *60 Minutes* described the video of the incident: "There is no mistaking Jeffrey Sonnenfeld for Fred Astaire or Baryshnikov as he bounces his way down the corridors of Emory's business school, legs flying . . . It didn't get him a job at the ballet, but it cost him his job at Emory. Based on this tape, Emory fired him and publicly disgraced him." But as *The New York Times* reported, "that accusation does not hold up."

Sonnenfeld found himself unemployed and his reputation in shambles. As he put it, "That was the entirety of what destroyed a twenty-five-year career, believe it or not, that is, that is it. Did it look a little silly? Yeah, there certainly was no damage, no intent to damage, and absolutely nothing that comes close to vandalism." During an interview with the *Observer,* he broke down and confessed that "every night I cry."

Rather than simply cowering, Sonnenfeld fought back. He reached out and asked for help from the powerful executives and politicians he had been helping for years. Hundreds of CEOs and university professors showed up to support him. Kent Nelson, the retired CEO of UPS, backed up Sonnenfeld, arguing that "Jeff has professed to have not done the things they said . . . it's inconsistent with my twenty-five-year relationship with him. And it's just not fair that those things can be said without proof. If there's proof, let's see it." The video Emory produced offered very little evidence. But the incident made Safer reflect that "the cutthroat politics that go on behind the doors of academia can make the cutthroat politics of Washington look positively benign." From the world of politics, former president Bill Clinton wrote Sonnenfeld and offered a signature phrase of his: "I regret what you've been through . . . I can feel your pain."

Sonnenfeld had powerful supporters to draw upon because many had been through similar adversities. Those adversities are what make great leaders.

One of the first people Sonnenfeld called when charged with vandalism was Bernard Marcus, the founder and former CEO of

Home Depot. Marcus said of Sonnenfeld during that period, "You know, he was very depressed. He was despondent, frustrated. Just absolutely beaten down." Describing a similar experience of his own when he was ousted as CEO of Handy Dan before founding Home Depot, Bernie recalled, "There was a lot of self-pity on my part . . . I was drowning in my sorrow, going several nights at a time without sleeping. For the first time in my adult life, instead of building, I was more concerned with surviving."

Common identity created through shared vulnerability catalyzes relationships. Built on those kinds of relationships, Sonnenfeld's network not only saw him through the darkness of the 1990s but has made his CEO summits a trusted ground for executives to discuss personal and business issues frankly. Attendees read like a list of who's who from the C-suite. Regulars include David Abney of UPS, Ken Chenault of American Express, and Indra Nooyi of PepsiCo.

Whether or not it is advisable to deliberately be vulnerable to create trust is debatable. But we all face true moments of crisis. When these come, being honest about them and candidly asking for help can transform something that seems dire into an opportunity to strengthen relationships and rebuild reputations.

Gossip

We usually don't make decisions about trust in social isolation. Ronald Burt, a professor at the University of Chicago and a leading figure in social networks research, and his colleagues argue that "trust is 60% network context." He came to this conclusion after studying 4,664 relationships among seven hundred entrepreneurs in China. Burt studied fifty-three different individual characteristics, ranging from how happy the entrepreneurs were to their age, education, family size, and political participation. Collectively, these individual attributes accounted for only about 10 percent of the difference in who was trusted and who wasn't. Network characteristics, including how frequently the entrepreneur was in contact and whether he or she was around during key events, were six times more important than individual factors for explaining trust.

While Burt and his collaborators drew the 60:10 conclusion from Chinese entrepreneurs, decades of research in settings ranging from families in the United States and employees in global corporations to Maghribi traders in the eleventh century has consistently found that network closure—when your friends are also friends with each other—leads to trust. Simply, conveners are more likely to be trusted and trusting.

Network closure creates an environment in which norms can be enforced and you are likely to hear if someone is engaging in dubious behavior.

Kids, particularly socioeconomically advantaged kids, whose parents have closed networks perform better in school. Convener parents can more easily monitor what is going on with their kids. In a study of around 20,000 youth in 144 schools, researchers found that for kids from more advantaged backgrounds, parental network closure is associated with higher high school grade point averages and lower levels of dropout. If you notice your friend's teen hanging around a shop when he should be in school, you'll probably mention it to your friend. The broadened monitoring and enforcement of a large parent mafia ensure that kids get their homework done and don't fall through the cracks.

This isn't just what is happening with kids on the block. Gossip is also key to doing business between Fifth and Sixth Avenue on 47th Street in New York City. On these two blocks, billions of dollars in diamonds—90 percent of the U.S.'s diamond imports—are traded each year. In a 2011 report from the New York Industrial Retention Network, the total economic impact was estimated to be around $24 billion. To put that number in context, it is not far off the annual revenue of Starbucks in 2018. Despite the enormous value being exchanged, most of the transactions on 47th Street are sealed with a handshake and the traditional phrase "Mazal and Bracha." The trust-based exchange, which has been called "the real treasure of 47th Street," depends heavily on the ultra-Orthodox Jewish community that dominates the diamond exchange. One diamond dealer, Philip Weisner, who was born into a long lineage of diamond traders, described the strength of the community's culture, avowing that "it is my blood; it is my fabric, whether I like it or not." The strong sense of community and history is augmented by Jewish laws against gossip, except gossip that is necessary or beneficial. The relative rarity and stature of gossip within the community gives it power. Any potential negative talk could easily lead to expulsion from both the community and business.

Gossip often gets a bad rap. People who gossip are frequently seen as weak and unlikable. This is particularly true for "high frequency negative gossipers." But as Professor Robin Dunbar succinctly put it, "Gossip is what makes human society as we know it possible." From an evolutionary perspective, gossip enabled humans to form large social groups because it allowed for policing and sanctioning of cheaters.

Like it or not, we spend an inordinate amount of time gossiping. More than 60 percent of time in conversations is spent gossiping, according to analyses of casual conversations captured in cafeterias, bars, and trains by Dunbar and his colleagues. The remaining third or so of conversation time is largely devoted to politics, sports, work, and the like. The amount of time people spend gossiping doesn't vary substantially by age or sex. It's not just old women who gossip.

We may be hardwired to gossip. When observing antisocial or unfair behavior, we often experience it physically—our heart rate rises and we become agitated. The ability to gossip has been shown by Matthew Feinberg, a psychologist at the University of Toronto's Rotman School of Management, and his colleagues to alleviate the uncomfortable physical manifestations of observing deceit. Three out of four people are even willing to pay money to be able to gossip about cheats and escape the emotional and physical discomfort.

Bandwidth and Booster Clubs

Convening networks are evolutionarily advantageous in part because they effectively make use of gossip. Their architecture—characterized by strong ties and redundant connections—provides protection from potentially nefarious others, and also helps generate trust and resilience. They are comfortable and safe.

They also have higher bandwidth. This bandwidth makes them better at conveying complex, tacit, and sensitive information. Strong and cohesive ties increase people's willingness and motivation to share information. A coworker who is also a friend is going to be more disposed to spend time and effort teaching you than a stranger. In industries in which sharing complex information is critical, this can be an important competitive advantage. Studies that examined collaborations among hundreds of scientists found that tie strength and cohesion—the hallmarks of convening networks—were associated with higher rates of knowledge sharing.

Beyond complex information, strong and cohesive ties make it more likely that people will share sensitive information, even with their competitors. Prices are a good example. In both the champagne and the hotel industries, pricing is somewhat arbitrary and a highly guarded topic. What is an empty hotel room worth? What is the difference between a $30 bottle of champagne and a $35 bottle of champagne? As one grower put it, "Price is not something people talk about in Champagne. It's a private matter. For some reason, it makes people feel uncomfortable."

But within convening industry networks where people are comfortable talking about prices and other potentially guarded topics, they benefit. Research on champagne growers by Amandine Ody-Brasier at Yale University and Isabel Fernandez-Mateo at the London Business School found that the strong informal relationships among female champagne growers allowed them to systematically charge higher prices. The same was true among hotel managers in Sydney. Each additional close tie a hotelier had with a competitor was worth an estimated $390,000 in revenue.

But not everyone benefits from the bandwidth of convening networks. This is why cartels—extreme examples of convening networks—are illegal. They harm consumers.

Higher bandwidth networks are particularly good for those on the receiving end of information. But according to a study conducted by Martin Gargiulo and his colleagues at INSEAD, such networks are less beneficial for employees who are principally responsible for transmitting information. They are also more efficacious in jobs in industries where approval and social support are essential. When reputations are valued and buy-in is critical, the dense strong ties of convening networks have been associated with higher bonuses.

Beyond business, convening networks may also increase resilience. To understand where resilience comes from, consider one anecdotal example. Monique Valcour looked at how female UN leaders working in areas of civil unrest, natural disasters, and armed conflict remained resilient in the face of constant instability and adversity. Social relationships were key. As she writes: "Positive, energizing connections to others are vital to resilience. They provide socioemotional support, a sense of belonging, and people to share experiences and ideas with. They infuse challenging situations with a sense of playfulness and optimism, heightening capacity to learn and perform. Positive relationships, both at work and in personal life, boost self-confidence, self-esteem, and resilience."

The resilience benefits of relationships often lead people to form convening networks after natural disasters. One study compared the Facebook networks of college students who were exposed to a natural disaster and others who weren't directly affected and found a greater increase in network closure in colleges impacted by the hurricane. This tendency persisted for more than two and a half years after the hurricane struck.

Linnea Van Wagenen, who works for the United Nations Integrated Peacebuilding Office in Sierra Leone, regularly convenes "an informal monthly lunch" in her community to help her remain resilient in the face of continual crises. In explaining why the lunches are so important, Ms. van Wagenen told Dr. Valcour, "It's an informal network that functions like a boosting club."

Mean Girls and the Mafia

While clubs can be great and a mafia of school parents can boost GPAs, high school cliques are arguably one of the most treacherous social topographies to navigate. Every school has cliques to varying degrees. George, a junior at Guilford High School in Guilford, Connecticut, puts it bluntly: "The day there aren't cliques in high school is the day high school doesn't exist."

During childhood, kids' social relations tend to focus on dyads—one-on-one social attachments. Parents and best friends tend to be the center of kids' social worlds. But in the move to adolescence, cliques start to appear and the pressure for friends to be friends increases. Beginning in middle school, teachers have to start rearranging classrooms and orchestrating mean girl bustups because Hailey and Emily have decided they don't get along. When that happens, all hell breaks loose because it no longer affects only Hailey and Emily but has ramifications that ripple through the social structure of the school.

Cliquishness may be at its peak in high school, but it persists throughout adulthood. Mom cliques permeate preschools and playgrounds. There are the breastfeeding, baby-wearing moms, the PTA moms rushing their six-year-olds off to Mandarin, the moms who've known one another since high school, and a half-dozen or so other clearly demarcated tribes. As Deborah Hurowitz, a Boston-based social worker and parent support group leader, reflected, "When you have a kid, it's like going back to high school . . . Everybody is scrambling to figure out who they are, how they'll fit in, and who they want to be friends with." Mom cliques can be savage and merciless. Amy Sohn wrote of navigating parenting in the treacherous waters of Park Slope: "Clique warfare in new-mommy circles makes high school look like fun."

Work doesn't always provide a safe harbor, either. In a survey of close to 3,000 employees by CareerBuilder, 43 percent of people reported that their workplace was populated by cliques. And in offices with cliques, nearly half of employees' bosses are a part of a clique. While office cliques don't change the behavior of the masses, one in five people report doing things they wouldn't have done otherwise—watching TV shows, making fun of someone, or smoking—to fit in at the office.

Think about how you feel when someone says, "Hey, did you see *Madam Secretary* last night?" Once you start watching the show, a line could be crossed. You've let the desire to fit in change your behavior—even outside the office. Before you know it, you may be hosting the season finale watch party and trying to decide whether to invite a coworker with an avowed distaste for political drama.

The golden years don't provide much respite. Cliques are pervasive in senior centers, assisted living facilities, and nursing homes. Marsha Frankel, a clinical director overseeing services for seniors, put it bluntly: "What happens to mean girls? Some of them go on to become mean old ladies." In residential settings for older adults, turf wars can turn public spaces like TV rooms into fiefdoms and exercise classes can get nastily competitive. Dr. Robin Bonifas of Arizona State University estimates that up to one in five elders in senior communities experience bullying—roughly the same rate observed in high school.

Cliques are ubiquitous because they fulfill deep psychological needs—a need for identity, familiarity, and social support. These are the same needs that lead to convening.

Group identification can form almost instantaneously over completely meaningless distinctions. The social psychologist Henri Tajfel demonstrated how little it took for in-group favoritism to form in a 1970s series of experiments known as the *minimal group studies*. In one of these studies, Tajfel and his collaborators put boys in a comprehensive school into groups randomly. But they told the boys the groups were based on their preference for certain modernist paintings over others. The boys had no interaction with other members of the group. The groups were completely meaningless. But the boys still favored members of their own group. Boys who favored Klee paintings awarded more points to others who also supposedly preferred Klee. The same was true of the Kandinsky group. They favored their "own."

Random and inconsequential group distinctions determined

by coin tosses, random shapes, and T-shirt colors have repeatedly been shown to invoke in-group favoritism in hundreds of subsequent experiments using a much more representative pool of subjects than teenage boys. People put into meaningless groups give members of their own group more money. They perceive their group members as more likable and cooperative even without meeting them. They even implicitly associate their group with words like *sunshine* and outsiders with *sickness*.

What is remarkable about these experiments is that they show that strong in-group favoritism develops without competition between groups or discrimination against other groups. One's social identity arises substantially from membership in a group. Such membership boosts self-esteem, something we can't do well without.

It doesn't take an enormous leap of the imagination to see how systematically favoring your own could be linked to intergroup conflict. Much of Henri Tajfel's work was motivated by a desire to understand where intergroup conflict and dynamics arise from. During World War II, Tajfel was taken prisoner by the Germans and had to decide whether or not to lie about being a Polish Jew. He admitted he was a Jew but claimed to be a French Jew. He survived the war in a POW camp but lost all of his immediate family during the Holocaust.

Call them cliques or call them convened groups—some are good and some are bad. But all groups provide support. Girls who aren't a member of a clearly defined clique in high school are twice as likely to consider suicide as girls in a tight-knit group. Even mafia networks, which epitomize social closure and corruption, come with enormous trust, coordination, and reputation benefits. As Joseph Bonanno, the longtime boss of one of America's most enduring mafia families, reflected, "Mafia is a form of clan-cooperation to which its individual members pledge lifelong loyalty . . . Friendship, connections, family ties, trust, loyalty, obedience—this was the 'glue' that held us together." And it is the same kind of glue that holds society together, albeit with different pledges and rules.

Why Andrew Is Likely to Marry Amy, Knows No Agnostics, and Is Work Friends with Allen

While tight-knit groups can form based on even the most arbitrary distinctions, a psychological need for familiarity leads relationships and groups to frequently form based on similarity. Spouses often have phonetically similar names. People are more likely to trust someone who orders something similar at dinner.

Friends are often similar—whether it be by class, race, age, musical preferences, values, or hairstyle. Hundreds of studies have confirmed that "birds of a feather flock together," a tendency known as *homophily*. Researchers have observed it in networks across the globe in settings from marriage to online friendship. In the roughly twenty years between 1985 and 2004, the propensity for friends to have a similar racial, educational, age, and religious background remained about the same. As researchers at Northwestern University wrote, "Homophily's potency as a social mechanism lies in its apparent universality."

Three-quarters of white Americans do not have one nonwhite friend. Among blacks, the tendency toward homophily is a bit weaker. According to the American Values Survey, a representative survey of 2,300 American adults, two-thirds of black Americans report that their closest confidants are all black.

Race may be the strongest social dividing line in social networks in the United States. Religion is likely second. Eighty percent of white evangelical Protestants' confidants are also Protestants. Seventy-two percent of Catholics' ties are to other Catholics. Religious chasms, however, are weakened by people without a religious affiliation, who seem to be much happier to hang out with people with different religious beliefs.

Politics doesn't divide networks quite as much as race and religion, but it's fairly rare for Republicans and Democrats to be friends. Both religion and politics raise an important question: Do we choose to be friends with, marry, and associate with people of similar religious and political beliefs, or do our beliefs converge over time?

This brings to the fore the more general question of whether self-segregation in networks is intentional or accidental. How much of it is based on choice versus circumstance? Do preferences, psychological need, and biases lead to networks built on self-similarity? Or do jobs, neighborhoods, schools, and voluntary organizations create limited opportunities for cross-group interaction and induce homophily?

It appears to be both—choice and circumstance. We've seen evidence from the Tajfel experiments that choice and in-group favoritism play an important role. And we've also seen that interaction spaces can have a huge impact on friendships and collaborations. In a small town with no library or clubs, the likelihood that you will befriend someone different from you is far smaller than in a diverse urban community with strong traditions bringing together neighbors from all walks of life.

The lines between mean girls, jocks, hipsters, and hippies are more strongly drawn in some schools than others. It isn't the students but the schools that determine the extent to which choosing a lunch table feels like taking a mafia oath. Larger, more diverse schools that give students a greater choice over the classes they take are more likely to have school social contours defined along clique lines. A study of social networks incorporating data from 75,122 students in 129 schools led by Daniel McFarland, a professor at Stanford University, found that school structures that force students to interact across groups—whether smaller schools, smaller class sizes, or simply enforced seating arrangements—made cliques less ubiquitous.

If homophily is a result of both choice and circumstance, it creates the opportunity for organizations to devise structures, programs, and practices that help avoid the creation of networks based solely on self-similarity. But simply having diversity isn't enough.

This is important because racial and gender homophily often reinforce patterns of stratification by providing unequal access to social capital. Even if they are in a richly diverse community, women and minorities in closed networks of similar others have a harder time finding jobs and are promoted at lower rates.

To be clear, there is no evidence that conveners necessarily have a preference for networks built on self-similarity. But the structure of conveners' networks can often become homophilious because people who wear expensive clothes are more likely to befriend others in designer duds, people who drive pickup trucks tend to associate with other truck drivers, and so forth. This can generate a dynamic where even a small amount of self-similarity becomes magnified. Before conveners realize it, without intention, all of their friends drive pickup trucks or wear fancy clothes.

Brian Uzzi, of Northwestern's Kellogg School of Management, and Shannon Dunlap developed a quick tool to assess the extent to which your network may be built on the principle of self-similarity. Write down the names of your closest contacts. In a column next to their name, write who introduced you to them. If you introduced yourself to them, make note of that, too.

Uzzi and Dunlap have found that if you introduced yourself to 65 percent or more of your contacts, then "your network may be too inbred"—whether by age, gender, sector, or role.

Two solutions to this problem are to try to develop relationships with brokers who can inject diversity into your network and to focus on shared activities. Emphasizing the power of shared activities, Uzzi and Dunlap write: "Shared activities also forge ties between diverse individuals by changing their usual patterns of interaction, letting them break out of their prescribed business roles of subordinate, relationship manager, aide, finance whiz, cognoscente, or president and stand out from the crowd." Shared activities, such as soccer leagues and bridge clubs, can quickly help move a network away from a tendency toward self-similarity while still fulfilling your psychological needs for familiarity and social identity.

Who Becomes a Convener, and
What Can We Learn from Them?

Age, gender, and race are poor predictors of who is likely to become a convener. Rather, a preference for convening seems to arise from subtler psychological predispositions deriving from a desire for safety and security.

Consider the following statements:

"I dislike questions that can be answered in many different ways."

"I think that having clear rules and order at work is essential for success."

"I think it is fun to change my plans at the last moment."

Agreement with the first two statements and disagreement with the last imply what psychologists call a need for closure—or a dislike of ambiguity. Research led by Francis Flynn of Stanford University, Ray Reagans, and Lucia Guillory found that people who prefer certainty have a view of the world in which networks are much more closed than they really are. The psychological need for closure likely reflects more general preferences for certainty and risk aversion. As we've seen, convening networks are safe.

One reason why people may want a safer and more secure network is that they are more sensitive to social rejection. In one study, Joseph Bayer, a professor at the Ohio State University, and his colleagues combined fMRI scans of the brain, psychological experiments on social exclusion, and analyses of Facebook networks to better understand the causes and consequences of convening.

In the study, participants engaged in a game of Cyberball.

During a round of Cyberball, three participants represented with avatars play a ball toss game. The game begins with everyone getting the ball in equal turns. But two avatars, who are presented as study participants but are really controlled by the computer program, start to exclude the participant. The game reliably induces social distress and feelings of exclusion.

Previous neuroscience research had found that certain regions of the brain light up when people experience social disconnection and social pain. Playing Cyberball activates these same regions. Professor Bayer wanted to know whether this differed for conveners, brokers, and expansionists. Bayer found that the social pain regions of conveners' brains were more active in response to social exclusion.

Sensitivity may also translate into more effective perspective taking. This ability is an important predictor of the number of strong ties in your network—another defining feature of convening networks. Can you intuit another person's feelings? What is it like to walk in their shoes?

To examine how perspective taking relates to the number of strong ties in someone's network, Professors James Stiller and Robin Dunbar asked sixty-nine participants to list those people they had contacted in the last month and whom they would turn to if they needed advice or support when facing a serious life problem. The participants were told seven stories involving complex social situations in which they had to deduce the thoughts and intentions of the characters.

Emma's dilemma is an example: "Emma worked in a greengrocer's. She wanted to persuade her boss to give her an increase in wages. So she asked her friend Jenny, who was still at school, what she should say to the boss. 'Tell him that the chemist near where you live wants you to work in his shop,' Jenny suggested. 'The boss won't want to lose you, so he will give you more money,' she said. So when Emma went to see her boss, that is what she told him. Her boss thought that Emma might be telling a lie, so he said he would think about it. Later he went to the chemist's shop near Emma's house and asked the chemist whether he had offered a job to Emma. The chemist said he hadn't offered Emma a job. The next day the boss told Emma that he wouldn't give her an increase in wages, and she could take the job at the chemist's instead."

After reading the scenarios, participants completed a questionnaire that gauged their ability to engage in perspective taking. The second level of questions asked what the participant thought the actor in the story thought. For instance, what did Emma want? Third-level perspective-taking questions asked what the actor thought another actor thought. Fourth-order questions asked what the actor thought a second actor thought another actor was thinking. An example of a fourth-order question would be: Did Emma think that the boss believed that the chemist wanted her to work for him? Questions continued to increase in complexity through the ninth order, though most people were unable to go beyond the fifth level.

There was a strong correlation between higher-order perspective taking, which is a bit like thinking through several moves ahead in social chess, and the number of strong ties in a network.

The link between the number of strong ties in someone's network and their perspective-taking capacity is consistent with a growing body of work in social psychology establishing that perspective taking promotes interpersonal understanding and encourages compassionate behavior and empathy. It helps reduce interpersonal conflict by allowing people to anticipate the feelings and reactions of others. And it fortifies social bonds by enabling us to see more of ourselves in others, as well as more of others in ourselves.

Perspective taking is not just a cognitive exercise, and it certainly isn't a fixed ability. You can learn to see the world as others see it by seeing more of the world. This is true in both our personal relationships and our relationships at work.

During his time as the CEO of Virgin Mobile South Africa, Peter Boyd kept hearing complaints from the director of Virgin's call center about employees repeatedly being late for the eight A.M. shift. After enough complaints, Peter decided to try to figure out what was going on. As he recalled, "What had I learned from the past? That you try to walk in someone else's shoes. You can't do that, but you can walk alongside them."

Rather than simply walking with them, he decided to commute home with them. Most of the call center employees lived in the township of Soweto, which was roughly forty kilometers from Virgin's office in swanky Sandton. There is no public transportation between Sandton and Soweto. On a Friday afternoon, Peter packed into a white Toyota van with a handful of men and women from the call center and passed his money forward to the driver. Two and a half hectic hours later, they finally made it to Soweto. The interchange in the central business district where they transferred vans was chaotic, almost to the point of physical aggression. Queues for the vans looked nothing like a normal taxi line. If a queue filled up, you had to pick a new line and hope this van wouldn't fill before you got on. It was completely unpredictable and emotionally exhausting. There was a huge margin for error in the grueling commute. It wasn't surprising someone would occasionally be fifteen minutes late.

The experience not only allowed Peter to understand a key managerial issue but also deepened his bond with his employees. They invited him out dancing with them that evening. Peter reflected, "That power of walking next to somebody is hopefully a humble power and one that is incredibly useful . . . Your willingness to give something of yourself, to open up, and say I want to understand and then be understood is incredibly powerful as a manager."

Perspective taking is a potent way to deepen social connections through greater insight into others. Self-disclosure also helps strengthen relationships by allowing others to see aspects of yourself that you usually keep hidden. The power of self-disclosure became wildly popular in early 2015, when *The New York Times* posted an article entitled "To Fall in Love with Anyone, Do This."

The article went viral, and within days potential romantic partners all over New York could be overheard asking each other a series of thirty-six increasingly personal questions that were the focus of the article:

3) Before making a telephone call, do you ever rehearse what you are going to say? Why?

13) If a crystal ball could tell you the truth about yourself, your life, the future, or anything else, what would you want to know?

36) Share a personal problem and ask your partner's advice on how he or she might handle it. Also, ask your partner

to reflect back to you how you seem to be feeling about the problem you have chosen.

After completing the thirty-six questions, Mandy Len Catron, the author of the article, and her partner decided to gaze into each other's eyes for four minutes for good measure. They fell in love. So also did two participants in the original lab study conducted by Dr. Arthur Aron.

The reliability of the exercise in producing lasting love is debatable. But the study did demonstrate that self-disclosure leads to interpersonal closeness. Of the fifty pairs in the experiment, those who completed the thirty-six questions reported significantly higher levels of closeness than pairs in the control group who engaged in small talk. "One key pattern associated with the development of a close relationship among peers is sustained, escalating, reciprocal, personalistic self-disclosure," according to the study.

Revealing your values, goals, beliefs, past mistakes, and fears can accelerate deeper feelings of intimacy. A meta-analysis that brought together the results from more than ninety separate studies found that self-disclosure reliably leads to connection. And the effect is causal—we are liked more when we share more of ourselves. It is not just that we reveal more to people when they like us.

But self-disclosure can also backfire. More than three out of five workers say they have a colleague who overshares at least once a week, according to responses from 514 professionals to a questionnaire conducted by SurveyMonkey Audience.

Amelia Blanquera was once the victim of an office oversharer. He would stop by her desk incessantly to complain about his nonexistent love life, grouse about his family, and describe in detail new yoga practices he was trying. She wore headphones and moved desks to try to get away. When he whipped out a book on tantric yoga, she pushed back. "He needed a therapist or a best friend or a companion, which ultimately he got." Just not from her.

Where is the line between positive self-disclosure and over-sharing? Disclosure has a more positive effect when it occurs in an ongoing relationship or is happening between cross-sex pairs. Revealing deeper truths about oneself is more likely to produce a sense of closeness than just disclosing a greater volume of information. Finally, and critically, interpersonal intimacy is greatest when disclosures are reciprocal. There needs to be turn-taking and a natural sense of deepening. Suddenly disclosing vulnerabilities about yourself to your boss probably isn't a great idea. This helps explain why the thirty-six questions work but Amelia's coworker was off-putting. When self-disclosure has depth and is reciprocal, it can quickly deepen the strength of our attachments. Too much disclosure to too many people can cost you your friends, and sometimes even your job.

Convening Cool

Anna Wintour has the Met Gala. Jeff Sonnenfeld hosts CEO summits. Linnea van Wagenen has her monthly lunches. By simply creating social events in which friends have the opportunity to become friends, one can become more of a convener. Part of what makes a convener is the depth and strength of their ties.

Perspective taking and self-disclosure create depth. The other hallmark is the fact that all conveners' friends are friends. Cliques are created by repeatedly bringing people together. Particularly for people who have a high sensitivity to social exclusion or anxiety, convening can be a powerful network building tool. But it can also be a divisive one. As Wintour put it, "On the whole, people who say demeaning things about our world, I think that's usually because they feel in some ways excluded or not part of the cool group, so as a result they just mock it."

Whether composed of cool kids, class clowns, or colleagues, the cliques of conveners have unparalleled trust and resilience. Conveners also are extraordinarily good at transmitting and receiving complex information because they have a high bandwidth and lots of redundancy in their networks. The downside is that they generally have little diversity. The information within cohesive networks often lacks novelty. Within convening networks, disagreement rarely surfaces and new ideas aren't readily flowing in. Many people live in an echo chamber of some sort, but conveners are at higher risk of having a louder echo chamber. This trade-off—the diversity-bandwidth trade-off—is at the heart of social networks. Conveners favor bandwidth and redundancy. Brokers are hot for diversity.

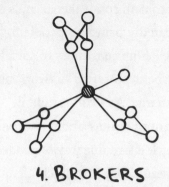

4. BROKERS

Foam margaritas overflowing from cubes of snow, liquid peas swirling like magic ink before congealing into solid ravioli, paella made from Rice Krispies. The mastermind behind these dishes, Ferran Adrià, has been called "the best cook on the planet" by French chef Joël Robuchon. He is one of the pioneers of molecular gastronomy and made surprise a hallmark taste. Willy Wonka and Salvador Dalí are frequent comparators.

The emotion and enchantment that transpired at Adrià's El Bulli helped it garner three Michelin stars and the coveted title of the best restaurant in the world a record five times. But El Bulli wasn't just a restaurant. It was an innovative madhouse full of delight, where soup becomes solid and food frequently explodes.

Ferran's ability to revolutionize cuisine is all the more impressive given how mundane food can be. We ingest it daily. Renowned chef and TV personality Anthony Bourdain described the feat, stating: "People say that when you are talking about cooking, you are talking about cuisine, that there is nothing new under the sun. That you can't reinvent the wheel, that you basically are reinventing the same thing over, and over, and over. Maybe adding a spoke here and there . . . but when you mention Ferran Adrià and what he is doing at his restaurant El Bulli, people tend to get confused."

Confusion and contrasts are part of Adrià's genius. He brings together hot and cold, soft and crunchy, solids and liquids, the familiar and surprising. In doing so, he tries to invoke what he refers to as the "sixth sense"—an introduction of irony, humor, and nostalgia into cuisine. Much of Ferran Adrià's brilliance comes from something quite simple—brokering. Bringing together concepts, ideas, and people from worlds that are normally far apart.

In Adrià's workshop, which was once a Gothic-era palace, are backlit displays of bottles; computers; notebooks filled with sketches, photographs, and diagrams; strange-looking equipment; and unusual vessels. There is surprisingly little food. As the equipment evinces, much of Adrià's genius can be boiled down to the application of chemistry to food.

Brokerage and recombination are at the core of innovation. Consider the printing press. A driving force behind the Scientific Revolution and Protestant Reformation, Johann Gutenberg's creation was just the combination of a coin punch and a wine press. Countless other innovations—from the Model T and hundreds of patents filed by Thomas Edison's group at Menlo Park to the discovery and understanding of DNA—have arisen from brokerage.

But Ferran's ability to broker, similar to that of Edison and many of his predecessors, required a diverse network of specialists with deep expertise. Describing the importance of his team,

Adrià emphasized, "One of the very important things is the team. Normally the chef is the center of the universe in the kitchen. I might be the media star . . . but they are part of the history of El Bulli. They participate in the creativity in the same level as [I do] . . . This is the big and great difference between El Bulli and other creative restaurants. They never say 'I.' 'I did.' 'I made.' It's 'we' . . . It's the team."

Adrià's team is as unusual as his workshop. There are the heads of the salty and sweet worlds. His brother Albert, Swiss industrial designer Luki Huber, organic chemist Pere Castells, partner Oriol Castro. In more recent human recombinations, he has delighted in bringing together a butcher, a scientist from NASA, and a Nobel Prize–winning economist.

Describing the logic of brokering, Adrià reflected, "One shouldn't speak only to other chefs; inbreeding is no good . . . It's also very important to be connected to other disciplines: the world of art, of design, of science, of history. When an architect designs a building, he has to work with engineers and people in new technologies. It's the same in cooking. We need experts in other fields. We turn to science, for example, to explain the 'why' of things."

Insular Islands

Brokerage is valuable because it is rare. People tend to be sealed off in dense convening clusters—their own little worlds. Chemists know other chemists. Chefs know other chefs. But it is relatively unusual for a chemist to work with a chef.

To understand why brokerage is rare, imagine entering a new social situation, perhaps starting college. Who do you think is likely to become your friend?

By far the strongest determinant of whether you are likely to interact with someone is whether you already have a close friend in common. A study of millions of emails sent by more than 20,000 university students found that having a strong tie in common more than doubled the chance that two people would interact. Having a close tie in common trumped being in the same class, being the same age, and having three mutual acquaintances as the strongest predictor of tie formation.

If we think of social structures as equivalent to the elements in the periodic table, this tendency for a friend of a friend to become a friend, which is known as *triadic closure*, has the elemental importance of oxygen. Just as oxygen makes life possible, triads make social life possible. The triad, a party of three, is the foundation of social structure. Only when you have a party of three does it become possible to form alliances, create a community, and engage in the dark art of social exclusion.

Imagine your network as a set of possible triangles. Take any two friends. Let's call the pair in the first draw from your network Stephen and Maya. If Stephen and Maya know each other, then the triangle created by you, Maya, and Stephen would be closed. If you repeated this for all possible pairs of friends in your network, you would have a sense of how much triadic closure there is in your network.

Since the celebrated sociologist Georg Simmel first introduced the idea of triadic closure more than a hundred years ago, studies of a variety of network types, such as core discussion groups,

Facebook networks, email exchanges, and scientific collaborations, have found that more than half of these triangles are closed. Our friends tend to be friends.

The tendency toward closure is partially created by circumstance. If you are friends with Stephen and Maya and see each of them frequently, chances are the two will meet—perhaps at a party you throw, a birthday, or a barbecue. They'll also probably meet on more than one occasion, increasing the likelihood of developing their own relationship. In cases when you have strong ties to both, triadic closure is particularly likely. The same doesn't hold for weak ties and acquaintances.

Another factor at play is a need for psychological balance. This has been described by the adages that a "friend of a friend is a friend" and "an enemy of an enemy is my friend." When this isn't the case, relationships become unstable. If two of our friends don't like each other, it's awkward. Someone becomes the third wheel. We're likely to either try to help them smooth things over or stop being friends with one of them.

Unsurprisingly, this tendency toward closure becomes stronger with social similarity. The same is true if your friends are from the same realm of your social life. The likelihood that your friends are also friends is 4 times higher if you all are coworkers than if you don't work together, 3.5 times greater if they are neighbors than if they are not, 52 percent higher if they are of the same race, 45 percent higher if they have the same religion, and 35 percent higher if they have similar levels of education.

Triadic closure creates a social world composed largely of islands of similar people. It creates conveners. In similar and familiar groups, we tend to have the same conversations (albeit with slight variations) over and over again. New information and ideas are rarely introduced. Instead, people tend to converge on the same opinions and views. They are reluctant to voice disagreement or question assumptions. These convening islands become echo chambers that inhibit creativity and innovation. But not everyone is stuck on an island. Frequently people will float between two or three. Brokers are the bridges between islands.

The Science of Creativity

Scientists, like most humans, tend to collaborate with the same people again and again. Multiple studies analyzing more than 6 million publications found high rates of triadic closure among researchers. In physics and neuroscience, more than half of the collaborative triangles are closed.

When Richard Freeman, an economist at Harvard, took a look at scientific labs, he noticed that they also seemed to be homogenous islands. Labs appeared to be disproportionately composed of people with similar ethnic backgrounds.

Richard and his collaborator, Wei Huang, analyzed 2.5 million research articles and found Richard's observation was accurate. There was significant homophily in research teams. Authors with European surnames tended to work with other authors with European surnames. Scientists with Korean surnames tended to have collaborators who also had Korean surnames. This pattern held for nine ethnic groups, and the effects were quite large. For seven of the nine ethnic groups, co-ethnic collaborations were more than twice as likely as what would be expected by chance.

But Freeman and Huang found that papers written by diverse teams were more likely to produce novel and important insights. They appeared in more esteemed scientific journals and were more likely to be referenced by other scientists.

More diverse teams are thought to be more creative because they provide groups with access to a broader range of information and perspectives. But when scholars from Columbia University, MIT, and Carnegie Mellon University analyzed 1,518 project teams, they found that the networks, not the demographics of the people in them, really matter for performance.

Brokers' networks tend to be more diverse and more creative because they span what University of Chicago sociologist Ron Burt calls *structural holes*. Instead of focusing on the islands and what type of people are on them, Burt argued, we need to pay attention to who creates the connections between them. The spaces between groups are what he calls structural holes.

In study after study examining the networks of mid-level managers and executives in industries from electronics to financial services, employees who bridge structural holes are more likely to receive positive outcomes such as favorable job evaluations, raises, larger bonuses, and early promotions.

To understand why the brokers were successful, Burt studied the networks of 673 managers in the supply chain at a large electronics firm. He mapped managers' networks by asking them whom they frequently discussed supply chain issues with. He collected data on salary, promotions, and evaluations. Finally, he asked managers to write down suggestions about how to improve the supply chain and had senior executives evaluate the ideas.

The best ideas came from managers occupying structural holes. The early promotions and better salaries they received were a result of their creativity. As Burt reflected, "The usual image of creativity is that it's some sort of genetic gift, some heroic act. But creativity is an import-export game. It's not a creation game." Since brokers sit at the intersection of multiple social worlds, they are exposed to novel ideas and perspectives. This allows them to excel at importing, exporting, and recombining ideas.

The link between brokerage and idea generation is one of the most robust findings in network science. Burt's discovery has been replicated in dozens of settings ranging from patent filings among inventors to product development at the renowned design firm IDEO. An analysis of the patents of more than 35,000 inventors found that collaborative brokerage was instrumental in innovation. When studying the firm IDEO, which helped develop Apple's first mouse and redesign baby food, Andrew Hargadon and Bob Sutton found that technology brokering was at the heart of the firm's innovative success. The genius of IDEO was creating "new products that are original combinations of existing knowledge from disparate industries."

Despite the value that can arise from brokerage, most people don't do it, largely because they are myopically focused on their own little island. "Often people are like sheep eating grass," according to Burt. "They're so focused on what's right in front of them, they don't look for the whole."

Edges

When Yo-Yo Ma, an iconic classical musician, looked around, he noticed that "the most interesting things happen at the edge. The intersections there can reveal unexpected connections." Within ecology, this is known as the *edge effect*. Where the edges of two ecosystems meet, there is the greatest biodiversity.

Yo-Yo Ma's human-scale experiment with the edge effect is known as the Silk Road Ensemble. The musical collective brings together everything from the Chinese pi-pa, Korean drums, the Persian kamancheh, and folk vocals from Azerbaijan. It's the musical equivalent of the diverse labs Freeman and Huang studied. And the experiment has been extraordinarily successful. They won a Grammy for their album *Sing Me Home.*

But Silk Road doesn't have a home. It is a journey. As the Galician bagpipe player Cristina Pato said, "In Silk Road, you also have to keep going and meeting new strangers, meeting new communities, meeting communities of people that you have never imagined of working with."

Unlike what happens at the edges of ecosystems, where biodiversity naturally emerges, successful brokers have to work to actively create connections. The tendency toward triadic closure makes brokerage positions inherently unstable. Silk Road is able to continually broker and innovate by appearing in various configurations with an ever-changing cast of members.

Some brokers—like Ferran Adrià and Yo-Yo Ma—purposefully create their positions. Like Yo-Yo Ma, Ferran Adrià worked to constantly generate brokerage opportunities. As Adrià wrote,

"We were very aware of the necessity to avoid falling into monotony. For this reason, we constantly changed the timetables, calendars, and the people on our team." Without such dedication, the structural holes they created would likely close.

Others become brokers by taking atypical career paths instead of focusing on edges. Within many organizations, there is a fairly conventional progression by which careers unfold. Lawyers move from associate to partner to managing partner. Investment bankers try to move through the ranks from analyst to associate to vice president to director to managing director. Although the sequence may not be as straightforward in other industries, some paths are more well-worn than others.

When careers wander, according to research by Adam Kleinbaum at Dartmouth's Tuck School of Business, professionals are more likely to be brokers. Take two employees described by Kleinbaum, Kellie and Sheryl, who worked at a large IT firm with the pseudonym "BigCo."

Kellie has spent nearly twenty years at BigCo. She works in middle management as a consultant in Louisiana. Over time, her work has become slightly more specialized, with an increased focus on serving clients in financial services. At the beginning of Kleinbaum's study, Sheryl's position in BigCo was similar to Kellie's. She had also been with BigCo for more than twenty years and was a similarly ranked consultant. But in 2002, their paths deviated. Sheryl moved into an executive administrative role in the technology consulting division. She was there for a year before moving into a marketing role in the same division. In 2006, she moved to company headquarters to work in the supply chain group.

Using networks created from emails exchanged among 30,328 employees and career histories constructed from human resources records, Kleinbaum found that employees like Sheryl were more likely to be brokers. Compared with her peers, Kellie (who remained in an increasingly specialized consulting role) ranked in the bottom 6th percentile of brokerage. Sheryl was in the 94th percentile of brokerage. Kleinbaum dubbed people with career histories like Sheryl's "organizational misfits." One potential problem with this type of research is that the type of person who is more likely to be an organizational misfit might also be more likely to become a broker. Even after Kleinbaum took this into account by comparing people with similar previous career trajectories, salaries, job functions, office locations, and so forth, misfits were still more likely to be brokers. The diverse contacts misfits make as they journey through uncharted organizational waters put them in an ideal position to broker.

But just because someone is in a position to broker doesn't mean he or she can do it well. You could put a lot of people in a room with a Persian kamancheh player and a cellist and they might create nothing but cacophony. So what makes a good broker?

Code-Switching

Brokers are adaptable translators. Can you blend in anywhere? Do you adapt what you say or change what you wear depending on where you are? Are you the friend that thrives at the random/assorted table at weddings or gets asked to tag along to potentially awkward fundraisers because your friends know that you can pretty much fit in anywhere? Would throwing a party and inviting all your friends be a potential invitation to disaster because they all know a slightly different version of you?

Or are you pretty much the same regardless of who and where you happen to find yourself? You say what you think and you think what you say.

Depending on your answer, you are what psychologists would classify as either a high or low self-monitor. According to Mark Snyder, a professor of psychology at the University of Minnesota who created a scale to distinguish between high and low self-monitors, "Self-monitoring gets at a fundamental difference between people, on whether your view of how to handle social situations is to fit yourself to the context and to play a role versus whether you view it as finding a way to do what you want, express who you are, show other people your true inner self."

High self-monitors are keenly aware of the image they are projecting to others. According to Snyder's research, which over the course of decades has involved tens of thousands of participants, high self-monitors find it easy to imitate others, can make "impromptu speeches" on topics they know little or nothing about, often defer to friends for choices about music and movies, and laugh a little harder when watching a movie with friends than when alone.

Consider the following situation posed by Snyder: It's a beautiful Sunday afternoon in September and you're looking for a partner for a round of tennis. Let's further imagine that you have a decent tennis game. "Let's say you have one friend who is a really good tennis player, but is actually not your favorite person—not the most likable person you know . . . And you have another person who is really likable—you share a lot in common with them—but they're not really a great tennis player," offered Snyder. Your likable friend is hilarious but may unintentionally garner some laughs for his enthusiastic but somewhat wild playing style. But you could count on the good player to behave appropriately and potentially improve your game. Whom would you invite to join you?

"The high self-monitor plays tennis with the person who's great at tennis, even if they're not the most likable," according to Snyder. "The low self-monitor plays tennis with the person who they just enjoy their company, even if they're not the best at that activity."

High self-monitors are keenly attuned to situational cues and social norms. When traveling, they quickly pick up that hugging in public is frowned upon in Qatar. One kiss is culturally appropriate in Colombia, two in Italy, and three in Slovenia. And they rarely face the awkwardness of inappropriately leaning in for an extra kiss.

Suppose you are trying to discern whether someone else fits into this category. High self-monitors often speak first in conversations and break silences. They use humor to lighten the mood, willingly reciprocate self-disclosures, and are less judgmental.

High self-monitors make great brokers. Of all of the personality characteristics that have been investigated as predictors of what position in a network someone will occupy, the relationship between high self-monitors and brokers is the most robust.

If someone wants to become a better broker, is it possible to learn to behave more like a high self-monitor? Professor Snyder's first response is that most people will not want to. They see their way of being as better. High self-monitors perceive their behavior as being more attuned, flexible, and adaptable. Low self-monitors, on the other hand, cringe at this approach and perceive it as inauthentic or fake.

When high self-monitors do it well, their behavior helps them broker. But if their behavior comes across as contrived, they risk being seen as doing "whatever it takes to enhance their social appearance in a given situation." Depending on the situation and interpretation, high self-monitors can either be seen as trying to get along or attempting to get ahead. It's the latter that creates problems.

Ultimately, high and low self-monitors have different conceptions of the self. Chameleonlike high self-monitors don't have a unified sense of self. They see themselves through the lenses of the roles they play—"I am a father, I am a media analyst, I am a host." Low self-monitors are more likely to have a unified and essentialist vision of themselves. They believe there is one true self. Neither way is right or wrong. But the different conceptions of self that high and low self-monitors have make it difficult to fundamentally change their approach. Anyone can become better at reading social cues and situations, but not everyone is willing to change.

Hongseok Oh and Martin Kilduff, researchers currently based at Yonsei University and University College London, who were instrumental in uncovering the relationship between brokerage and self-monitoring, offer another piece of advice: "There is a route to brokerage . . . that does not involve attempting to alter their characteristic dispositions: They can develop many acquaintances."

The Power Paradox

While high self-monitors are more likely to be effective brokers, people in power are more likely to think that they can broker. Power, which psychologists often define as having greater control over valued resources in a relationship, has a paradoxical effect on brokerage. Power makes it more difficult to identify brokerage opportunities, but simultaneously increases people's willingness to broker. It makes people willing to act with an inaccurate map.

Powerful people tend to feel more psychologically distant from others. When people are primed to feel less powerful, they tend to be more empathic and sensitive to others' emotions.

Power also promotes abstract thinking. These propensities, which Pamela Smith and Yaacov Trope documented in a series of studies, lead powerful people to think about their friends and colleagues in a more removed and heuristic fashion. For instance, one mid-level manager described her feelings about her new position to the researchers, stating: "It's like I have to think differently, to use a different part of my brain, now that I'm a supervisor . . . I'm thinking about the agency's five-year plan, not just what I need to do to get through the week. But I feel so removed from what's going on in the office." In contrast, people who feel less empowered tend to pay more attention to relationships and are more accurate in their perceptions of social ties.

In general, people are extraordinarily inaccurate when it comes to perceiving their networks. Overestimating triadic closure is one of the most common biases people default to when guessing what networks look like. They assume that if two people are friends, their friends are also going to be friends. This predisposition to see triadic closure in networks makes people miss brokerage opportunities.

While most people are pretty inaccurate when it comes to identifying opportunities to broker, powerful people are the worst. In a study of more than 160 employees at a media firm led by researchers at University College London, employees were asked to respond to a series of items on a Sense of Power scale. The items included measures of high power, such as "I can get them to listen to what I say," as well as statements like "Even when I try, I am not able to get my way," meant to capture low power. Blaine Landis and his colleagues then mapped the network of the organization, which allowed them to know where opportunities for brokerage really existed. They then compared this map to employees' perceptions of the network. The more powerful employees perceived themselves to be, the less likely they were to see brokerage opportunities. This effect held in a second experiment in which 330 participants were randomly assigned to either a high-or a low-power role and then were asked to identify brokerage opportunities on an imaginary network. Even when people were simply randomly assigned to a high power position, their brokerage perception was impaired. Power made people more likely to fill in social blanks where they actually existed, but it didn't make them more likely to engage in other errors in network perception. This suggests that the cognitive shortcuts people take when they are feeling powerful—using abstract reasoning rather than empathic social perception—blind them to brokerage opportunities. Perhaps this is the root of the folk wisdom that power corrupts.

Despite their impaired perception, when people were primed to feel powerful, they were more likely to try to control information regardless of whether or not people were actually disconnected. Imagine the following scenario: Intoxicated with a little bit of power, a newly appointed manager overhears from Naomi that the research division has finished testing a new product that looks incredibly promising. The manager immediately realizes the potential value of the product to Kevin. Rather than putting Kevin directly in contact with Naomi, he tries to describe the new product and mentions that he might be able to help him get an early account. But he bungles the new product's specs. And he doesn't realize that Kevin and Naomi frequently get together for coffee and have been talking about the product for months. He's left with egg on his face.

Even among parties who were already connected and therefore wouldn't benefit from brokerage, high-power individuals were almost 20 percent more likely than low-power individuals to try to control information. These misguided brokerage efforts not only consume unnecessary effort but can also create reputational risks. Trying to act as an intermediary between people who don't need it can come across as nothing but selfish obstruction.

Ferran Adrià keenly understood the potentially devastating

effects that power could have on brokerage opportunities He began a lecture on cooking and science at Harvard University by pulling out an orange. After acknowledging that everyone knows what an orange is, he asks a question: "What type of orange is this?" This deflates egos, since no one can identify it by visual inspection, even in rooms full of chefs. There are more than 2,500 types of citrus in the world.

Adrià explains that, "To know about citrus, probably you would have to live many lives. Probably it is impossible . . . It is impossible to know about everything." Adrià argues that you need "a lot of humility or you are dead." Without humility, you *are* dead, because "to create, you have to have the willingness and desire to be challenged—to be learning."

Power and Politics

The only citrus on the table when Anthony Bourdain and Barack Obama dined on noodles in a Hanoi hole-in-the-wall may have been lime in the sauce for Vietnamese bun cha. Bourdain captioned the photo he tweeted of their dinner together: "Low plastic stool, cheap but delicious noodles, cold Hanoi beer." According to *Rolling Stone,* "Obama and Bourdain appear to be the only Westerners in the frame, but they blend in effortlessly."

That ability to blend in effortlessly is a hallmark of high self-monitors. The combination of brokerage and adaptability is critical for political success. Barack Obama adapted a professorial air during fundraisers in New York, responded "Nah, we straight" when asked if he needed change at Ben's Chili Bowl, and boogied on *The Ellen DeGeneres Show* in front of a group of mostly white women. Bill Clinton—like Lyndon Baines Johnson before him—would adopt a southern drawl when visiting below the Mason-Dixon Line. In Taiwan and Canada, politicians change the language they speak depending on the audience. Politicians routinely get called out for code-switching—changing the way they talk to different audiences.

It's not just how they say it. It is also what they say. A field experiment conducted by researchers at the University of Southern California, Stanford Graduate School of Business, and University of California, Berkeley, found that U.S. senators tailor response letters to constituents depending on which side of an issue constituents supported in their original letter reaching out to the senator. Those senators who sent tailored responses were viewed more favorably, particularly by those who disagreed with their position.

The political power of being able to tailor messages and messaging to different audiences isn't something new. Studies examining political coups from Cosimo de' Medici's rise to power during the birth of the Renaissance state to the successful implementation of reforms within the UK's National Health Service repeatedly find that brokers make great change agents because their actions and words are interpreted differently by audiences with different agendas.

The Medici family were the precursors to modern-day politicians. Decades after Cosimo's rule ended, Machiavelli still held them in "awe—attributing both all good and all evil in recent Florentine history to Cosimo's deep and ruthless machinations." A well-known study of marriage, political, familial, and trade networks among Florentine elite families revealed that Cosimo de' Medici's power arose from an obfuscated brokerage position at the center of these overlapping networks. Cosimo hardly ever gave a public speech, and he did not hold formal office for a long period of time. Rather, his power came from his ability to use his brokerage position to apply the principle of *divide et impera* (Latin for divide and conquer) that Machiavelli would later write about. According to John Padgett, a professor at the University of Chicago, and Christopher Ansell, a professor at the University of California, Berkeley, who analyzed the Florentine networks, Cosimo's sphinxlike character was as critical as his network position for his ability to consolidate power and create the Renaissance state. Padgett and Ansell referred to this sphinxlike character as *multivocality,* or "the fact that single actions can be interpreted coherently from multiple perspectives simultaneously."

In its extreme form, if used without empathy or morality and for personal gain, this form of brokerage gives rise to the eponymous personality trait of Machiavellianism. A defining trait of Machiavellianism, for instance, is to "never tell anyone the real reason you did something unless it is useful to do so." But what about more benign forms of adaptation?

Because brokers sit at the intersection of non-overlapping social worlds, they can change what they are saying to different audiences without worrying about offending constituents who have a different world view. Obama could emphasize one aspect of a policy to the New York fundraising crowd while accentuating another on Ellen's show without worrying too much that the audiences would overlap and notice contradictions.

That tactic can work equally well closer to home. Kids frequently try it with their parents. And parents who successfully navigate their school's parent-teacher association (PTA) often deploy multivocality adeptly. In many ways, a school's PTA is the embodiment of local politics. And frequently the organization draws a disdain typically reserved for politicians. Even a super socially savvy mom lamented, "I have PTA PTSD." Terry Haward described her unsuccessful efforts to ingratiate herself with the PTA: "There was also a smugness, a closed-circle 'we're inside and you're not' attitude. They knew things that I would never know, and I couldn't tell if these were things I needed to know. They were the school's Power Moms, and they held that power close."

However, when I reached out to several of the heads of the PTA in the country's most successful school districts, the majority self-identified as brokers. The "Power Moms" may think they rule Haward's school, but that is because they largely live on their own island. When Jordan Rosenfeld confronted her stereotypes of the "Perfect Type A" and became involved in her local PTA, she "found a much wider array of parents than I expected: A mom who had to bring her groping toddler along, hair frayed at the edges in a shirt half-arranged from breastfeeding. A mom who was there on her lunch break from work at a local grocery store. A former schoolteacher who wanted to stay involved. These moms (and a few dads) were a lot more diverse than I had expected."

Diversity makes brokerage critical for successfully mobilizing and creating change—particularly when change is contentious.

Take a movement in a small town to implement what would seemingly be a straightforward improvement for high schoolers—

pushing back school start times. Far from being straightforward, it ignited a town-wide fight that has gone on for years. As Dr. Craig Canapari, a pediatric sleep specialist, described: "When I moved to town, I was shocked to see high schoolers getting on the bus at 6:20 A.M. on my block. As a sleep physician, I was aware of the overwhelming evidence which shows that early school start times cause harm to teenagers by resulting in chronic sleep deprivation. The American Academy of Pediatrics, the Centers for Disease Control, and many other organizations recommend that junior high and high school start times start no earlier than 8:30 A.M. . . . I brought my concerns to the local board of education, and they were very receptive to the information and expressed interest in making a change. This was five years ago, and we have yet to implement a meaningful change. The scientific evidence was so overwhelming I thought that this would be easy, but I was wrong."

Successfully navigating the political perils of the PTA requires the same political acumen as creating change in the workplace or getting a bill through Congress. Changing bell times is politically fraught because it is a personal issue for families. Some needed earlier start times to ensure they could get to work on time. And still others were against the change because it would mean they wouldn't get home from sports until late. Evidence alone doesn't create change.

In a town just sixty-five minutes to the south, the high school headmaster spoke to proponents of a later start time. He listened to the concerns of opponents. After acknowledging arguments on both sides, he made a case for small changes in a letter to the editor of the town newspaper. He did so even though it was not his "usual practice to express my perspective through the press on a topic currently under review." But after careful consideration, he thought it was time to try to publicly broker a compromise by making "commonsense adjustments that will allow us to benefit from the later start time and address some of the negative impacts of the change." Since he was not firmly entrenched in either camp, he could speak to both sides. He needed to appeal to parents whose kids' athletics were a priority, while addressing other parents' personal pain points. In the face of what had previously been seen as a zero-sum game, a compromise was reached.

Describing how she effectively brokered a potentially treacherous workplace change, a nurse in a study conducted by Julie Battilana and Tiziana Casciaro recounted how she tried to get support from hospital management. She "insisted that nurse-led discharge would help us reduce waiting times for patients, which was one of the key targets that the government had set. I then focused on nurses. I wanted them to understand how important it was to increase their voice in the hospital and to demonstrate how they could contribute to the organizational agenda. Once I had their full support, I turned to doctors." Expecting strong resistance, she argued the new discharge process would reduce their workload while putting them more in control of the time spent with patients. One by one, the nurse went to different factions with different appeals. When Battilana and Casciaro studied more than five dozen change initiatives implemented within the United Kingdom's National Health Service, the researchers from Harvard and the University of Toronto repeatedly found that brokers were more successful at implementing disruptive changes. They could use brokerage and message tailoring to their advantage.

Whether in the PTA, the workplace, or the realm of politics, brokers can effectively help move contentious change forward by tailoring their message, controlling who knows what, choosing the order in which they engage with consistencies, and carefully deciding when to bring different camps together or keep them apart. This isn't an option for conveners, whose connections are already connected and who are usually deeply embedded on a side.

Arbitrage or Cooperate?

Brokers are faced with a choice: do they bring together disconnected parties and make introductions, or do they play a game of arbitrage?

To distinguish between cooperative and arbitraging brokers, Giuseppe Soda, a professor at Bocconi School of Management, and his team, presented more than 460 employees in the human resources department of a large global consumer product company with the following scenario:

Consider the situation in which you have been appointed to accomplish *an important organizational task*. This task requires specific knowledge that you don't have, but two of your contacts (let's call them Mike and Jenny) do have. Mike and Jenny do not know each other, or, if they do, they don't usually work together;

however, thanks to your credibility, you are in a position to ask Mike and Jenny for help, and access their knowledge and expertise.

They then asked participants how they would approach the task. Would they (a) try to put Mike and Jenny in touch with each other and find a time they could all work together? Or would they (b) think that working with both Mike and Jenny would be inefficient? It would make more sense to just meet with them individually and combine their insights.

Option A is a cooperative approach. It was the approach favored by 85 percent of respondents. Option B is an arbitraging orientation and was preferred by 11.5 percent of respondents. The remainder preferred a middle ground.

Soda and his collaborators also collected information on employees' network positions, supervisors' evaluations of respondents' job performance, work experience, education, job rank, and the type of work the respondent did. Consistent with previous studies, brokers were found to have better job performance.

Arbitraging brokers—despite being in the majority—performed much better than cooperative brokers. Brokers with an arbitraging approach were 14 percent *more* likely to have above average job performance. Conversely, cooperating brokers were 16 percent *less* likely to have above average job performance. Arbitraging brokers control information flows, have the ability to exploit information gaps, and can distort information. Whether it is Cosimo de' Medici or PTA parents, brokering can be politically advantageous.

But it can also be morally perilous. This was foreshadowed by Ron Burt a quarter century before it was studied as he laid out the idea of structural holes—disconnects in who knows and talks to whom—writing: "The information benefits of structural holes might come to a passive player, but control benefits require an active hand in the distribution of information." An arbitraging broker is an "entrepreneur in the literal sense of the word—a person who generates profit from being between others."

While an arbitraging approach affords power and control benefits for *individual* brokers, cooperative approaches are more likely to produce innovations that benefit *the group*. When studying seventy-three innovations that arose during the five-year process of designing a new vehicle for a Detroit auto manufacturer, David Obstfeld found that people who don't feel the need to control information flows and simply like to cooperate instead were more likely to be involved in major product and process innovations. One employee described his intuitive understanding of cooperative brokering to his boss, Ed. He said, "Ed, I create these networks . . . That's half the battle. Half the battle is creating the networks. I've created the networks between functional specialists and my staff. I created the drivetrain and chassis [connection]." And these connections were critical to the successful design of the vehicle.

The potential to create value for everyone involved by cooperatively joining disconnected parties isn't new. Headhunters, agents, and matchmakers all exist to ideally create mutual benefit.

Marriage matchmakers existed in early Aztec civilizations and in ancient Greece and China. Even in an era in which getting a date can be as easy as swiping right, the market for matchmakers continues to grow. Matchmakers focus on finding the right person rather than on generating endless possibilities. They also provide quality assurance in a realm in which assessing whether someone is embellishing or outright lying can be difficult. Almost everyone who has dated online has discovered that their date is a little older or less attractive than their picture promises.

While cooperative brokerage can produce a happy marriage brimming with love—or at the very least benefit multiple parties—arbitraging brokers can infuriate people who feel manipulated or taken advantage of. Arbitraging brokers may not make good friends.

Tortured Brokers

Most of us have had to suffer an intolerable colleague or a frenemy. There are all sorts of reasons relationships hit rough patches. With colleagues, turf wars over resources or fundamental differences in approach can generate entrenched battles in the office. Incompetence can evoke indignation. Lives diverge. Jealousy can creep into friendships. But occasionally colleagues and even friends have a character flaw. Some people just seem like assholes.

Brokers are more likely to be pegged as assholes. When asked to name "people who make life difficult," a study of approximately seven hundred Chinese entrepreneurs found that difficult colleagues were disproportionately brokers. Ron Burt and his colleague Jar-Der Luo of Tsinghua University wondered why this was the case and looked into the reasons people cited for calling a colleague difficult. It tended to be factors like they "say bad things to stir up employees," "[they] secretly stir up trouble with the government," or they steal things. Comparatively rarely were factors related to competence cited. It was their duplicitous, conniving, and deceitful character that made brokers unlikable.

Due to their location in networks, brokers are at higher risk for misunderstandings and conflicts of interests than conveners or expansionists. But it is a particular type of broker—one that connects to a weaker tie (shown with a dotted line) in a convening network—that Burt and Luo found was particularly vulnerable to "character assassination." Within convening networks, negative sentiments about the broker's character tend to become amplified as sympathetic friends weigh in.

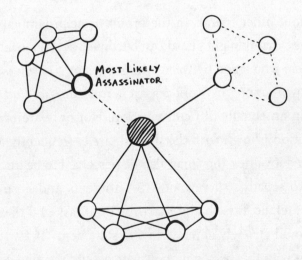

Consider the following example of a drunk night guard on the edge of a dense convening network, provided by Burt and Luo:

When the respondent tells his friends about the night guard who was drunk on the job when a major theft occurred, his friends share sympathetic stories about the irresponsibility of such employees. "I had an employee just like that. I fired him on the spot, but I'm still recovering from the damage done." The function of the stories is to display empathy, letting the respondent know he is not alone. Deepening their social support, friends in convening networks embellish the stories about such drunks, shading ambiguous behavior into malignant intent. Over time, the repeated stories create a shared feeling of having had more experience than has actually occurred, amplifying negative opinion of the drunk employee, justifying angry rhetoric deriding the employee's character.

Without other friends in the group to help dampen the dynamic, the drunk night guard can become a social pariah.

Brokers who stand between two groups of conveners, a position known among network researchers as *the ties that torture*, can be in an equally difficult position. Not only are brokers in this position (shown with the shaded circle) frequently tortured by divided loyalties, they may also be perceived to be uncaring.

In two separate surveys of MBA students and hospital employees, Stefano Tasselli and Martin Kilduff asked if the respondents would strongly agree with the statement "If I shared my problems with this person, I know (s)he would respond constructively and caringly," for each person in the student and employee network. Tortured brokers were thought to be devoid of empathy.

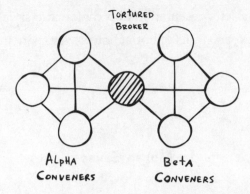

TORTURED
BROKER

ALPHA
CONVENERS

BETA
CONVENERS

The most untrustworthy of the tortured brokers were blirters. BLIRT is an acronym for Brief Loquaciousness and Interpersonal Responsiveness Test. It is a measure of how much of a filter someone has. Blirters agree with statements like "If I have something to say, I don't hesitate to say it" and "I always say what's on my mind." Generally speaking, blirters are perceived to be smarter, more likable, more attractive, and more interesting. While blirtatiousness can be a good thing, it creates problems for tortured brokers. Blirtatiousness, like convening networks, is an amplifier of human traits. Brokers are typically treated with suspicion due to their structural position, but it's worse if you are a blirter. Among tortured brokers, blirters at the hospital were around a full point lower than non-blirters on a seven-point trust scale. Blirters at the business school saw an even bigger impact. Blirters can't be trusted to act with discretion—and this is precisely the characteristic that brokers spanning cliques need.

Chameleonlike high self-monitors, on the other hand, face no trust penalty for being in a brokerage position. They are trusted even more than non-brokers, according to Tasselli and Kilduff.

Their flexible self-presentation and diplomatic style allow them to meet the expectations of both cliques they span and avoid distrust.

Mogao Caves

For brokers of all types—from investment bankers to online avatars in virtual games to marriage matchmakers—the rewards from brokerage have repeatedly been shown to be contingent on reputation. Sitting between two groups in a network makes someone vulnerable to being seen as being "two-faced." It isn't that brokers lack empathy or diplomacy. But their network position naturally presents them with a choice: to either cooperate or arbitrage.

Yo-Yo Ma's Silk Road is emblematic of cooperative brokerage. As Yo-Yo Ma described, "At Silk Road we build bridges. In the face of change and difference, we find ways to integrate and synthesize, to forge relationships, to create joy and meaning."

Jeffrey Beecher stands in a full-size replica of one of the Mogao cave temples, and the top of his double bass reaches the shoulder of an open-palmed Buddha flanked by two imaginary lions. The replica caves are adorned with thousands of colorful earth-toned Buddhas and bodhisattvas, many playing instruments. Fellow Silk Road member and tabla player Sandeep Das reflects on the bridging of religious traditions within the caves' imagery: "Of course, all these caves include so many things that I've literally grown up with. One of the major images in Cave 285 is Shiva and

Ganesh on one side, and Vishnu on another. To me the blurring of lines between what is Buddhism and what is Hinduism is so obvious. It's just amazing to see them all there—the same names, just looking different."

The original art-filled grottoes, also known as the Caves of the Thousand Buddhas, served as a central node on the Silk Road. As Yo-Yo Ma wrote of the Silk Road playing in replicas at the Getty Center, "The murals and sculptures owe their existence to people who followed the best human instincts: openness to the unknown and an inclination to meet, connect, and create—the values that can shape a world guided not by fear but by empathy and commitment to the results of radical collaboration." The murals owe their existence to cooperative brokers.

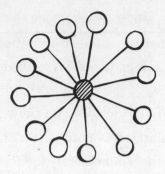

5. Expansionists

After a spectacularly unsuccessful first, and last, day of work at Los Padrinos Juvenile Hall, Shep Gordon pulled into a modest and off-the-beaten-track hotel in Los Angeles. The Landmark Motor Hotel was, unbeknownst to Shep, a regular stop for rock stars looking for privacy in Los Angeles. A Jewish kid from Long Island who "never had a friend over" growing up, Shep took to hanging around the hotel pool with fellow residents Jimi Hendrix, Janis Joplin, and Jim Morrison.

He got his start when Jimi Hendrix asked him, "What's your real job?" (He didn't have one.) "You Jewish?" According to Shep, he "had no idea that would be the luckiest moment of my life." Hendrix told him, "You're Jewish, you should be a manager."

Shock rocker Alice Cooper became Shep's first client. He also managed everyone from Groucho Marx, Blondie, and Kenny Loggins to Luther Vandross. Sylvester Stallone, Tom Arnold,

Willie Nelson, Mike Myers, and the Dalai Lama were close friends and associates. He shared custody of a cat with Cary Grant.

Emeril Lagasse, another client, credited him with inventing the celebrity chef. As TV personality and renowned chef Anthony Bourdain said, "Shep has been there at so many titanically significant moments in cultural history (and he's been in many cases, responsible for them): the birth of theatrical shock rock, the demise of the exploitative 'chitlin' circuit,' the celebrity chef phenomenon, some really great indie films, and so much more. There's no one like him. He knows everything and everybody. He can walk through walls. And he's the most loved guy I've ever known."

Part of Shep's success has been a deep understanding of the dynamics of popularity. He understands that popularity is a self-fulfilling prophecy. He frequently hired photographers with no film in their cameras to follow clients around relentlessly snapping shots. He also understands the value of creating a buzzworthy spectacle. When trying to launch Alice Cooper's career, Shep had him booked to play Wembley Arena—a venue with more than 10,000 seats. Just days before the show, they "had only sold fifty tickets." With little time and no budget for traditional marketing, Shep needed media coverage. He needed to get people talking. What people tended to talk about in London at the time was traffic. So Shep hired a truck to display a billboard with a photo of Alice naked except for a snake wrapped around his genitals. He then arranged for it to "accidentally" break down in Piccadilly Circus, a main intersection in London. The press called the moment a "landmark in the decline of the British empire," the show sold out, and Alice's song "School's Out" went to number one in England and then around the world.

Shenanigans involving snakes are only a part of what has made Shep so successful. Reflecting on his career, Shep "looked for some common threads linking the events in my apparently accidental life. One of the things people seem to respond most strongly to . . . [is] that I've managed to become successful in the cutthroat worlds of the music and movie businesses while staying a nice guy, and apparently a happy one. It's not something we are used to seeing." For Shep, that's been possible because he practices "compassionate business." He tries to ensure that deals make everyone better off. He looks for win-wins. Part of that philosophy is his coupon system. "When somebody does me a favor, I feel I am obligated to return that favor. I say they have a coupon with me. They can redeem that coupon anytime, in any way, and I will honor it. That's win-win too."

Shep's principles and personality have garnered him the nickname Supermensch. Mike Myers, his good friend, the *Wayne's World* star, and the producer of a laudatory documentary about Shep, put it simply: "Shep Gordon is the nicest person I've ever met—hands down."

Despite his famous friends, after an illness left him with a slim chance of survival, it was his longtime assistant who sat vigil. "After the surgery, I would just sit by the bed and hold his hand," recalled Nancy Meola. "But he finally looked up and I could see in the fogginess he was looking for someone else to be there . . . I felt really bad for him that the person sitting there was me, his paid assistant. Going through that experience you would want it to be your life partner, and there it was me. And I felt really, really lonely for him."

Mere Mortals and Super Connectors

Shep is a force, an inspiration. He embodies many of expansionists' greatest qualities: generosity, an uncanny ability to read others, and social competence. He is both popular and likable. When those two traits come together, they are potent. But you don't need one to have the other.

While most mortals have networks that conform to Dunbar's number, a cognitive limit on the number of relationships we can maintain, a few outliers are super connectors. Shep is one of those people.

Expansionists' power comes from knowing many times more people than the average person. The average person knows approximately 600 people. Super connectors can know 6,000 or more. Their unimaginably large networks roughly follow a power-law distribution. This means that while most people know hundreds of others, there is a long tail to the distribution where a small percentage of individuals know orders of magnitude more.

Many of the phenomena in the world we are familiar with follow a bell-curve distribution. Height, for example: most of us know a few people who are under five feet and one or two who are over six and a half feet. But most of the people we encounter are in the range of five and a half feet to six feet tall, right in the middle of the distribution. If height followed a power law, at least one person on the planet would be more than 8,000 feet tall.

Popularity follows a similar distribution. It is hard to know how many people have heard of Barack Obama, but he has almost 108 million Twitter followers. Eight sheep even recognize his face. In an era that predated social media, Franklin D. Roosevelt amassed more than 22,500 acquaintances. And while social media makes it much easier to collect acquaintances and followers than it was in FDR's era, only 1 percent of LinkedIn users have more than 10,000 connections. These extreme outliers—at the very tail of the distribution of network size—are the social equivalent of the 8,000-foot-tall person.

Expansionists live on the tail end of the distribution of network size. This position is associated with popularity, status, and power. Expansionists can inspire.

Popularity comes with a whole host of perks. Popular teens are better paid than socially excluded peers almost forty years after high school ends. A study of 4,330 men who graduated from Wisconsin high schools in 1957 found that men who were more frequently nominated as friends by their peers had higher wages decades later. And the effects can't be explained by IQ or social background. Moving from the bottom 20th percentile in popularity to the top 80th percentile would have yielded a 10 percent increase in earnings.

Even as adults, popularity comes with privilege. At the office, popular adults perform better and are more successful. A meta-analysis of more than 130 studies confirmed that the larger the network someone has, the more rewards they get from work. Expansionists also have a more pleasant experience at the office.

Popular employees—not just those who are liked more—are more likely to get help and are more welcomed. They are less likely to be belittled, treated rudely, or ignored.

In certain domains—such as public relations, marketing, or entertainment—having a large network isn't just nice. It can be essential.

Good Luck, Good Looks, and Good Genes

Is there something different about expansionists that put them on a path to develop inordinately large networks? Was there something predestined about Shep Gordon? Perhaps it was his generosity? His likability? Common sense suggests that personality and good looks probably play a role. But maybe it is simply chance?

It isn't possible for scientists to randomly assign popularity advantages when kids enter school or to give people initial boosts in their career to see whether luck can make someone popular. Princeton sociologist and network scientist Matthew Salganik conducted an online experiment with songs by unknown artists to see whether he could make *something* popular.

Matt and his colleague Duncan Watts, who's now at the University of Pennsylvania, asked more than 12,000 participants to listen to songs and download the ones they were interested in. For several weeks, they allowed the preferred song ranking to emerge naturally and provided the ordered list to participants.

They then presented the same list to new participants but reversed the order. The most popular song, "She Said," became the least popular song. The least popular song, "Florence," was presented to new participants as having the most downloads. For the majority of songs, this false ranking of the popularity of the songs continued. It became a self-fulfilling prophecy. Telling people that songs were popular made the songs popular. It's likely the same is true for people.

Both songs and people have the peculiarity that there are huge disparities in popularity.

These disparities are created by a phenomenon known as the Matthew effect. The name arises from Matthew 25:29 (KJV): "For unto every one that hath shall be given, and he shall have abundance: but from him that hath not shall be taken away even that which he hath." Or more colloquially, the rich get richer (and the poor get poorer). As its appearance in the Bible evinces, people have intuitively recognized the cumulative advantage process underlying the Matthew effect for millennia.

The renowned sociologist Robert Merton gave the phenomenon its name in the 1960s. But it has been independently identified by scientists in a range of fields from statistics to political science. British statistician Udny Yule discovered it in 1925. The American social scientist Herbert Simon noticed it in 1955. The British scientometrician Derek Price rediscovered it under a different name again in 1976. But it was the physicists Albert-László Barabási and Réka Albert who explained why we observe such extreme disparities in network popularity.

The Barabási-Albert model shows that if one person in a network has twice as many connections as another person, then they are twice as likely to be befriended by someone new entering the network. Put simply, the more connections you have, the easier it is to grow your network.

This process of preferential attachment means that even small early differences in popularity can generate large inequalities in subsequent fame. This is where Shep Gordon's publicity genius comes into play. His stunts, which frequently relied on using the fame of friends to make new clients famous, would set off cascades of visibility and popularity for his clients.

Getting a large network going is difficult. But after a certain point, expanding your network is pretty much effortless. The work becomes figuring out how to manage it, not grow it.

When people try to understand success, they frequently underestimate the role luck plays. Instead, they tend to look back on an outcome and attribute it to characteristics that seem obvious in retrospect. It is a great song, obviously destined to be a hit. Of course she won—she is clearly more talented. Naturally he has a ton of friends—he is incredibly charming. She couldn't help but become famous—just look at her.

This tendency, which is frequently referred to as hindsight bias or the "knew it all along" effect, is particularly acute when events are unpredictable. And long-tail events are particularly unpredictable because it is hard to know in the beginning what is going to take off. But what happens early on sets the course for outsize gains through cumulative advantage. These dynamics make understanding what content will go viral or who will become popular nearly impossible, despite the billions of dollars advertisers spend on identifying influencers and trying to develop the next hit song, shoes, and drug.

This isn't to say that expansionists aren't special. Dozens of studies have found that popularity can be reliably predicted as early as age three. How popular someone is at three remains a remarkably accurate predictor of popularity beyond elementary school and into adulthood. It even persists across contexts as people move from place to place. At the same time, some people aren't so popular in school and find great popularity as adults. As Lyle Lovett croons, "Well, I went to high school and I was not popular. / Now I am older, and it don't matter." It isn't just Lyle Lovett. Taylor Swift, Lady Gaga, and Adam Levine all weren't popular on the playground.

Whether expansionists are simply lucky beneficiaries of preferential attachment or are exceptionally socially skilled, though, depends on how you define luck.

Are genetics luck? Winning the genetic lottery can help make you popular according to research done by scholars at the University of Groningen who identified a polymorphism within the $5HT_{2A}$ serotonin receptor gene that they believe is the "secret ingredient for popularity."

To find out just how much genetics matter for popularity, James Fowler, Christopher Dawes, and Nicholas Christakis studied 1,110 twins. Twin studies determine how heritable characteristics are by comparing same-sex identical (monozygotic) and same-sex fraternal (dizygotic) twins. Identical twins share close to 100 percent of genetic material. Fraternal twins share closer to 50 percent. By comparing how frequently identical and fraternal twins are expansionists, researchers can make a rough estimate of the expansionist trait's heritability. When looking at the twins' networks, Fowler, Dawes, and Christakis found strong evidence that both expansionist and brokerage tendencies are inherited. Genetic factors accounted for almost half—46 percent—of the variance in network size.

But maybe genes aren't capturing popularity itself but something else that is hereditable—like looks? We know that physical characteristics are inherited. Perhaps similar looks give twins similar networks? Common inherited personality traits? Or behaviors?

Children that are physically attractive are twice as likely to be popular than their less attractive peers. A similar but slightly smaller effect persists in adults. To examine the power of beauty, scholars have used a variety of methods from having coders rate photographs to relying on computer-generated faces that represent beauty ideals. The latter approach is particularly interesting because it also reveals the two key dimensions of beauty— symmetry and averageness. Work done by the University of Texas at Austin professor Judith Langlois, and her colleague Professor Lori Roggman, has found that faces generated by taking photographs of multiple people and repeatedly morphing them together results in mathematically "average" faces that are by no means average—they are perceived to be beautiful. Beauty has a powerful influence on individual experience and is strongly correlated with the number of positive and negative social interactions a person has and their social standing.

Children's attentiveness to attractiveness suggests that we may be hardwired, rather than socialized, to privilege beauty. In studies where infants were held by their blindfolded parents and presented with two faces, the babies paid more attention to the more attractive face. When the attractive images moved from one screen to the other, so did the infants' gazes. In a separate study, a professional actress donned theatrical masks made from a mold of her face but with slight adjustments to one mask—the eyes were narrowed, the eyebrows lowered, and the nose lengthened—to make it slightly less attractive but still within normal range. The masks were constructed to feel the same on the inside and any mirrors or other signal of which mask was worn were hidden from the actress to ensure it didn't affect her behavior. When she wore the more attractive mask, the one-year-olds were significantly more likely to use a positive affective tone and play with the actress.

Physical attractiveness gets our attention. But so does popularity and status.

This is true for humans and monkeys. In an experiment in which monkeys were rewarded with sips of juice if they looked in certain directions, male rhesus macaques were willing to sacrifice fruit juice to gaze at the face of popular group members. (They would also forgo juice to look at the booty of a female.) But they required extra juice to look at low-status monkeys' faces.

A study that followed preschoolers for nine months found that kids with the most friends were more likely to be watched by other children in the classroom. This is also true for adolescents. When shown pictures of popular and unpopular classmates, tweens were more likely to look at pictures of popular kids first and stare at them for longer. So perhaps it is not surprising that adults tend to visually fixate on more popular adults. This remains true even after taking into account physical attractiveness. While popularity and beauty are clearly related, beauty alone can't explain popularity.

The first response, looking at the popular face first, suggests that part of the response to popularity is unconscious. But continuing to look at it means that even once the more conscious part of our brains are activated, popularity still has an effect.

Perceiving Status

While we are evolutionarily predisposed to pay attention to popularity, expansionists are particularly attuned to status signals. Their brains are more likely to light up at the sight of someone who is popular.

To understand the neural processes that track popularity, a study led by Noam Zerubavel and Peter Bearman of Columbia University compared the functional MRI (fMRI) scans of popular and unpopular group members. The research team assessed popularity by asking members of two clubs how much they liked each group member. By aggregating everyone's scores, they were able to devise a popularity rank ordering. They then put the club members in an fMRI scanner to see what happened to their brains when they were shown pictures of group members who varied in their position in the social hierarchy.

Two areas of the brain activated when group members saw pictures of popular people: first the neural valuation system, which in turn engaged the social cognition system. The neural valuation system has previously been shown to register the rank of primates in monkey studies. The social cognition system is involved in making judgments about others' mental states and intentions. The study was pathbreaking in showing that human brains encode and value social status. These status valuations then guide our behavior. We are wired to read networks.

Popular people were better at detecting status differences. And at a neural level, expansionists recognized and valued status more. This puts them at an advantage.

Being able to identify who's popular is valuable because unlike in high school, when it is fairly easy to tell who is popular (because they are frequently bestowed with titles like Prom Queen and Prom King), a variety of psychological biases frequently lead people to misjudge their popularity.

One fact that makes accurately assessing popularity difficult is that your friends are almost always more popular than you are. Rather than being the result of some warped social reality, this is due to a phenomenon known as the *friendship paradox*. Discovered in the early 1990s by the sociologist Scott Feld using data on adolescent school friendships in the sixties, the friendship paradox has been shown to hold in studies of more than 700 million Facebook users and close to 6 million Twitter users. It also applies to networks ranging from sexual partners—your sexual partners will typically have had more sexual partners than you have had—to scientific collaborators.

Take Facebook friends as an example. You could spend much of your free time posting, stalking, and friending, but your friends would likely still have more friends than you on average. A team composed of researchers from Facebook, Cornell, and the University of Michigan studied the networks of all active Facebook users—close to 10 percent of the world's population at the time of the study—and compared the popularity of each user to the friend count of others in their network. More than 90 percent of the time, users had fewer friends than their friends had on average.

How? It goes back to the power-law distribution. In social networks, many people have a few friends, but a few people have a very large number of friends. It's your friends at the tail of the distribution—the extreme expansionists—who create the paradox. People with lots of friends are more likely to be in your friendship network in the first place. And they have a disproportionate effect on the average number of friends your friends have.

Expansionists' ability to accurately assess popularity may help explain why they are popular in the first place. If you know who's in and who's out, you can arrange to be seen with the in-crowd. There is a halo effect.

Shep Gordon calls it "guilt by association." As he described it, "If you take somebody really famous and put them next to someone else, that other person melts off the fame." And he used it to make Canadian folk singer Anne Murray's career. The fresh-faced Murray arrived in Los Angeles, white-bread and almost completely unknown. She even appeared on stage wearing Raggedy Ann overalls. To gain publicity for the folk singer, Shep literally got on his hands and knees and begged Alice Cooper, John Lennon, and other members of the Hollywood Vampires to take a photograph with her. The Vampires acquiesced. According to Murray, "That picture has had more mileage than any other picture that I have had taken in my career . . . I was all of the sudden the it girl."

Reading and Misreading Others

Expansionists are extraordinarily good at being able to read others. They excel in one-on-one interactions and understand how to make an instant connection. Perhaps this makes them more likable?

Decades of research in psychology has found that humans send strong social signals through verbal cues and nonverbal behavior. From very short observations of interactions, known as *thin slices*, it is possible to accurately predict everything from salary negotiation outcomes to teachers' ratings at the end of the semester.

In a study of more than 900 speed dates, Stanford University professors Dan McFarland and Dan Jurafsky found that a handful of behaviors predicted the likelihood of successfully landing a follow-up date. What were some of the best predictors of interpersonal attraction? Men signaled interest by laughing. When women were excited about a prospective male partner, they spoke louder and talked about themselves.

In an entirely different instance of trying to win someone over, MIT professor Alex (Sandy) Pentland found that a third of the differences in salary negotiations for new employees can be explained by the degree to which two people mirror each other in the first few moments of negotiations. Our tendency to mimic or mirror people we trust begins in infancy.

Mirroring is just one of four cues that reveal how well a social interaction is going. According to Pentland, consistency, activity, and influence are the others. The degree to which someone's voice is a monotone or fluctuates between higher and lower pitches—its consistency—is a good marker for how mentally focused they are. More consistency equates to more focus. Their overall level of physical and verbal activity is a great barometer for their level of interest and excitement. More activity, more interest. Finally, influence can be detected from how frequently one person can induce another person to copy their way of speaking.

In a competition at MIT in which executives pitched business plans, Pentland and his colleagues asked competitors to wear sociometers. The cellphone-sized sensors detect face-to-face interactions, sample speech, and measure physical activity. They also asked the executives, who had more than a decade of working experience, to rate one another. Collectively, consistency, mimicry, and influence accounted for close to a third of the difference in assessments of pitch persuasiveness. In a different study, they found that the same factors have similar explanatory power in job interviews.

Expansionists are extremely adept at reading body movements, interpreting the *ums* and *aahs* of conversation, and following the rhythm of conversation. They also have specific social signatures. In order to understand the conversational cues and behavioral characteristics that allow expansionists to develop inordinately large networks, my colleagues and I studied interactions among hundreds of professionals in thirteen different offices, showed that expansionists speak in longer segments, talk more frequently than their peers, and are less likely to interrupt. This is our verbal equivalent to chimpanzees standing up straight, hunching shoulders, and hurling rocks.

The importance of volubility and speech also helps explain the puzzling finding that personality explains very little of who is likely to be an expansionist. As you might expect, extroverts who are more sociable, outgoing, and assertive are more likely to be expansionists. But the effect is, at most, fairly small. In a study of hundreds of MBA students, for instance, extreme extroverts have only twelve more friends than extreme introverts.

It isn't extroversion itself that matters so much. Extroverts and introverts communicate differently. Extroverts use a stronger voice and talk faster. When strangers watch a short recording of someone speaking, they can accurately guess their level of extroversion.

Much of the verbal fluency of extroverts appears to be developed rather than innate. A study by researchers at the University of Helsinki asked the parents of more than 750 seven- and eight-year-olds to rate the level of extroversion of their children. Parents' perceptions of how extroverted their child was predicted the child's popularity the following year. But the effect was largely explained by teachers' assessments of the children's oral ability. How well and how easily they communicated their ideas, not just personality, made them popular.

Once again, this becomes a self-fulfilling prophecy. Small initial differences in verbal and social skills in childhood have positive effects on the number of social interactions a child has and their popularity. In turn, this gives them the opportunity to practice more frequently and develop social confidence, which leads to social competence.

Being Loud Is More Important Than Being Right?

It isn't just competence. Confidence makes people more popular. Cameron Anderson, a psychologist at the Haas School of Business, University of California, Berkeley, made this point by giving 243 MBA students a list of items and asking which ones they were familiar with at the beginning of the semester. Included along with real names, events, and concepts were some fictitious ones like Windemere Wild and Queen Shaddock. This allowed Anderson and his colleagues to see how much the MBA students overestimated their knowledge. After the semester ended, they assessed the students' popularity. Students who reported knowing more about the fakes were more popular at the end of the semester.

It isn't just in MBA classrooms (where we might expect overconfidence to be valued) that this holds. Business schools are arenas where young professionals who have already experienced extraordinary success duke it out to reach the top rung of the next ladder. Many of them have never failed at anything, but suddenly they are pitted against one another for a few select spots at McKinsey and Goldman Sachs. In a world where everyone is talented, sometimes confidence literally pays. It does for pundits as well.

Jim Cramer is the epitome of brash overconfidence. On March 11, 2008, the CNBC *Mad Money* host responded to a question from a viewer named Peter about pulling money out of Bear Stearns. Cramer literally screamed, "No. No. No. Bear Stearns is fine."

Six days later Bear Stearns's stock was down 90 percent. The funny thing is that in the world of punditry, accuracy doesn't matter. *Mad Money* viewership increased substantially after Cramer's disastrous Bear Stearns prediction.

Being loud is more important than being right—for pundits at least. Two economists currently at the University of Nebraska Omaha and Pennsylvania State University analyzed more than a billion tweets from the 2012 baseball play-offs. After filtering out tweets that did not make predictions, each tweet was coded for its level of confidence. Words like *annihilate* and *destroy* were given higher scores than *beat*. Using words that exuded confidence increased the number of followers a pundit had by 17 percent—far more than being right. In comparison, if a pundit were to correctly predict the outcome of every game, it would have increased their following by only 3.5 percent.

Displays of overconfidence—cocksure expressions, expanded postures, a calm and relaxed demeanor, speaking a lot and using a confident tone—make people more popular. It is often possible to know who among the MBA students will get a coveted job and become the class president within the first week of classes. And it frequently isn't their skills or intellectual acumen that matter. Overconfidence is often falsely mistaken for competence. As a consequence, it leads to higher status because even when overconfidence is exposed and real ability is revealed, groups still reward the overconfident. This helps fuel the relationship between overconfidence and popularity.

Mr. Nice Guy

Expansionists are not only confident. They are surprisingly generous.

In his role as CEO of the accelerator program at Y Combinator, which has helped launch more than 2,000 start-ups collectively valued at over $100 billion, including Airbnb and Dropbox, Michael Seibel spends most of his day helping others. "Founders are always surprised that I answer their emails and that my email address is in my Twitter profile. Helping each other is a core value in the tech start-up world. Everyone should practice it. The start-up community is a family—we should look out for one another."

Seibel isn't alone in his policy of trying to help strangers by answering their emails. Adam Rifkin has a similar policy. He calls it the five-minute favor. This idea is simple. "You should be willing to do something that will take you five minutes or less for anybody," according to Rifkin.

Rifkin and Seibel may not fit your vision of an expansionist. Rifkin is frequently likened to a shy panda bear. He has an affinity for *Star Trek,* anagrams, and tech. Yet he has been named one of the best networkers by *Fortune* magazine and was featured in Adam Grant's book *Give and Take* for building an extraordinarily successful network through generosity.

Keith Ferrazzi probably is closer to the stereotype of an expansionist. He wrote the bestselling networking book *Never Eat Alone.* When he walks into a room he's usually flashing a huge smile, quickly begins engaging in rapid-fire conversation, and exudes so much energy it can be almost exhausting just to watch him. Despite a difference in disposition from Seibel and Rifkin, Ferrazzi has a similar message: "It's better to give before you receive. And never keep score. If your interactions are ruled by generosity, your rewards will follow suit."

Shep Gordon put it even more simply: "Do something nice for someone today." He embraced this motto in spite of Alice Cooper's hit "No More Mr. Nice Guy."

The advice given by Gordon, Rifkin, Seibel, and Ferrazzi is borne out in research. It is the same sage advice that appears in Luke 6:38: "Give, and it shall be given unto you." Givers have larger networks.

There are many ways to give. You can informally provide advice or emotional support to individuals. Or you can more formally give to organizations, volunteer, or donate blood. People rarely do both—except expansionists.

A study that analyzed the networks and prosocial behaviors of close to 1,000 respondents found that conveners with dense networks of strong ties frequently provide social support. But they rarely engage in organized prosocial behavior. Expansionists, however, were more likely to be there for the people they know and were also likely to give their time, money, and blood to voluntary associations.

Perhaps not surprisingly, expansionists appear to be more likely to give in public than they are to give in private. In a study of popularity and the giving behavior of more than 200 kids, how likely popular kids were to hand over one or more of four colored wristbands depended on whether the decision was made in private or in public. Popular kids were more likely to share their wristbands—

but only when asked to do so in public. Unpopular kids didn't significantly change their behavior in public or private. Perhaps understanding the value of publicly showing prosocial behavior is part of what allows expansionists to build large networks.

The nature of expansionists' networks also makes giving easier. An extensive network makes it easier to learn about potential opportunities to provide social support and advice. Their wide networks also make expansionists likely targets for volunteer recruitment. About two-thirds of people who volunteer didn't begin doing it on their own initiative but were recruited by others. Not only are expansionists more likely to be recruited, but their networks make them more valuable recruits. A similar dynamic works for charitable giving. Most charitable donations are given in response to a direct request. When people were asked why they had made their most recent contribution, about 80 percent said they did so "because someone asked me." Since expansionists simply know more people, they are more likely to be asked to give. And the more they give, the larger their network and reputation for generosity become.

This also puts them at risk for generosity burnout. Adam Grant's book highlights one of the puzzles of generosity. Givers such as Gordon, Rifkin, and Seibel who want to help others regardless of anticipated payback are more likely to get ahead. But they are also more at risk of failure and victimhood. Compared to takers, who prefer to get more than they give, givers earn 14 percent less, are twice as likely to be targets of crimes, and are perceived to be less powerful. Yet a meta-analysis of dozens of studies representing thousands of business units has consistently found that giving is associated with greater financial success, efficiency, customer satisfaction, and lower turnover. Givers who can successfully prevent burnout and being taken advantage of succeed. Those that don't are worse off than those who are more selfish.

Successful giving requires self-preservation. In order to give effectively, expansionists in particular need to be careful to avoid burnout.

Expansionists can help stave off giving burnout by being careful about setting boundaries. Rifkin has the five-minute favor—not the five-hour favor. Shep Gordon tries to do something helpful for someone each day. He doesn't try to help everyone every day.

According to Grant, a second possible strategy is to chunk giving. If you set aside a chunk of time specifically devoted to giving, your giving becomes more focused and efficient and the psychological rewards that come from giving are amplified.

Finally, and somewhat paradoxically, a study led by Cassie Mogilner Holmes, currently at UCLA's Anderson School of Management, found that giving more of your time can actually make you feel like you have more time. Participants who were directed to use that time to help others instead of wasting time or doing something for themselves subjectively perceived themselves to be more time affluent.

Creating More Time

But changing perceptions of how much time you have available is quite different from actually creating more time. And as we have seen, time and cognitive capacity are the two biggest constraints that limit the size of someone's network. Expansionists are frequently great at *establishing* social connections, but have a harder time developing and maintaining them. As a result of their difficulty cultivating deep social relationships, they also have difficulty getting value from their network.

Effective expansionists have a system. Vernon Jordan had rows of black three-ring binders with home phone numbers, cellphones, and information about contacts' families. David Rockefeller had his note cards with details of past meetings. Ronald Reagan kept note cards with quotes and jokes.

People who work in an office receive an average of 200 emails a day and spend more than 12.5 hours a week on email. In 2018, people spent an average of 142 minutes a day or more than 16 hours a week on social media. Expansionists have substantially more traffic.

Expansionists make the unmanageable manageable by setting up systems. They use customer relationship management tools, typically used by sales forces to store contact information; keep call logs; create task lists; set reminders to touch base; and keep detailed notes about past meetings and personal information. Most of this can also be done with a simple Excel spreadsheet— but if you want to maintain a large network, it needs to be maintained meticulously and consistently.

The same goes with dealing with incoming emails. There is usually a system (and an assistant) in place. For instance, Michael Seibel usually responds to emails with only one or two sentences, rejects practically all public speaking requests, and uses a scheduling tool to allow people to sign up for a limited number of phone call slots each week. He writes blog posts that answer the most frequent questions he gets and then just points people to them. "And I just kind of realized that ninety percent of the value is that someone replies."

Keith Ferrazzi doesn't just keep track of the people he knows, he keeps a list of "aspirational contacts," people he wants to know. "I'm constantly ripping out lists in magazines . . . I had been ripping out forty-under-forty lists for years and continue to do so. Those are individuals who somebody has spent enough time to identify as an up-and-comer, a mover, an intellectual, and these are the kinds of people I want to surround myself with. I rip out lists of top CEOs, most admired CEOs, regional lists." Ferrazzi or his assistant then enters the lists into a database, along with background research on each of the individuals. Ferrazzi then creates call sheets by region.

The idea of creating calling lists isn't a recent development. America's elite have had one in the form of the *Social Register* since at least 1887. Louis Keller, whose obituary described him as "known to more persons here and abroad than any other one resident of New York," began the *Social Register* with the names and addresses of America's most prominent families. Keller's original list of 2,000 families now contains around 25,000 entries with information on their primary residences, the location of their summer homes, the names of their yachts, and a code that denotes memberships. ("Sfg" denotes the San Francisco Golf Club, "BtP" represents the Bath and Tennis Club of Palm Beach.) For decades, "It used to be if someone wasn't listed, you just didn't know them," according to Brooke Astor.

Stretched Too Thin

When signing new artists, Shep Gordon sits down and warns clients, "If I do my job perfectly, I will probably kill you." Popularity and fame have a lot of pitfalls. Picking up any celebrity gossip magazine will confirm the seriousness of Shep's warning.

In personal relationships, there is a danger of spreading one's self too thin. Research by Christina Falci and Clea McNeely found that having too many "friends" increases risk of depression. (Having too few friends has the same effect.) Relationships come with a set of expectations and obligations. As the number of relationships a person is embedded in increases, so do the expectations and obligations. This can eventually produce a phenomenon known as *role strain,* in which expansionists simply cannot fulfill the demands of their multiple roles. In turn, this leads to depression and burnout.

Having too many friends may also increase the risk of depression and loneliness because we face trade-offs between the strength of our ties and the number of relationships we have. A study led by James O'Malley at the Dartmouth Institute for Health Policy and Clinical Practice and Samuel Arbesman found an inverse relationship between the number of contacts someone has and how close they feel to the rest of the people in their network. This was confirmed in another study using an entirely different data set. People with small networks considered roughly 6 percent of their non-family relationships to be "very close." For expansionists with much larger networks, the figure was less than half of that.

This can create a situation where expansionists know a lot of people but feel like they don't have any friends. As Selena Gomez, the singer and actress, puts it: "I know everybody, but have no friends."

At work, too, popularity can lead to collaborative overload and burnout. Using research done in more than 300 organizations, Adam Grant, Reb Rebele, and Rob Cross found that 3 to 5 percent of employees provide 20 to 35 percent of the value added in collaborations. These employees are unsurprisingly highly desired and popular collaborators. But they are disengaged and the least satisfied with their jobs.

While having an extremely large network isn't without its downside, University of North Carolina professor Mitch Prinstein argues in his book *Popular* that there are two kinds of popularity. The one we've been talking about, which Prinstein would call *status,* is the most damaging one. It reflects our "visibility, power, and influence." It is why Dale Carnegie is creepy. It helps explain why pushy MBA students aren't the ones who are invited to their classmates' weddings.

But there is another form of popularity, *likability,* which is far more positive. Prinstein argues that most people spend their life pursuing the wrong type of popularity.

What makes someone likable as a child is also what accounts for likability decades later. There is an incredible persistence to likability. People who are likable, according to Prinstein, aren't aggressive. They listen. They aren't always the first ones to jump into a conversation. They make other people feel valued and welcome. They aren't domineering.

A study that followed more than 14,000 Swedish adolescents

for forty years found that the most likable children turned into the most successful adults. Even after one takes into account cognitive ability, socioeconomic status, parental mental health, misconduct, and a host of other factors that one would think would matter for long-term success, likable kids are more likely to graduate from high school and college and succeed in the workplace. They are less likely to face economic hardship and struggle with depression, anxiety, and addiction.

Most of the time, likability isn't related to popularity or network size. Only about 30 percent of people with high network-based status are also likable. When children are young, the two are linked to each other. But with the onset of neurological changes during puberty, status seeking takes root and the two begin to diverge. As cumulative advantage sets in, there becomes increasing opportunity for divergence between the underlying human characteristic that set off popularity—likability—and popularity itself.

The most effective and enduring expansionists, like Shep Gordon, manage to remain likable while becoming unimaginably well-known. But even Shep didn't avoid all the pitfalls of popularity.

When Shep was sitting in his hospital bed, his loneliness activated his ego. And as he put it, "I think my ego probably said, because I was feeling sorry for myself, I said, 'Yeah, yeah, maybe that's a good way to come out of this thing. If I live, let's do the movie.'" After ten or twelve years of saying no, he finally let Beth Aala and Mike Myers make a documentary about him. If the movie hadn't been made, Shep would likely have remained in relative obscurity.

While the actual making of the film might have been initially motivated by a momentary need to inflate his ego, what comes through in the movie is Shep's generosity, his willingness to help others. After a screening of the movie in the Midwest, he was approached by a couple. "They said, 'We're so thankful. We wanted to talk to you. We just moved here from Saint Thomas and our children are grown up and we're empty nesters. We came back and we realized we have so much to be blessed for. We just don't do enough good stuff. Watching the movie made us realize we have to change that in our lives.'"

Giving, service, and gratitude guard against loneliness. Through renowned chef Roger Vergé and His Holiness the Dalai Lama, Shep learned "how to live a happy and fulfilled life in service to others." He learned how to be likable and popular.

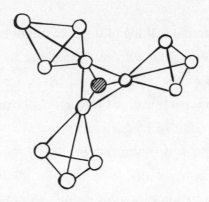

6. In the Mix

Everybody has a longing for belonging . . . Deep in the human spirit is a longing for belonging. It's why the worst kind of punishment is solitary confinement. We're made for relationships . . . That's why people will join all kinds of stupid causes just because they want to belong," preached pastor Rick Warren, who is better known by his congregants at Saddleback Church as "Papa Rick."

Warren was called to Orange County, California, to plant a church for people who didn't like church. When he arrived in a U-Haul from Texas with his wife and four-month-old baby, he knocked on doors asking people why they didn't go to church. The answer was partially sociological. As he put it, "If a young couple walk into a church, the first question they'll ask is: 'Are there any other young couples here?' If all they see is gray hairs, they're not staying."

He wanted to create a church where everyone could find community, a place where worship was accessible and entertaining. Rather than an organ or a choir, Saddleback has a rock band. It also has a "Praise" tent with gospel music, a "Traditions" area featuring old-fashioned hymns, "Overdrive" blasting heavy Christian rock, and Spanish language services. People come in jeans and have a place for their kids to play. Baptisms on the beach are often followed by barbecues.

As a teenager, Papa Rick grew out his hair and aspired to be a rock star. A conversion experience drew him to ministry. Saddleback began as a Bible study in Rick and his wife Kay's home. To recruit new members, Warren penned a letter. He and Kay along with his tiny congregation hand-addressed the envelopes and sent the letter to more than 15,000 community members. On Easter in 1980, the church's first official service at the Laguna Hills High School Theater drew 205 people.

Today Warren is a rock star in the world of evangelical megachurches. His services draw close to 22,000 people a week. One in nine people in the area consider the church their religious home. Saddleback is "one church in many locations," including places as far-flung as Buenos Aires and Berlin. Warren's book *The Purpose Driven Life* has sold more than 34 million copies.

"Churches, like any large voluntary organization, have at their core a contradiction. In order to attract newcomers, they must have low barriers to entry. They must be unintimidating, friendly, and compatible with the culture they are a part of. In order to retain their membership, however, they need to have an identity distinct from that culture. They need to give their followers a sense of community," wrote Malcolm Gladwell in his article on

Saddleback. Warren overcame this tension, which also confronts expansionists and conveners, by using small prayer groups.

Small groups consist of three or more who come together to socialize and worship. They are dense convening networks. On a typical Wednesday in Los Angeles, there are more than a hundred small-group meetings. There are meetings for military personnel, fifth graders, Spanish-language speakers, moms and toddlers, Bud's Beach Buddies, the Notorious Sinners, and Praying Pickles groups.

Small groups are what have made Warren America's most successful "pastorpreneur." His success is network genius. Malcolm Gladwell dubbed the model "the cellular church." These small prayer groups came at no extra cost to the church. Worshippers were free to pick whomever they felt most comfortable with. Gladwell believes that the forty million Americans now in these small religious groups have brought about "a profound shift in the nature of the American religious experience."

The cellular model, which is really a network of networks, overcomes many of the limitations that are inherent to conveners, brokers, and expansionists by mixing elements from all three configurations. It allows for extraordinary network growth while still retaining a sense of community. It accommodates people's preferences to affiliate with others who are like themselves, while still allowing for an extraordinarily diverse network that encompasses everyone from Praying Pickles to Notorious Sinners.

It is the same model that has sustained Alcoholics Anonymous, an organization that has as a defining principle that it "ought never be organized," for more than eighty years. The Communist Party was similarly structured.

A few extraordinary individuals—Rick Warren, Vernon Jordan, and Heidi Roizen among them—have been able to build networks that simultaneously maximize the benefits of brokerage, convening, and expansion while minimizing the downsides. While most people don't need a network capable of recruiting a megachurch, understanding the potential value of combining and mixing multiple network styles can help you make the most of your network.

There is no one best or right network. Based on my analysis of close to a thousand individuals' networks, I've found that one out of three people don't have a clearly defined style. An additional 20 to 25 percent have a mixed style—they are simultaneously brokers and expansionists, conveners and expansionists, and so forth. An ambiguous or blended style, as we will see, can be an asset.

The most appropriate network is the one that matches your personal goals, career stage, and needs. The visibility, popularity, and power benefits that accrue to expansionists are often most valuable early in a career or to professionals who need to see and be seen. The innovation benefits that accrue to brokers are greatest in creative industries or arenas that privilege unique work. Conveners' trust and reputational benefits help ensure emotional well-being, guard against loneliness and burnout, and are advantageous in arenas with a lot of interpersonal uncertainty. Different moments and challenges require different networks. Just as your emotional, social, and work needs change over time, so can your network.

Turbulent Times

Leaving his house at five thirty each morning, Marvin Powell made his way to Pontiac, Michigan, where he worked at the Pontiac Assembly Center on the line for Chevy Silverados and GMC Sierra pickup trucks. Marvin, a tall, stocky African American man approaching his forties, followed his father into the auto assembly industry. "It's not a glamorous job, to say the least," reflected Marvin. But it allowed him to buy a home in the racially integrated middle-class neighborhood of Kingsley Estates, take his children to Disney World, and order takeout on the weekends.

Marvin was among the last six hundred employees at Plant 6. Close to 3,000 employees there manufactured 1,300 trucks a day in 2003. But two hours into Powell's shift on a Monday in 2009, the line was stopped for an all-company meeting. The plant would be closing.

Powell is an optimist and a man of faith. "Over time, I think I'll be okay," he said. He planned to look for a job on another auto assembly line nearby. But Jonathan Mahler, the author who profiled Powell for *The New York Times Magazine,* "was constantly torn between marveling at his faith, his stubborn belief that everything was going to work out, and the urge to tell him to look around, to read the paper on any given day, to see the train that's heading straight for him and so many others and try to make a viable plan for his future before it's too late."

Mark Gorham, a former vice president at Hewlett-Packard and a Harvard Business School graduate, was laid off around the same time as Powell. Gorham took a different approach. Upon the advice of his personal job coach, Jeffrey Redmond, he set out to figure out how to network. He contacted three people a day. His goal was to reach out to sixty people a month. His first cold call was to a colleague he hadn't spoken to in almost a decade. He rehearsed the call with his job coach for weeks and then practiced at least five more times before picking up the phone.

"Part of the dread was saying I didn't have a job. I've never not had one," recalled Gorham. "But I realized, I wasn't calling to say, 'Hey, can you hire me.' I basically was letting him know what's going on and getting his advice on my plan. He was very engaged and threw out a bunch of ideas. He said, 'Let's get back together.' Afterward I wondered why was I so worried."

Marvin Powell's and Mark Gorham's stories were invoked by researchers Ned Bishop Smith, Tanya Menon, and Leigh Thompson to show the contrasting cognitive responses people have when faced with job threat. While Marvin turned his focus to friends and family, Mark began to work his extended network.

The researchers were interested in whether the network winnowing and widening that Marvin and Mark experienced were generalizable. They were also curious about whether people's network responses differed if they were of higher or lower socioeconomic status. A large body of research in social psychology has demonstrated that people with power are more likely to be optimistic and confident in the face of risk. In contrast, people who lack resources are less likely to ask for help because it heightens feelings of powerlessness. This may make people with relatively little power more likely to default to the security of the smaller denser convening-like parts of their networks.

They first confirmed their hunch by looking at survey data.

After taking into account that people with greater resources have larger and more far-reaching networks to begin with, they looked at the size and convening tendencies of 806 respondents in the face of job threat. Respondents with greater power had larger and broader networks when they thought they were likely to be laid off sometime in the next year. Potentially losing their jobs was associated with network broadening. Faced with the same possibility of getting laid off, people without power constricted their networks. Their networks were smaller and took on greater convening tendencies.

The researchers also wanted to see if the relationship was causal—if it really was the threat of job loss that was causing changes in people's perceptions of their networks. They recruited 108 participants who were about to graduate and begin new jobs to come into the lab. They then randomly assigned half of the participants to imagine a scenario in which after a year of working at their job, they were informed the company would be downsizing. They would lose their job. After imagining the scenario with a high threat of job loss, participants were asked to write about how they would likely feel if confronted with the unfortunate situation. The other half of the recruits were simply asked to think and write about how they would feel if they were to land their ideal job. There was no mention of potentially losing it. Both groups were then asked to list whom they spoke to about important issues and what relationships existed among their contacts.

Once again, the trio found that lower status participants were more likely to recall smaller and more convening-like networks when faced with job loss. When confronted with the same threat of job loss, higher status participants perceived their networks to be larger and broader. Mentally, people with greater resources and financial security recalled networks that would be more advantageous when looking for a job.

Network winnowing in times of uncertainty can be particularly detrimental. Dense convening networks can provide important psychological support during uncertain times, but larger, more diverse networks are more likely to yield potential job leads.

It isn't just the threat of job loss that seems to lead to network narrowing. Difficulty, uncertainty, and negativity lead people to perceive that their networks are smaller and more convening-like than they really are. When asked to recall negative, positive, and neutral life experiences, people randomly assigned to think about their worst moments recall networks that are more convening-like. Since they were randomly assigned to recall different life experiences, it isn't that their underlying networks or experiences are different. They aren't necessarily conveners to begin with. But the negative emotional experiences lead them to recall denser parts of their network. In turn, this is whom they are likely to reach out to. From moment to moment, our networks change based on our emotional states.

In some difficult circumstances, as when one is dealing with an ill spouse or depression, focusing on the densest convening-like parts of one's network can be helpful. The security of convening clusters can provide needed emotional support. But in situations of uncertainty or threat, broker-like networks with their information benefits are more likely to yield solutions. When employees are facing rounds of layoffs, organizations are suddenly confronted with new competition, law enforcement officials are searching for a terrorist, stock prices tank, or doctors are trying to figure out what is causing an outbreak, networks "turtle." People focus on their densest, strongest ties. They go inward. And it's precisely the opposite of what they should do.

If powerlessness is part of the problem, one seemingly reasonable solution would be to try to create a sense of empowerment. Perhaps recalling a time in which one was powerful might generate the confidence necessary to think beyond the dense convening-like subparts of one's network? This approach can backfire.

When Tanya Menon and Ned Bishop Smith asked people to "recall a particular incident in which you had power over another individual or individuals," they found that empowerment led to network winnowing for those who typically don't have a lot of power—the people who most needed network widening. It conflicted with their identity and their experience. Being told they had power when they were used to having none created more threat and uncertainty.

Rather than prompting power, confirming one's identity proved to be a more successful strategy. According to the researchers, "the emotional signature of having a confirmed identity is feeling comfortable and in control." Control was more important than power. Power just provided the illusion of control. Focusing on aspects of the situation that one might be able to change is a better way to override the psychological tendency to convene when faced with uncertainty.

Turbulence and fear can lead people to squander their network resources. It isn't that their networks are actually smaller or more convening-like during difficult times. People just perceive them to be. Rather than trying to build new relationships in times of difficulty, one should access the more diverse, far-reaching parts of one's network—reach out, rather than turtle in.

Acting Your Age

At different moments in our lives and at different points in our careers, it can make sense to turtle in. When Ron Burt, the University of Chicago professor who first discovered the value of brokerage, began to investigate brokerage's returns over the life course, a distinct pattern began to emerge. Studying the networks of close to 2,200 managers working in computer manufacturing, human resources, financial services, banking, supply chain management, and software engineering, Burt found that brokerage was most common mid-career. Managers who were in their late thirties and early forties were most likely to be brokers.

The greatest returns for brokering also accrue to middle-age managers. For brokers to be successful, they need to come up with good ideas, but they also need enough stature or respect to get those ideas implemented. Even if new employees have groundbreaking ideas, chances are they will likely have a hard time getting them implemented. They don't have the political clout to see an idea through to implementation. In some divisions and sectors, those that focused on human resources and computer manufacturing, Burt found that the advantages of brokerage arrived a little later. But young employees were never the biggest beneficiaries of brokerage.

For the young, a very large network is likely to yield the biggest benefits. Imagine being a recent college graduate. You are likely entering a firm with little experience, close to the bottom of the organizational hierarchy. You probably wouldn't have access to a lot of resources, and you are unlikely to have a lot of power. Anyone you meet is likely to have more power than you. They are also more likely to have better information and more resources. So the more people you meet, the better.

Over time, this changes. Assuming you do well, you and your peers will become better resourced. Fewer and fewer people have the resources and information you need. The pyramid gets narrower. Instead, people are trying to get your time and attention to see if you can help them out. As you move up the social pyramid, you need equally or better resourced contacts to help you out. And there aren't that many of them. As a result, being an expansionist becomes less valuable.

At the same time, brokerage networks can become quite unwieldy. It is possible to imagine brokering between three or four social realms with relative ease. Five or six might even be a possibility. But beyond a certain point, no one, no matter how adept he or she is, can continue to act as a broker across a multitude of social circles. At that point, you need people you can trust to act as liaisons. You need a network of networks.

Without them, you may fall into one of the common network traps that Rob Cross, a professor at Babson College, identified over the course of studying the networks of thousands of mid-level managers and executives. Many of the traits that initially allow managers to succeed—they are smart, accessible, willing to offer help, and responsive—can eventually lead to collaborative overload. This is especially so because many of the collaborative

tools that exist make it easy to reach out to managers instantaneously. If mid-level managers and executives can't figure out
how to network down—create connections between others be-
neath them—they will eventually drown.

Heidi Roizen reached that point in the middle of her career
when working as the worldwide head of developer relationships
at Apple. She was in meetings for eight to ten hours a day while
hundreds of emails piled up. Even with two assistants, she
couldn't keep up. As Royal Farros, a friend from college, put it, "I
could tell Apple was getting overwhelming based on the length of
emails Heidi sent me. When she started there, she would send me
emails that were at least a paragraph long. Then a few months
later, her emails changed to short sentences. By the end of the
year, she was simply using incomplete phrases."

Heidi Roizen is one of the best-networked women in Silicon
Valley. Harvard Business School wrote a case study about her networking prowess. Over the course of her career, she has worked
as an entrepreneur, a technology executive at Apple, and a venture capitalist. Whether intentionally or accidentally, Heidi created a textbook example of how a network successfully evolves
over the course of a career.

After graduating from Stanford, Heidi began her career writing a company newsletter. It may seem like a bit of an odd choice.
But as she explained, "It's difficult to develop a professional relationship with anyone, let alone a senior-level executive, when you
have no reason for interactions. So it would be tough to start
working at a company and say, 'Gee, I think I'll get to know the
CEO.' That's probably not going to happen unless the CEO has

some reason to interact with you. As the editor of the internal newspaper, there was a good reason why the CEO was going to talk to me—I was one of his main communication vehicles to his employees. Now you could either take the opportunity and not run with it, or you could take it and say, 'This is a rare opportunity for me to demonstrate my performance and consistency, to deliver on promises, to put my best foot forward . . . and to build my reputation.' I chose the latter approach."

Heidi's first jobs—in communication at Tandem Computers, as a founder of one of the first spreadsheet software companies, and as the VP of worldwide developer relations at Apple—gave her extraordinary reach into tech networks. Many of the early contacts she developed, including Bill Gates, became household names. "It took a long time to build that network. I don't think you can expect that you are going to suddenly have this network of super important people . . . Not all those people were that important when I first met them. They may be important now, but they weren't that important back then. Neither was I."

As a venture capitalist, Heidi was able to capitalize on those relationships. A good venture capitalist acts as a broker between a business founder and the people they need to know to be successful—whether technology or industry experts, other investors, advisers, potential high-value employees, or customers.

But it became too much. She was receiving hundreds of emails and close to a dozen business plans a day from people she knew or who were referrals from people she knew. To manage that complexity, she had to become more efficient.

Brian Gentile, a former work associate of Roizen's, described the transition: "Constellations form, which are comprised of many different networks . . . There are very few people who become the nucleus of a network. Heidi is one of those people. As the nucleus of her own network, Heidi will forge a deep relationship with the nuclei of other networks within her vast constellation, which allows her to keep in touch with all the people in those other networks. I can only imagine how many networks Heidi touches."

Trajectories and Oscillation

Over time, networks evolve, sometimes naturally and sometimes purposefully. New relationships form, old relationships fade away. Some individuals experience continuous gains in network status. Others take reputational hits and lose stature. Brokerage opportunities disappear and people who were previously brokers become conveners. A move or a transfer from one division to another can turn a convener into a broker. Heidi Roizen transitioned from an expansionist to a broker to a convening nucleus.

Ron Burt and his collaborator, Jennifer Merluzzi, studied 346 bankers and documented common network trajectories. Over four years, the majority of bankers experienced considerable churn in their networks—they established new connections while other relationships faded. Close to 20 percent experienced a continuous increase in status, 13 percent saw their prominence diminish over the four years, and 40 percent saw their status fluctuate from year to year. Similarly, roughly 10 percent saw an increase in brokerage opportunities, 13 percent lost their ability to broker, and 45 percent experienced ebbs and flows in brokerage.

The most advantageous of these trajectories were oscillations between brokerage and convening. Higher compensation was linked to going deep into convening relationships for several months, then focusing for several months on brokering, then switching back to convening, and so forth and so on.

Oscillating helps overcome the trust issues that pure brokers routinely face. In fact, brokers benefit most from oscillating. Another potential reason that oscillating is advantageous is that it promotes fluidity and flexibility in identity. Children who grow up in multiple countries, for instance, have an easier time shifting between languages and culture. The same is true for employees. As Burt and Merluzzi wrote, "Experience with change is preparation for change." This flexibility may allow for more rapid adaptation when circumstances change in social circles at work.

It's possible to switch network styles by changing either your situation or your behavior. Moving between project teams or taking part in a rotation program can encourage oscillation at work. Joining seasonal sports teams or a volunteer project can produce the same effect outside of work. While moving between interaction spaces is the easiest way to encourage oscillation, you can also change your network by modifying your behavior. Self-disclosure, perspective taking, and vulnerability can encourage convening. Working on translating between groups can help someone become a better broker. Another approach is to use your network to change your network—that is to say, to enlist the help of others.

Make New Friends but Keep the Old

Remember that guy who used to live down the street from you? He may be able to give you better insight than your most trusted adviser. Daniel Levin, Jorge Walter, and J. Keith Murnighan asked hundreds of managers in their executive MBA classes to reconnect with former colleagues whom they hadn't spoken to in at least three years. The researchers called these folks *dormant ties*.

Either in person or via the phone, the managers were to ask dormant ties for advice about an ongoing project. As you might imagine, the executives weren't thrilled about the task of reconnecting. As one put it, "If there are dormant contacts, they are dormant for a reason, right? Why would I want to contact them?" Another described the potential awkwardness: "When I thought about reconnecting . . . I found myself feeling very nervous. Some thoughts that ran through my head were: What would be the best way to make first contact with little chance of being rejected? What if they do not return my call? Will they be uncomfortable reconnecting after so long? How do I begin the conversations? What if there are awkward moments during the conversations? What if they do not want to help me with this project?"

But reconnecting paid off. Compared to current strong and weak ties, dormant ties provided more useful and novel knowledge.

Old contacts provide more valuable insight because they have novel perspectives and are less likely to be in your echo chamber. They provide the same benefits that arise from brokerage. What's more is that the trust and shared perspective you have with former friends and colleagues whom you once had a strong relationship with doesn't disappear over time. Strong dormant ties provide both the novel insights that arise from brokerage and the trust benefits of convening.

Reaching out to dormant ties is a way to blend network styles within your current network.

Most people have thousands of acquaintances and even formerly close friends they are no longer in touch with. Expansionists have even more. Which one should you reach out to? Maybe the one who has truly excelled and is now at the top of his field? Another tactic might be to reach out to the person who you think is most likely to be willing to help. Or the person you've known the longest or used to interact with most frequently.

To see which cold connections people were most likely to reach out to, as well as who actually enriched one's life, the trio of researchers conducted a second study. They once again recruited executives who were taking MBA classes, 156 this time around. The managers were asked to list and rank-order ten dormant ties whom they could possibly reconnect with. Of the ten, they were asked to reach out to two—their top choice and one that was randomly picked from the remaining nine on the list by the researchers.

When they had the opportunity to choose for themselves, the executives reached out to people whom they had known the longest or previously interacted with most frequently. But those former colleagues didn't prove to be the most valuable. The most useful knowledge came from former coworkers with the highest status who were perceived to be trustworthy and willing to help. But pretty much all of the dormant ties that came to mind were worthwhile.

If there is so much untapped value in relationships that have faded away, why are people so hesitant to reconnect? Part of it is simply finding the time to reconnect. Feeling embarrassed about not keeping up is another common obstacle. Others don't want to impose or are hesitant to ask. But the primary reason is that people are afraid it will be awkward.

As the executive who previously expressed his hesitance attested, "From a personal standpoint, I believe that I completely underestimated their reactions to assisting me with my project and hence was worried for no reason . . . Though nervous at first, I am now looking forward to maintaining both these connections, since I believe it will be beneficial for all of us—on a business and personal level." A year later, he was still in touch.

Go ahead and pick up the phone. Or draft an email if you are feeling timid. It isn't nearly as awkward as you think. If an old associate whom you consider a friend reached out to you, wouldn't you be happy to hear from them?

Finding a Network Partner

When asked for a loan by an acquaintance, financier Baron de Rothschild purportedly said, "I won't give you a loan myself; but I will walk arm-in-arm with you across the floor of the Stock Exchange, and you soon shall have willing lenders to spare." Rothschild understood the value of association. How we are perceived by others is deeply influenced by the people and things we are connected to—even if we did little or nothing to contribute to their success.

Men who are randomly paired with an attractive "girlfriend" are perceived more favorably than those seen with someone more homely. If they were able to land such an attractive date, they must be smart or successful, right? Or at least have some redeeming quality?

You've almost certainly been in a conversation when a friend or an acquaintance name-dropped a connection to someone famous or quasi-famous. Or perhaps talked about the time they were eating at a restaurant and a celebrity was dining nearby. In an attempt to bask in the reflected glory of their team, university students are more likely to don sweatshirts and T-shirts with their school's name or mascot after the school's football team has been victorious. They are also more likely to use *we* when talking about the team's victory than the team's loss. Following elections, yard signs for winning candidates stay up longer than signs for losers.

A long line of research has confirmed the notion that we are judged by the company we keep. A study of the British village of Winston Parva conducted in the late 1950s and early 1960s, entitled *The Established and the Outsiders*, illustrates the truth of the assertion. "Newcomers who settled in the 'good streets' of the 'village' were always suspect unless they were obviously 'nice people.' A probationary period was needed in order to reassure the established 'good families' that their own status would not suffer by association with a neighbor whose standing and standards were uncertain," wrote the cultural sociologist Norbert

Elias. "The ostracised 'black sheep' was in this case a woman who had recently moved into the neighbourhood and who made the following comments when she herself was asked about her relations with her neighbours: 'They're very reserved. They speak on the street but nothing else.' She then told how she had asked the 'dustmen in for a cup of tea one cold day,' soon after she had arrived . . . 'They saw it. That shocked them round here.'"

Just as inviting a garbage collector in for tea can apparently ruin a reputation, affiliating with someone of prominence can elevate it. Employees who have an influential boss, for instance, are more likely to develop large networks.

Network researchers Martin Kilduff and David Krackhardt, who are professors at University College London and Carnegie Mellon University, were curious about whether the status of an employee's colleagues and work friends affected how he or she was perceived at work. In particular, Kilduff and Krackhardt were interested in how perceptions of networks impacted perceptions of job performance. They collected data on the employee's friends, as well as to whom they turned for advice. But they also asked everyone in the organization whom they thought their colleagues would turn to for advice and whom they would consider a friend. For instance, they would ask Steve for the names of his friends. But they also asked Steve for the names of those he thought Maria would consider a friend. This allowed them to construct actual friendship and advice networks within the organizations, as well as create a network based on perceptions of relationships.

Perceptions were far more important than the actual friendships within the firm. Thinking that Maria had powerful friends made Maria more powerful. It didn't matter that she wasn't actually friends with them. So it seems that Rothschild was right. Perception matters—perhaps more than reality.

Halo effects like the one Kilduff and Krackhardt observed likely have the strongest effect in large organizations or communities where people might not know one another well. Their study took place in an organization with roughly thirty-five employees. When or where coworkers or potential friends have less information, halos are more likely to glow. These are also the situations in which frequently being seen with someone who is popular might make you more powerful.

Beyond prominence, it is possible to seem more trustworthy by creating relationships with the right colleagues. The most obvious way to gain your coworkers' trust (other than by earning it) is by getting your team's formal leaders to trust you. Studies of trust found that more than 7 percent of how much your colleagues trust you is explained by whether or not you help them. By comparison, 6 percent of trust can be chalked up to whether the group leader trusts you. Interestingly, it doesn't matter how much the group itself trusts the leader—having his or her trust is still an endorsement. Having the trust of the team leader is especially important if your team isn't performing well. If everything is going smoothly and your team is performing great, your teammates are more likely to trust the judgment of their fellow coworkers. But if there is turmoil or uncertainty, they look to the group leader.

It's also possible to garner trust by relying on advocates. The best advocate is a convener whose contacts do not overlap with yours. The denser your advocate's network, the more influence they will have. When studying managers in a very large firm that provides emergency response services, research led by Sze-Sze Wong found that the best backers frequently provide advice to people who wouldn't normally turn to you for advice. This helps extend your reputational range by increasing the number of people who might hear about your good deeds and strong character. The value of an advocate whose network spans parts of the organization that your network doesn't reach is huge. If your advocate's network is large and spans multiple parts of the organization, your peers trust you 70 percent more than if your advocate's network was large but confined to your mutual department.

However, Wong and her coauthor caution that "managers should not view advocates as a substitute for providing support. Rather, advocates are complements to their own reputation-building efforts." Helping behaviors were more important than supervisor support. Trust—unlike prominence or popularity—has to be earned. It can't be achieved solely through halos. But it can be augmented and extended by carefully cultivating promoters.

Borrowing brokerage is more complicated. As we've seen, brokers frequently encounter reputational challenges. The nature of their position—spanning different social circles—makes them inherently suspect—sometimes for good reason. Brokers can strategically withhold information. Even when they share information, their contacts might not benefit. Many of the innovation benefits of brokerage come from recombining specialized knowledge. But the broker, who isn't necessarily an expert, may have difficulty translating and sharing information with his or her peers. The potential benefits get lost in translation. Even when information is shared and effectively translated by the broker, it may be disregarded, since there is a well-documented tendency for conversations to focus on shared or common knowledge.

Studies in contexts ranging from headhunters to inventors have found a dark side to being connected to a broker. In a network of more than 18,000 inventors in thirty-seven pharmaceutical firms, University of Minnesota professor Russell Funk found that scientists who established a relationship with a broker were subsequently less likely to file patents or invent new drugs. In headhunting, there is also a price to pay for brokerage. London Business School professor Isabel Fernandez-Mateo shows that brokers often favor one party over another and treat them more favorably. The other party suffers as a consequence. In other settings, brokerage doesn't seem to cause problems for the parties being brokered. But it doesn't produce advantages, either. Only the broker benefits.

One exception seems to be if the broker is your boss. Being connected to a senior broker can help you help your colleagues. According to a study of more than 2,200 bankers by researchers at INSEAD and Singapore Management University, being connected to a broker who is of your same stature or a subordinate doesn't allow you to add more value to someone seeking your advice. But if your boss or a higher ranked contact is a broker, you add more value to those around you.

Bosses are more likely to be beneficial brokers because they are more motivated to cooperate and share information. While a competitive peer broker might withhold information, your boss's success is likely to depend at least partially on your success.

Put differently, brokerage is most likely to be beneficial when it is combined with cooperative motivation. One arrangement that produces this potent combination is when the broker is your boss or someone higher up in the organization who is less likely to be threatened by your success. Another beneficial combination that rests on the same logic is when the broker's associates are conveners.

Beyond business, it is reasonable to imagine that similar combinations of brokerage and convening could be advantageous. Many of the psychological tensions that come from brokerage—role strain and illegitimacy—can be offset by relationships with conveners, who are more likely to offer emotional and social support. Child translators who act as a go-between—interpreting messages from doctors, schools, and other institutions for migrant parents—are a good example. Anne Chiew, whose parents moved from China to Australia, recalled going to the bank with her parents and trying to open an account: "I remember being on my tippy-toes, trying to see over the teller counter, that's how small I was still . . . It did cause a lot of stress, because if I didn't know something, I didn't know who to turn to for help." Some of the potential stress arising from brokering can be offset by strong relationships at home and support at school or other outside institutions. Research finds most children who act as go-betweens don't buckle under the strain and continue to be steadfastly devoted to their families.

Under the right conditions, alliances between brokers and conveners can be mutually beneficial. But cooperation and trust are essential.

Six Necessary Partners

When studying the networks of managers, Rob Cross and Robert Thomas found executives who were consistently in the top 20 percent of company rankings of well-being and performance had networks with a very specific set of characteristics. They typically have a core network of twelve to eighteen contacts and with six kinds of critical connections.

At least one person within their inner circle offers:

1. Access to information
2. Formal power
3. Developmental feedback
4. Personal support
5. Sense of purpose
6. Help with work/life balance

One person within their inner circle could fulfill multiple roles. The key is that they don't try to fulfill any themselves.

The first three roles are key to professional success. Mentors and sponsors, as we will see in chapter 9, can be instrumental in providing access to information and formal power, as well as developmental feedback. Beyond success, the most satisfied executives also have people in their inner circle they can vent to, who will listen to them and provide support—protégés, bosses, clients, friends, or family members who help them find meaning in their work and reorient them toward a primary purpose. Lastly, they have supporters who remind them of their values and hold them accountable to maintaining a life outside of work. Whether it's activities that support mental, physical, or spiritual well-being, without someone to encourage you to sign up for a new art or music class, show up at the gym, or volunteer, it is easy for work to take over your life.

Beyond these roles, according to Cross and Thomas, "what really matters is structure: Core connections must bridge smaller, more-diverse kinds of groups and cross hierarchical, organizational, functional, and geographic lines." There are brokers within your convening core.

The fluidity of networks allows them to transform as our lives, emotional needs, and work demands change. What may be the optimal network structure for those in sales early in their career likely won't meet the demands of their work once they are in senior management. The expansionist network of a mid-twenties social butterfly isn't likely to provide the social support she needs to get her through the loss of a spouse. Moves, layoffs, and children all require adaptation.

While networks are perpetually evolving, there are a few constants: the people we need in our lives and emotional rewards that can come with even the briefest of encounters. In the next chapter, we move from looking at more enduring network structures to what defines the quality of our interactions in any given moment.

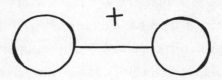

7. In the Moment

Sit three feet apart. Try to gaze between the brows. Maintain direct eye contact. Don't touch. Sit in silence. Be still and slow your breath "until it is 'almost unnoticeable.'" At least an hour of uninterrupted gazing is ideal, according to Marina Abramović. She spent eight hours a day, six days a week, for nearly three months staring into the eyes of over 1,500 strangers at the Museum of Modern Art (MoMA) in New York as part of her performance The Artist Is Present.

"Nobody could imagine . . . that anybody would take time to sit and just engage in mutual gaze with me," reflected Abramović. People camped out on 53rd Street to get a chance to sit with the striking Serbian performance artist. Many cried. Some laughed. A few put their hands on their hearts. One man commemorated the twenty-one times he sat with Marina with a tattoo.

"There was so much pain and loneliness. There's so [many] incredible things when you look in somebody else's eyes. Because in the gaze with that total stranger, that you never even say one word—everything happened." Abramović believes our lack of eye contact is socially crippling. That we should set up "eye-gazing stations" in hotel lobbies and shopping centers. "It was [a] complete surprise . . . this enormous need of humans to actually have contact."

Humans have a profound need to feel seen, heard, and understood. But it is a privilege we are not frequently granted. "What is so beautiful about the MoMA performance," according to Klaus Biesenbach, the former chief curator at the museum, is that "she's treating, actually, every human being she encountered with the same attention and same respect. That is pretty shocking. And some people are shocked by this. And some people think they deserve this attention and they are finally where they should be. And others fall in love with her."

How is it possible to fall in love with someone without ever speaking to them? Love, according to Barbara Fredrickson, who is the Kenan Distinguished Professor of Psychology at the University of North Carolina at Chapel Hill, is an emotion. Like all emotions, it is created in brief ephemeral interactions.

Fleeting moments—like those Abramović sought to create— determine the quality of our interactions. Jane Dutton, a professor emerita at the University of Michigan, calls these interactions *high-quality connections*. According to Dutton, John Paul Stephens, and Emily Heaphy, they arouse or increase energy, positive regard, or mutuality. As therapist Lisa Uihlein says, "It is this sense of your aliveness, your beingness, your presence. That's what in my experience is so enriching about being with another and being in relationships. It is really the wow-ness of being alive in the present moment." Unlike love, these interactions aren't necessarily positive in the usual sense. They aren't necessarily happy. But they have a high emotional carrying capacity. This allows them to hold more emotion, both positive and negative, than typical interactions. It makes them resilient and allows them to bounce back.

Our bodies respond physically when we are in high-quality interactions: blood pressure lowers, heart rate slows, oxytocin is released. You can literally feel a high-quality connection. This may help explain why more than half a million people gathered to witness Abramović connect with strangers.

The ephemeral potential of connections—a fleeting interaction in an elevator can produce the same effect as a beloved's kiss upon the forehead—helps explain one of the more puzzling features of social life. Even short interactions can have a transformative effect on our life and sense of well-being. While our networks are the constellations created through repeated interaction, brief moments are central to our emotional experience.

Imagine going to order a coffee. You approach the barista, ask him how his day is going, make eye contact, and smile as you hand over your credit card. Now picture going for a coffee, but being in a hurry. You order and pay as efficiently as possible. A study by Gillian Sandstrom and Elizabeth Dunn at the University of British Columbia randomly assigned people to one of these two scenarios. Having a brief social interaction with the barista made people happier, largely because they felt a stronger sense of belonging.

A glance and a smile from someone while you are walking down the street can have the same effect. At a Midwestern university, a research assistant walked by 282 strangers and either looked them in the eye and smiled, looked them in the eye without smiling, or looked in the direction of the person but past them. In German there is an expression for the last behavior: *wie Luft behandeln,* "to treat like air." A second experimenter then approached. Without mentioning the look or lack thereof, the experimenter asked the unsuspecting walker, "Within the last minute, how disconnected do you feel from others?" Being acknowledged with a smile, even by a stranger, led to a greater sense of social connection—but only among participants who were aware of the smile. For the 55 percent of people who didn't notice the smile and gaze, their sense of social connection was no different than if they had been looked at as though they were air.

Spending a couple of minutes casually interacting with a stranger or barista can make us as happy as spending the same amount of time with our romantic partner. A study led by researchers at the University of British Columbia found that conversing with a stranger can be as pleasant as communing with a loved one because we tend to try to put our best foot forward when interacting with a stranger. The very act of trying to seem pleasant actually makes us feel pleasant.

Innately, we have the capacity and know how to have transformative connections, even with strangers—when we try. Things that we do every day are at the heart of powerful social connection. But we rarely take the time to reflect on them. Truly seeing, hearing, and listening to another leads to connection. Too often, however, we are either too hurried or afraid to deeply connect.

Good Samaritans, Clowns, and Other Distractions

In Luke 10:25–37, Jesus tells a parable about a traveler who is making his way from Jerusalem to Jericho. Along the way, the man is robbed. He is stripped of his clothes, beaten, and left by the side of the road. Two men, first a priest and then a Levite, walk past the injured man. They offer no help. Finally a Samaritan approaches, bandages his wounds, and carries him by donkey to an inn, where he leaves money with the innkeeper to look after him.

In the 1970s, two psychologists restaged the parable near Green Hall at Princeton University. They wanted to understand why the priest and the Levite walk by the man without helping. Perhaps the priest only espoused religious values but didn't really believe in them? Or maybe the intrinsic nature of the Samaritan's values made him more willing to act?

John Darley and Daniel Batson recruited forty-seven priests in training from the Princeton Theological Seminary to help them untangle what led to helping behavior. Under the guise they were studying placement opportunities for seminarians, the professors asked half of the group to prepare a lecture on job opportunities and half of the group to prepare a talk on the Parable of the Good Samaritan. After preparing their remarks, the volunteers were instructed to head to the building next door to record their sermons.

Along the way, they encountered a man hunched over on the ground in a doorway. The victim's head was down and his eyes were closed. As the seminarians walked by, he coughed twice and moaned.

Who stopped? The priests reminded of the parable and asked to prepare a lecture on it weren't more likely to stop. As the researchers reported: "Indeed, on several occasions a seminary student going to give his talk on the parable of the Good Samaritan literally stepped over the victim as he hurried on his way!"

Whether the men were told to hurry because they were late made a huge difference. Only 10 percent of seminarians who were told they needed to hurry because they were late stopped to make sure the injured man was okay. When there was no mention of urgency, 63 percent stopped.

Close to a quarter of Americans always feel like they are in a rush. "The world is moving so fast now. People barely have an attention span at all," noted Chrissie Iles, a curator at the Whitney Museum of American Art, when describing Marina Abramović's work. "She slows everybody's brain down. She asks us to stay there for quite a length of time, which we are not used to doing. She transforms us as a result."

When we are in a rush, our ability to connect with others—whether friends, family, colleagues, or strangers—is impaired. Being hurried and harried impairs our ability to read and understand others' emotional expressions, from their gaze to their verbal intonation. When people are distracted, stressed, or under time pressure, they are much more likely to be self-absorbed and egocentric. They don't have the ability to read others well.

Now imagine that the seminarians of the study had had a cellphone in their hand. Chances are they might not even notice the man in need of help. Cellphone use induces what researchers call *inattentional blindness*. Unless people are devoting their full attention to who and what surrounds them, they often fail to notice unexpected stimuli that are in plain view. It's hard to imagine that you might miss a clown cycling by on a unicycle, for instance. But in a study of inattentional blindness, only one in four cell-phone users noticed a clown unicycling right by them. More than two out of three people talking with another person noticed the clown.

Even when we are with others, we often aren't fully present. Almost 90 percent of smartphone users confessed to using their phone during their most recent gathering. One in ten adults even check their phone during sex.

Our divided attention makes it difficult to notice what is going on around us, impairs our ability to read the emotions of others, and ultimately makes us socially disconnected. Even when we set out to spend time with those close to us, our phones can impair our ability to connect. As they entered a museum in Vancouver, researchers asked parents to participate in a study in which they were randomly assigned either to use their cellphone as much as possible or to avoid using it. Following their museum visit, parents who were asked to use their phones reported feeling 23 percent less socially connected than parents who put their phones away.

A phone's simple presence can deleteriously affect your relationships. A study that randomly assigned three hundred friends and family members sharing a meal to either leave a cellphone on a table or put it away found that simply having a phone on the table made the meal less enjoyable. While the effect wasn't huge, it was measurable and significant. Once you take into account what people are talking about, you find far larger effects. For instance, one study asked half of the participants to have a casual conversation about plastic holiday trees, while the other half were instructed to discuss the most significant events in their lives from the past year. For those engaged in casual conversations, the presence of a phone didn't have much of an effect. When a phone was present during a meaningful conversation, however, the overall quality of the conversation was perceived to be much lower. Perceptions of trust and empathy declined. If a phone was present—even if you weren't using it—you would have been better off talking about plastic Christmas trees than trying to engage in a more meaningful conversation.

While phones may seem trivial, the cumulative effect of cellphone snubbing can harm even the most enduring and persistent relationships we have as adults—marriages. A study titled "My Life Has Become a Major Distraction from My Cell Phone" found that perceptions of overall relationship quality were lower in couples in which one partner frequently checks his or her cellphone during meals or keeps it in a hand when the couple is together. The decrease in marital satisfaction was largely due to conflict over cellphone use. Fighting over cellphone use led to a decline in marital satisfaction, which in turn was associated with lower life satisfaction and higher rates of depression. It is almost hard to believe that picking up your phone could have such a huge effect, but a follow-up study conducted among 243 Chinese adults also found that phone use impacted marital satisfaction and ultimately resulted in feelings of depression.

Of course, people in unhappy marriages or unhappy people may be more likely to use their cellphone to numb and distract. Cellphones have even been shown to be effective anesthesia. Patients undergoing medical procedures without a cellphone were more than six times more likely than patients who were allowed to text a stranger to need supplemental fentanyl to reduce pain.

But it isn't just the numbing effects of cellphones or the conflict that they can induce that can lead to poorer social connections. It's the distraction. When examining why parents using their phones at the science museum or couples having dinner found their social interactions to be less pleasant, researchers in both studies found that people felt socially disconnected because they were distracted—much like the priests.

Staring at Strangers

Imagine you are walking down a sidewalk after leaving a coffee shop on a brisk fall day. A stranger walking alone is roughly twelve feet away from you on the uncrowded sidewalk. The person isn't on his phone, smoking, or eating. He's just walking. You stare at your shoes and don't look at him. Will he look at you? Marina Abramović would probably guess no.

Strangers look less than half the time. What if you glance at them? Their chances of looking at you now increase to 55 percent. If you look at them and smile, the odds that they will make eye contact are close to 2.75 times higher than if you stared at your shoes.

If you are in Japan, rather than, say, Saint Louis, the chance of your glance eliciting a smile plummets. In Japan it is 2 percent. In general, how welcome eye contact is differs by culture. However, an analysis of ethnographies from 306 cultures across the globe, one considered the "gold standard" for cross-cultural studies, found that eye contact was the most frequently mentioned cue of attraction. In cultures ranging from Imperial Romans to Iranians, Javanese to Jívaro, Turks to Trobriand Islanders, eye contact was positively associated with liking. In only one case (the Zulu) did eye contact have a negative connotation.

What is the optimal duration of eye contact? When people encounter strangers in malls, in hotel lobbies, or on the sidewalk and glances are exchanged, they are usually short. People feel most comfortable with roughly three seconds of eye contact. Any shorter and you seem shifty. Any longer and you may come across as overly intimate or domineering.

People are two to three times more likely in a conversation to initiate eye contact when they are listening than when they are speaking. When people are discussing intimate matters, there tends to be less eye contact. People look at each other more when they are cooperating than when they are competing.

When someone is looking straight at you, they are hard to ignore. From birth, infants prefer a direct mutual gaze over averted eyes. A direct gaze is detected faster, generates more physical arousal, and makes hearts race. Joint attention, empathy, and memory all increase when we look straight at each other. Individuals who make direct eye contact (within reasonable limits) are perceived to be more likable, intelligent, credible, attractive, and powerful than people who look away.

Couples who are deeply in love spend 26 percent more time gazing at each other in conversation than those who are less smitten, according to a classic study by Harvard psychologist Zick Rubin.

In a subsequent study entitled "Looking and Loving," researchers wanted to know if they could induce feelings of love in strangers by having them stare into each other's eyes. Ninety-six strangers were randomly paired to a member of the opposite sex and assigned to either look at their partner's hands, look at their eyes, or count how many times their partner blinked for two minutes. This was all done under the ruse that the various gazing exercises were preparation for the real experiment, which would be coming later. Feelings of respect and affection were significantly higher among pairs in which both participants were instructed to gaze into each other's eyes instead of having one partner look at the other's hands or count blinks. It isn't just that we like to look at those we love, looking itself can make you fall in love.

Whether it's affection, amusement, arrogance, or annoyance, our eyes convey how we feel. And the ability to read another person's eyes is one of the best predictors of a person's social intelligence. Simon Baron-Cohen initially developed the "reading the mind in the eyes" test to diagnose autism in the late 1990s. (You can take the test here: http://socialintelligence.labinthewild.org.) The test presents thirty-six black-and-white photographs of the eyes of actors and actresses who are conveying different emotional states. For each photograph four potential emotional states are presented. Is the man with the furrowed brow upset or annoyed? Is the man with the cocked bushy eyebrow uneasy or friendly? The better you are at inferring someone's mental state by looking at their eyes, the more likely you are to be prosocial, perform well in groups, and respond empathically.

So look into someone's eyes, but don't look for too long. The psychologist Giovanni Caputo found that ten minutes of mutual gazing in low illumination can lead people to lose their connection with reality. It also produces odd sensations. Among those recruited to engage in prolonged staring, there were frequent reports of facial disfigurations and "hallucinatory-like phenomena of strange-face apparitions." Reports of time slowing down were also quite common. Perhaps it is worth a try?

The Most Powerful Question

You walk into a cocktail party. Drink in hand, you approach a high top and introduce yourself to a stranger who has just finished eating a pretzel. Your cellphone is buried in your bag and you've made perfect eye contact—not too long, not too short. Now what do you say?

In his classic book *How to Win Friends & Influence People*, Dale Carnegie advised: "Ask questions that other persons will enjoy answering." More than eight decades later, a research team at Harvard confirmed the wisdom of Carnegie's advice. Asking questions leads to connections.

Testing Carnegie's assertion, Karen Huang, Michael Yeomans, Alison Wood Brooks, Julia Minson, and Francesca Gino investigated the relationship between the number of questions that someone asked and how much they were liked by their conversational partner. In one study, four hundred participants were recruited to have a fifteen-minute online chat in the researchers' behavioral lab. After pairing participants, one person in the duo was randomly assigned to ask either no more than four questions or at least nine questions. (The thresholds were based on a previous study.) People who randomly received many questions liked their partner roughly 9 percent more than people who were on the receiving end of only a few questions.

Taking the research outside the lab, Huang and her colleagues also examined question-asking among 110 speed daters. The speed daters each went on fifteen or so dates, each lasting four minutes. Microphones captured conversations during the speed dates. Again, they found that people who asked more questions were more likely to make a connection with a stranger. More questions were associated with a higher likelihood of getting a second date.

But not all questions have the same effect. The psychologists considered six different types of questions: introductory questions, full switches, partial switches, follow-ups, mirrors, and rhetorical questions. An example of an introductory question is the perfunctory "How are you?" Full switches and partial switches change the topic. For instance, the stranger eating pretzels is telling you about her job as an accountant and you interject to ask her about her hobbies. That is a full switch. Follow-up questions ask about something your collocutor was just discussing. A mirroring question is similar in content to the question just asked of you but now turned toward the questioner. If someone asks you how many kids you have and you respond, "I have three kids. How about you?" you've asked a mirroring question. Mirroring questions differ from follow-up questions because they are preceded by a question rather than a statement.

Follow-up questions were the elixir. They explained almost all of the benefits of asking questions.

While follow-up questions are undoubtedly potent, people tend to fail to recognize their power. When asked to recall how many questions were asked during a conversation, people have surprisingly good recall. But they don't link questioning to likability.

Rather than asking questions, people tend to talk about and try to sell themselves in conversations. This is particularly true in job interviews, first dates, and new social situations. In doing so, they sell themselves short. Questions, and particularly follow-up questions, help establish rapport through their focus on the other and by evoking self-disclosure. Conversational behaviors that are other-focused—saying their name, matching their language style, affirming their statements—have all been shown to increase liking.

People also get intrinsic pleasure from being able to talk about themselves. In experiments, people are even willing to sacrifice money to answer questions about themselves and will sacrifice even more money to have those answers disclosed to another person. We've previously seen the power of self-disclosure when talking about conveners. Arthur Aron's thirty-six questions followed by the four-minute stare laid the groundwork for the power of questions. But what Aron missed was the magic of the follow-up question.

The First Duty Is to Listen

Part of the follow-up question's magic is that it shows you were listening. We spend close to 44 percent of our time listening. But it is rare for someone to be truly heard.

Being listened to is a gift. As Thích Nhất Hạnh, the Vietnamese Buddhist monk, wrote: "The best gift we can offer our beloved is our true presence, our true listening." The theologian and philosopher Paul Tillich similarly remarked, "The first duty of love is to listen."

Carmelene Siani recalled a transformative conversation with a friend that prompted her to commit to listening more deeply. Carmelene's friend had been badly scarred during an accident as a child. Her friend revealed why she had decided to refuse further treatment. Each skin graft—she had endured fifteen—brought her back to the trauma of her childhood. Each cut made her feel more alone, as if she were at the "bottom of a deep well. I'd look up and see my mother and my family on the edge of the well peering back down at me," she told Carmelene. "'We're here for you . . . We love you,'" they would repeatedly tell her. "But they never left the rim of the well. Not one of them ever came down *into* the well with me." She quietly continued, "I wish they had listened to me . . . I wished they had let me be, exactly as I was; afraid and in pain. I wish they hadn't told me the pain would go away, that I would feel better some day. I wish they had just let me talk about what it was like for me and even though I was little, to not deny my experience."

Sometimes people don't want advice or reassurance.

Listening can literally make pain go away. Multiple clinical trials have found that listening reduces patients' physical pain. Effective listening improves leadership ability, sales performance, school outcomes, marriage, dealing with adolescents and crying children, and hostage negotiations, among other outcomes. When employees feel like their boss is listening to them, they are less likely to be emotionally exhausted and less likely to quit. When people feel listened to, they are more likely to trust you, like you, and feel motivated.

Yet, listening can be deceptively hard. As clinical psychologist Richard Schuster has written: "Although this requirement appears to be extraordinarily easy to accomplish, in reality it continually slips through our fingers. We all seem to know how to listen, yet many of us (even trained psychotherapists) fail to listen correctly." Because we have two holes in our head through which sound enters, people think they know how to listen.

And almost everyone thinks they are good at it. A survey conducted by Accenture that included more than 3,600 professionals from thirty countries found that 96 percent of respondents thought they were a good listener. Anyone who has spent a day in an office knows that this isn't true. Even the respondents themselves admitted to being highly distracted and multitasking.

It's the psychological phenomenon of positive illusion—people's unrealistically positive assessment of their self—once again.

Viewers who just watched the evening news recall less than a quarter of the content. Listening, it turns out, is extremely difficult. A typical conversation unfolds at 150 words per minute, while the average person can comprehend speech at a much higher rate. This leaves a lot of time in conversational space for our minds to wander. A study by Matt Killingsworth and Dan Gilbert used cellphone technology to ping participants to see how frequently their minds wandered. According to their study, we spend 47 percent of our waking hours thinking about something other than what we are doing.

Who is a good listener? Ralph Nichols, a professor at the University of Minnesota, had the feeling that his students weren't listening in class and set out to answer this question. He recruited schoolteachers for classes from first grade through high school to help him figure it out. Each teacher was asked to occasionally interrupt their class and ask their students: "What was I just talking about?"

As he wrote in his book, *Are You Listening?*, written with Leonard Stevens, "If we define the good listener as one giving full attention to the speaker," it turns out that "first-grade children are the best listeners of all." This may be difficult to believe if you have young children, but the answers revealed that first and second graders were listening 90 percent of the time. Among middle school kids, less than half of the students were listening. Less than three out of ten high schoolers were listening.

How is it possible that children are better listeners than adults? Attention spans increase throughout the school years, and typically won't begin to decline until much later in life. So, it isn't that elementary schoolkids are more attentive.

Many years after Nichols, "the father of the field of listening," began investigating what was going on in Minneapolis classrooms, another study examined self-perceptions of listening skills across the life course. Across the age groups, from elementary school to the elderly, most people thought they were "able listeners." But children have a quality that was perceived to be the single most important criterion for effective listening—being open-minded. Younger minds are more open, intrinsically flexible, and exploratory, according to research led by Alison Gopnik at the University of California, Berkeley. Kids are also "less biased by their existing knowledge." Perhaps this is why elementary schoolkids were found to be better listeners?

Open-mindedness is an asset when one is listening, because people frequently hear only what they want to hear. According to Nichols and Stevens, this is one of the biggest impediments to effective listening. "Listening ability is affected by our emotions," he wrote. "Figuratively we reach up and mentally turn off what we do not want to hear. Or, on the other hand, when someone says something we especially want to hear, we open our ears wide, accepting everything—truths, half-truths, or fiction. We may say, then, that our emotions act as aural filters. At times they in effect cause deafness, and other times they make listening altogether too easy."

This all begs the question of what it means to be an effective listener. Within the field of listening research, there are at least sixty-five different ways of measuring listening. But these can be boiled down to a few essential dimensions. There is a cognitive element: Are you actually hearing sounds and remembering what you hear? ("I understand.") A behavioral factor: Do you engage in and convey the behaviors that are typically associated with being a good listener, like making eye contact and smiling and nodding? ("I do.") There is also an affective component: Are you grasping the meaning and emotion of the conversation? ("I value.") And what has been dubbed the "ethical" dimension—whether you are listening without judgment.

It is estimated that less than 2 percent of the population have participated in organized listening training. Of that 2 percent, the vast majority have been trained in styles like active listening, which focus on cognitive and behavioral components. Many people think that effective listening is nodding, smiling, asking open-ended and probing questions, and paraphrasing. That it is understanding and doing.

But listening is about more than comprehending words. It is about suspending judgment. A team at the University of Minnesota called this form of listening *deep listening*, which "is a process of listening to learn."

Focusing on the actions of being a "good listener"—making sure that you smile when you should smile and thinking of follow-up questions—can distract you from actually listening. Silence can tell us as much as focusing on the nodding, smiling, and *uh-huh*ing. A study of 167 students compared the effects of a twelve-hour imposed period of silence to those of a short course on listening that included information about listening types and common obstacles to listening. The two groups performed similarly on a listening assessment. But students who observed the period of silence had insightful revelations about their behavior. As one participant reflected, "It is hard to listen because I dwell on my own thoughts." Another realized, "The quieter I am, the more people around me want to open up." And very aptly, "People want to talk more than they want to listen."

It doesn't take twelve hours to achieve the same effect. Many of the same insights can be gleaned in less than twelve minutes. Find a friend or colleague and take just two minutes to listen to him or her respond to the simple question "What is it like to be you today?" without any form of interruption. Don't ask questions or provide advice or affirmations; just listen.

The experience is usually quite uncomfortable in the beginning. Notice any inclinations you may have to want to interrupt.

At what point do these arise? Why? Are you thinking about what you want to say before the speaker has completed their turn? Do you want to jump in with your own experiences?

Understanding your conversational habits is essential to becoming a better listener. As the saying goes: name it, claim it, tame it.

For the speaker, the opportunity to be listened to in this way can be cathartic. On more than one occasion, I've seen executives brought to tears by this simple exercise. It is unusual to be given the space to speak and be heard. Strangers frequently remark that they learned more about each other in 240 seconds than they otherwise would have in two weeks.

This practice is a form of deep listening. According to Thích Nhất Hạnh, "Deep listening is the kind of listening that can help relieve the suffering of the other person. You can call it compassionate listening. You listen with only one purpose: to help him or her to empty his heart . . . Even if he says things full of wrong perceptions, full of bitterness, you are still capable to continue to listen with compassion. Because you know that listening like that, with compassion, you give him or her a chance to suffer less. If you want to help him or her to correct his perception, and then you wait for another time. But for the time being, you just listen with compassion and help him or her to suffer less . . . One hour like that can bring transformation and healing."

When we listen deeply, our brains synchronize with the person we are listening to. In a pathbreaking study, researchers at Princeton University found that a neural dance unfolds to match conversational flows. While a woman told an unrehearsed story of a prom date gone wrong, Uri Hasson and his colleagues used an fMRI machine to see which areas of her brain activated as she told the story. They then recruited eleven people to listen to a recording of the story in fMRI machines. The brains of the listeners and the storyteller were coupled. The same areas of the speaker's and the listeners' brains were activated during similar points in the story. When the story was told in Russian (which the participants didn't speak), there was no synchrony. The same was true when the speaker told a different story than the one participants listened to—no synchrony. It was mutual understanding that created the neural coordination. What's more, the coupling was strongest for listeners who were listening more deeply. Their brain activity even occasionally preceded that of the speaker. They knew where the speaker was going before she even got there.

Listening deeply allows people to reveal themselves through words and tone. As Ralph Nichols wrote, "The most basic of all human needs is the need to understand and be understood. The best way to understand people is to listen to them."

It's Touching

I recently counted how many times someone purposefully touched me at work. It happened twice in three days. And it was the same person. Touch is one of our most neglected senses. This is as true in science as it is in life. "Over the past fifty years, there have been probably a hundred papers about vision for every paper about touch in the scientific literature," according to David Linden, a professor of neuroscience at Johns Hopkins University and the author of *Touch*. Beyond science, touch has no real art. All of the other senses have a devoted art: the eyes feast on paintings, drawings, and sculpture; music for ears; the tongue has gastronomy. Even the neglected nose has perfumes. There isn't an equivalent for touch. Unlike voice and sight, which can be conveyed through audio recordings and video, we also don't have an artificial way of conveying touch.

But touch is our first sense to develop. It is estimated that the sense of touch begins as early as the first trimester in utero. The average adult has twenty-two square feet of skin. It is the physical edge of our being. And according to Dacher Keltner, a professor at the University of California, Berkeley, "Touch is the 'primary moral experience.'" He elaborated, "Skin to skin, parent to child, touch is the social language of our social life. It lays a basis for embodiment in feeling."

Matthew Hertenstein, along with Keltner and other colleagues, wanted to see whether it was possible to convey emotion through touch alone. In a slightly weird setup, the team erected a barrier between two strangers. One person stuck an arm through the barrier. The other person was provided a list of emotions to try to convey to the stranger on the other side only through touch. The researchers assumed there was a 25 percent chance that the person receiving the touch would guess the right emotion just by chance. Astonishingly, participants were able to identify gratitude, anger, love, and sympathy by a simple touch more than 50 percent of the time. Sympathy was conveyed by stroking and patting, fear with trembling, anger with hitting and squeezing.

What's more, love and gratitude could be differentiated through touch—something that people typically can't do well through facial expression and vocal communication. When trying to guess the emotions of love and gratitude based on short vocal clips, people are correct less than 20 percent of the time. Touch was far more telling. Equally revealing are the emotions that people *couldn't* convey through touch. Embarrassment, surprise, envy, pride, and other self-focused emotions weren't readily identifiable through touch. Touch seems to be a medium of social, not self, expression.

If you want someone to do something, touching them at the right moment also increases the likelihood they will comply with your request. Whether you are asking someone to divulge personal details, dance at a nightclub, lend you some change, sign a survey, give a good tip, or sample pizza, touching them makes them more likely to say yes.

People are more likely to acquiesce to requests when touched because they have more positive evaluations of the person touching them. Regardless of whether the person was a teacher, librarian, or server, multiple studies in both touch-friendly and touch-averse cultures have found that positive perceptions of touchers explained why recipients were more likely to comply. Touchers are seen as more friendly, sincere, agreeable, and kind. This was even true in an experiment with a used car salesman—an occupation typically greeted with suspicion where one would imagine touch wouldn't be welcome. The car salesman was seen as 28 percent more friendly, 38 percent more sincere, and 34 percent more honest by men he touched on the forearm for one second than by men he didn't touch.

The benefits of touch sound like a modern-day cure-all: it reduces stress, lowers blood pressure, and slows the heart. Prior to stressful events from surgeries to public speeches, holding someone else's hand or receiving a hug reduces anxiety, lowers blood pressure, and reduces levels of cortisol, which are a biomarker for stress.

A hug or a handshake can boost your immune system and help fight the common cold. Researchers at Carnegie Mellon University, the University of Virginia Health Sciences Center, and the University of Pittsburgh asked more than 400 adults to document every social interaction they had, including fights and hugs. They then quarantined them on an isolated hotel floor and exposed them to a cold virus. (They also took blood before exposing them to the virus to make sure they were not already immune.) Then they waited to see who would become ill. A little more than 30 percent of the participants got sick enough to meet the clinical criteria for illness. But those who had more social support were less likely to catch the cold. And hugging accounted for almost one-third of the effect of social support. While we often think of hugs as a way of catching colds, they can be surprisingly good at preventing them.

And the right kind of touch—whether a caress, a cuddle, or a clasp of a hand—feels good, can create synchrony with those around us, and eases pain.

After observing that holding his wife's hand during the birth of their daughter seemed to provide some relief from the pain for her, Pavel Goldstein undertook an investigation that demonstrates the profound effects of human touch and has begun to illuminate why it may have so much social power.

Goldstein and his colleagues recruited twenty-two couples who had cohabitated for at least a year and observed their brain waves, heart rates, and breathing. The couples were put into one of three situations: sitting in separate rooms, sitting together but not touching, or sitting together holding hands. Just being in each other's presence, regardless of whether they were touching, led to increased synchronization of the alpha mu band (the alpha mu band is associated with perception and empathy of pain), as well as of their breathing and heart rates.

When heat was administered to the woman's forearm to cause pain, the brain coupling, breathing, and heart rates of couples who couldn't touch each other became asynchronous. But among couples that were holding hands, synchronization increased and the woman's pain diminished. The stronger the coupling of the couples' brain waves, the more relief the woman felt.

And the more empathic the man, the more the couples' brain waves synchronized. Men who identified with statements like "I would describe myself as a pretty soft-hearted person" were more likely to synch with their partner. Science around touch, empathy, and pain is still in its infancy, so it is hard to know how brain synchronization with an empathic partner reduces pain. But Goldstein and his colleagues offer a potential explanation: "One possibility is that observer touch enhances coupling, which increases the tendency of the target to feel understood." Previous research has found that empathy and feeling understood reduce perceptions of pain and increase feelings of pleasure. "You may express empathy for a partner's pain," according to Goldstein, "but without touch it may not be fully communicated."

Getting touch right, even for the empathic, is surprisingly complicated from a biological and neurological perspective. A soft caress feels like a soft caress only if it is applied at the right speed with just the right amount of pressure. Too slow, and it feels like a bug crawling. Too fast, and it's superficial.

The perfect touch according to neuroscience? "Warm skin, . . . moderate pressure, [and] moving at one inch per second."

Touch isn't a single sensation. According to David Linden, it is created by multiple sensors working in parallel. Nerve fibers exist for cold, pain, itch, vibration, and pressure. Different parts of your body have different densities of nerves, which make them more or less sensitive to certain types of touch. Your fingers are especially sensitive to pressure. It's one reason why a hand massage feels good. The same massage on your thigh or eyeball wouldn't have the same effect.

Nerve endings specifically attuned to interpersonal touch were discovered by Håkan Olausson and his colleagues at the University of Gothenburg in Sweden. These caress-sensing fibers, which are known as C-tactile fibers, are distinctively slow. The signals registered by caress-sensing fibers send signals to the brain at a relaxed rate of 2 miles per hour. Other sensors, like those that register vibration and pressure, transmit information sixty times faster, at around 120 miles per hour. Caress-sensing fibers are moving at the rate of a mother pushing a stroller, while other tactile sensors are closer to a race car.

These two different touch systems send their signals to different parts of your brain. Caress-sensing fibers activate a region of the brain that helps distinguish between positive and negative emotions. The body's capacity to separate out affective and emotionally laden touches from neutral touches is somewhat miraculous. Without it, a sneeze and an orgasm would feel quite similar.

It also highlights the contextual nature of touch: the same touch could feel welcome or repulsive depending on if it was delivered by a friend or a stranger. And it isn't just the context that is different; the touch itself actually feels different.

Context also matters. In Italy, you are likely to see people greeting one another with a hug and a kiss (maybe even two). In Japan, there is a bow and no physical contact. Over the course of an hour a study found pairs in coffee shops in England didn't touch at all. In the United States, people were relatively touchy-feely. They touched twice. In Paris, there were 110 points of contact in an hour.

While considerable differences exist in the frequency of touch in high- and low-contact cultures, there seem to be universal norms about who can touch whom and where people feel comfortable being touched. A study of close to 1,400 individuals in five countries used a map of the human body to see where people would feel comfortable being touched by a stranger, acquaintance, friend, cousin, parent, or partner. Unsurprisingly, more of the body was available for touch when people were closer. This was true whether the respondent was from Finland, France, Russia, Italy, or the United Kingdom. Partners could touch pretty much anywhere, while the head and upper torso were available to friends and relatives. Strangers were restricted to the hands.

Ambiguity over the appropriateness of touch often reflects ambiguity over where you are in a relationship. In America, this often translates into the awkward hug versus handshake dilemma. Consider the question posed by Shane Snow that led to a heated debate on the internet: "When I run into a male acquaintance in a work setting, I know exactly how to greet him: shake his hand." But with females, "I often feel like I'm trapped between two walls of a deep-space garbage compactor . . . On the first meeting, we shake hands. Easy. But the next time we cross paths? Is a handshake now too formal (especially if we got along well in the first meeting)? Will a hug be awkward?" The answer seemed to boil down to the need for one person to be assertive and make the call. The worst case is two tentative huggers.

Our complicated relationship with touch is evidence of its power. As Tiffany Field quoted in her book *Touch*: "Touch is ten times stronger than verbal or emotional contact, and it affects damned near everything we do. No other sense can arouse you like touch . . . We forget that touch is not only basic to our species, but the key to it."

Nothing

During her three months at MoMA, Marina Abramović broke protocol only once—when Ulay, her former romantic and artistic partner, came to sit across from her. Marina and Ulay marked the end of their twelve-year relationship in 1988 by walking from opposite ends of the Great Wall. They had intended to marry there. Instead they broke up because he impregnated his translator. Years of acrimony followed.

When Ulay sits, Marina smiles. He takes a breath and shakes his head to the left, which says something only she seems to understand. Maybe it's an apology? She searches for breath, then reaches across the table and holds his hand. The conversation, during which she never says a word, lasts less than two minutes. "We came to this moment of really peace," Abramović said.

Two minutes can have more transformative power in a relationship than the previous twenty-two years. While our networks are the constellations created by enduring patterns of interactions, the quality of our relationships is determined in the moment.

In each moment, we have the choice of whether and to what extent to connect with the person before us. Sometimes it can take enormous courage to show up and be present for someone else. In moments of hardship—a friend has lost a parent or is going through a divorce—you don't always know exactly what to say. At other moments, it requires self-forgetting—when you have a million things to do but someone catches you in the hallway and asks for a couple of minutes.

Regardless of whether it is the person you love most or a complete stranger, the intensity of a social interaction happens only in the moment. It happens through our most basic human senses—seeing, hearing, and feeling. While tomes have been written about how to enhance charisma, relationships, and love, arguably doing nothing is the best way to have more meaningful connections. As Abramović reflected, "The hardest thing is to actually do something which is close to nothing [because] it's demanding all of you."

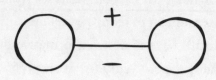

8. Human Design

It's dark outside. I can see the lines of lights down below from roads and this thing suddenly lurches and there's a big bang. And then there's another big bang. At that point it started lurching around all over the sky. That was horrendous and my skin just absolutely crawled because . . . we weren't anywhere near the ground," recounted Chris Thompson, a father of one, who was on a flight returning from a boat show in London. He was seated in 1E.

After the plane began to jerk violently, smoke poured into the cabin. Captain Kevin Hunt, a forty-three-year-old veteran pilot, calmly announced that the right engine was experiencing difficulty. He was going to shut the engine down and make an emergency landing at East Midlands Airport. The smoke began to clear. The crew started cleaning up trays and tidying the cabin in anticipation of the landing.

Passengers, particularly those seated at the back of the plane, were confused. Among those worrying that the pilot might be making a mistake was Mervyn Finlay, a bread deliveryman who was returning to his wife and son. He was seated in 21A. He wasn't confused about why the pilot was shutting off the engine. He was confused about which engine. Smoke and fire were pouring from the left engine, not the right.

"We were thinking: 'Why is he doing that?' because we saw flames coming out of the left engine. But I was only a bread man. What did I know?" recalled Finlay.

The passengers didn't say anything. The flight attendants, who could see fire emanating from the left engine, also didn't speak up. Minutes later the Boeing 737 crashed onto the motorway outside the hamlet of Kegworth, less than a thousand meters from the runway. The front section of the plane ripped off as the plane plowed through a field, hitting trees and plunging into an embankment. Luggage flew out of the overhead bins, causing head injuries to most of the 118 passengers. Seats thrust forward, crushing legs. Mervyn Finlay and Chris Thompson were among the survivors of the Kegworth disaster, which killed forty-seven people on January 8, 1989. Mervyn Finlay's "spine was 'left hanging by a thread.'" Both of Chris Thompson's legs were shattered.

If the flight attendants or one of the passengers had spoken up, nearly fifty lives could have been saved. But no one did. The pilots had tried to restart the functioning engine that he shut down during the final moments of the flight, but it was too late. The investigation into the crash concluded, "Had some initiative been taken by one or more of the cabin crew who had seen the distress of the left engine, this accident could have been prevented."

Human error is the most common reason planes crash. Of

accidents caused by pilot error, 84 percent occurred because junior officers were afraid to raise concerns or contradict senior pilots, or there was a lack of monitoring, according to an analysis of crashes between 1978 and 1990 by the U.S. National Transportation Safety Board. To try to prevent tragedies like the one that occurred at Kegworth, crew training programs that encourage lower-ranking crew members to speak up have become commonplace. But they don't seem to be that effective. In roughly half of the cases where flight attendants, pursers, and pilots felt it was necessary to speak up because of safety, they didn't say anything.

Why do people remain silent even when silence can be deadly? Why do they fail to make some of the most urgent immediate human connections they need to make?

Fear. According to Nadine Bienefeld and Gudela Grote, professors of management at ETH Zürich, flight team members do not speak up because they are afraid of damaging relationships and afraid of punishment. As one flight attendant put it, "I didn't want to get into trouble and risk a negative entry in my personal file. I am sure she [the purser] would have gotten angry if I had told her it was a violation of safety procedures. So I just hoped that I would never have to fly with this one [purser] again."

It isn't just in aviation that there is a fear of speaking up. In a study of professionals working in industries ranging from financial services to pharmaceuticals, 85 percent of respondents reported that there had been at least one instance in which they didn't feel comfortable raising an important issue at work. The reasons they gave were similar to those offered by the airline crews: fear of being seen as a troublemaker, damaging a relationship, and experiencing retribution.

Whether people are in the air or at the office, a fear of being seen negatively prevents them from speaking up. Most people want to seem friendly, competent, and smart. While this completely normal human tendency may serve someone well in airport lounges, it can be detrimental or deadly at work. At the same time, negative interactions have a disproportionate effect on a team's productivity, creativity, and well-being.

How can organizations, leaders, and team members create teams in which candor trumps fear? Where positive interactions prevail over negative ones? Where speaking the truth doesn't damage relationships? Where things get done and people get along? Outside of our families, we are most likely to face our greatest relationship challenges at work. So let's begin by looking there.

The Perfect Team

If fear and silence can have disastrous consequences for teams and organizations, what is the antidote? If we were to create a network map of interactions within the perfect team, what would it look like?

In a project code-named Project Aristotle, Google set out to create the perfect team. The project, which studied 180 teams for two years, was given its moniker after Aristotle's famous quote "The whole is greater than the sum of its parts." In an era when many companies are embracing big data to try to figure out how to make their employees more productive (and sometimes happier), Google is a leader.

To build the perfect team, Project Aristotle analyzed everything from how often people ate together to whether teams were composed of introverts, extroverts, or a mix. All told, it conducted more than 200 interviews and analyzed more than 250 team attributes.

As Julia Rozovsky, a researcher on Project Aristotle, put it, "We were pretty confident that we'd find the perfect mix of individual traits and skills necessary for a stellar team—take one Rhodes Scholar, two extroverts, one engineer who rocks at AngularJS, and a PhD. Voila. Dream team assembled, right? We were dead wrong. *Who* is on a team matters less than how the team members interact, structure their work, and view their contributions. So much for that magical algorithm."

As the team began to dig deeper, it was clear high-performing teams had different cultures. They felt different. But *culture* is a somewhat amorphous term. It is even harder to measure than it is to define. Some effective teams hung out together outside of work. Others saw one another only at the office. Some of the best-performing teams had a strong manager. Others were less hierarchical.

Ultimately, Project Aristotle identified five keys to a great team: something psychologists call *psychological safety*, dependability, structure and clarity around goals and roles, the discovery of personal meaning in work, and the belief that the work the team is doing matters. "Psychological safety was far and away the most important of the five dynamics we found—it's the underpinning of the other four," according to Rozovsky.

Psychological safety is a climate in which people feel safe to speak up and take interpersonal risks. It isn't about friendship or liking one another, it is freedom from interpersonal fear. It is a shared feeling that exists in the group, not something an individual has. When team members feel that they can take risks in their team, they can bring up problems and tough issues, people on the team don't undermine their efforts, they can make mistakes without its being held against them, they can ask for help, and their skills and talents are valued, teams have psychological safety.

Fifteen years before Project Aristotle kicked off, Amy Edmondson, who is now a professor at Harvard Business School, stumbled upon the value of workplace psychological safety. During graduate school, Edmondson was studying high-performing hospital teams. She administered surveys to capture how well teams worked together and observed them in action. Reasonably, she expected that high-performing teams would have fewer medical errors. But when she analyzed the data, she found just the opposite. The teams who worked together well had the highest error rates. And the difference was huge. Edmondson was puzzled. Why would better teams have higher error rates? Eventually she realized that the good teams weren't necessarily making more mistakes but were simply more likely to admit to errors, discuss them, and learn from them.

In retrospect, Edmondson thinks *psychological safety* might not be the most apt term. It is too warm and fuzzy. It feels too nice. Psychological safety isn't about being nice. "What it's about is candor," according to Edmondson. "What it's about is being direct, taking risks, being willing to say, 'I screwed that up.' Being willing to ask for help when you're in over your head."

Over the next twenty-plus years, Edmondson and collaborators building on her work studied psychological safety in hospitals, schools, government agencies, and factories. Dozens of studies have found that in companies where there is ambiguity, volatility, complexity, or uncertainty, psychological safety saves lives, makes employees more engaged, and increases profitability.

Yet only 30 percent of working Americans feel that their opinion is valued. Doubling that number could reduce safety incidents and turnover by 40 percent and 27 percent, respectively. Productivity could increase by 12 percent.

Psychological safety makes companies and teams more successful because it facilitates innovation and learning. In studies of teams working in environments ranging from German industrial and service firms to Taiwanese technology companies, researchers have found that in the absence of psychological safety, employees are unwilling to put forth new ideas because they are afraid of being rejected or embarrassed.

Fear impedes learning. It can be an effective short-term motivator. If you need quick and specific action, fear can be helpful. But the physical and cognitive demands that arise when we are frightened—heart racing, palms sweating, rapid breathing—make ingenuity and innovation difficult. When we are panicked or frightened, physiological resources are diverted from the parts of the brain that manage working memory and process information to deal with what the body deems are more pressing issues.

Ending the Blame Game

In neonatal intensive care units (NICUs), teams work around the clock to save the lives of tiny patients whose eyes are often still fused, their skin translucent. The smallest of babies can fit snugly in its father's hand. The technical work is exacting. A blood transfusion of two teaspoons can save a life, but an equally small mistake can end one.

On September 14, 2010, at Seattle Children's Hospital, critical care nurse Kimberly Hiatt turned panic-stricken to nearby staff when she realized she had given Kaia Zautner, an eight-month-old baby, ten times too much medication. It was the only major mistake she'd made in her twenty-four years as a nurse. But it left her "devastated," according to Kim's partner and co-parent. Ultimately, Kim couldn't live with the mistake and took her own life. The anguish over her mistake led Kim to become the "second victim" of the medical error.

Imagine the difficulty of admitting a mistake in an environment in which the stakes are so high. In order to help prevent further tragedies like the one that killed Kimberly Hiatt and Kaia Zautner, Amy Edmondson and Ingrid Nembhard, a professor at Wharton, wanted to understand how to create psychological safety. They studied 1,440 physicians, neonatologists, nurses, respiratory therapists, social workers, and other health care professionals in the neonatal intensive care units. If it is possible to create psychological safety in such extraordinarily difficult and demanding circumstances, it should be possible in much more mundane milieus.

Edmondson and Nembhard found that leaders need to invite participation. They need to go out of their way to ask what their coworkers are thinking. They need to be approachable and accessible and to acknowledge fallibility. In huddles and meetings, they need to ask the opinions of others before speaking to make sure they don't have undue influence.

When Julie Morath joined Children's Hospitals and Clinics in Minneapolis as their new chief operating officer, she began trying to lay the foundation for more open discussion of errors in order to meet her ultimate goal of 100 percent patient safety. She acknowledged that the health care system in which doctors, nurses, and medical assistants worked was complex and error prone. Rather than asking people if they had seen problems or errors, she invited participation. She asked, "Was everything as safe as you would like it to have been?" She replaced blame with curiosity.

Isn't blame necessary? Won't work turn into a free-for-all without it? Is it possible to have accountability without blame? This is a question that Edmondson hears a lot. No doubt some failures *are* blameworthy. Purposefully deviant or clearly fraudulent behavior deserves blame. If an employee is repeatedly careless, they are probably culpable. Somewhere in the middle of the spectrum from blameworthy to praiseworthy failures are tasks in which the process itself, not the employee's skill, created the error. Individuals aren't really at fault if the complexity of the problem or the challenge of the task leads to errors. Finally, when experimentation creates failures that teams or companies can learn from, those failures should be celebrated.

"When I ask executives to consider this spectrum and then to estimate how many of the failures in their organizations are truly blameworthy, their answers are usually in single digits—perhaps two percent to five percent," said Edmondson. "But when I ask how many are *treated* as blameworthy, they say (after a pause or a laugh) seventy percent to ninety percent. The unfortunate consequence is that many failures go unreported and their lessons are lost."

By clearly delineating what types of failures are blameworthy and which are praiseworthy, leaders create boundaries that increase psychological safety. But it isn't only leaders who can help create psychological safety. Teams themselves can be the architects of psychological safety.

When teams are psychologically safe, their relationships resemble the network of a convener. A study that followed sixty-nine teams working on government community projects for ten months found that teams with higher levels of psychological safety had dense networks in which coworkers more frequently collaborated with one another.

This isn't all that surprising given that convening networks are safe and imbued with trust. But trust and psychological safety aren't the same thing. While they are related, trust is about a relationship between two people or two parties. Is someone trustworthy or not? Psychological safety is about the group. There is usually consensus about whether the group has a climate of psychological safety, even when there may be disagreement over how trustworthy various members are. Trust is also about the future. Do you expect that someone will fulfill their obligations or be true to their word? Psychological safety is an immediate experience. In this moment, do I feel like I can say something?

Given their commonalities, though, it makes sense that networks high in trust and high in psychological safety would look similar.

Imagine being a part of a team in which everyone, regardless of rank, felt that their opinion was valued; in which saying "I made a mistake" wasn't preceded with hours of anxiety. The phone wouldn't feel like it weighed a hundred pounds when you had to pick it up and ask for help. In such a world, it is easy to imagine that coworkers would more readily turn to one another for advice.

When Mathis Schulte, a professor at HEC Paris, and his collaborators at Wharton began studying how networks within teams and perceptions of psychological safety unfold over time, they found that this was the case. How much psychological safety there was in a team predicted whether the team would become a convening team. Further, as connections within a team became stronger, team members began adopting one another's perceptions of psychological safety.

Psychological safety is contagious. When people think their team is psychologically safe, their colleagues start thinking it is psychologically safe, too. It becomes a self-fulfilling prophecy.

The contagion of psychological safety can be accelerated by seeding teams with conveners. Conveners can help create the connections necessary for psychological safety to take root. More connections leads to more candor.

There is a moment of opportunity when teams are first formed to make them psychologically safe. If that window is missed, it can literally take years for the team to become safe again. A study of 115 research and development teams found that psychological safety is highest in new and old teams—teams that have been together a moderately long period of time fare worst. On average, teams won't see the same level of psychological safety that they experienced at six months again until they have been together for close to six years. Taking advantage of this window of opportunity, ensuring that a convener is on the team, and creating participatory norms can help ensure that a team is as well engineered as possible.

Jerks at Work

All it takes is one snide comment to destroy psychological safety. Imagine you've been working closely with five people for a couple of months. Your team has established practices and principles to help ensure that everyone feels like their voice will be heard and respected. Colleagues listen to one another and question with genuine curiosity; there is a clear understanding of what is and what isn't blameworthy. It's a Monday and you are brainstorming process improvements. You pitch a new idea. In response, you get a "seriously, that will never work." Or maybe a "we've already tried that." Perhaps even just a sideways dismissive glance. If you are like most people, you'll keep thinking about the incident long after the meeting is over. You might be rehashing the conversation in your head, saying what you wish you would have said or ruminating about what a jerk one of your teammates is. You'll probably also think twice before making another suggestion. Other team members will, too. The team's psychological safety has just taken a hit.

Something as seemingly benign as a rude remark can have life-threatening consequences. In twenty-four NICU teams in four hospitals, thousands of miles from where Edmondson studied psychological safety, a team of researchers observed the potential consequences of toxic collaborators. After randomly assigning physicians and nurses to teams, the teams were told they were being observed by an expert in the United States. Embedded in a longer set of remarks, the "expert" made a number of rude remarks, including a mention that other teams he'd observed "wouldn't last a week" in his department. In the control condition, he didn't say anything nasty. After listening to the "expert," the teams were presented with a case of a baby who was several months premature and had a bowel that was rapidly failing.

Teams that heard the rude remark were less likely to share information and ask for help. As a consequence, they were less likely to accurately diagnose the infant's condition. They also were less likely to ask for the correct lab tests, perform resuscitation well, and give the right medications. All told, rudeness accounted for more than half of the variance in diagnosis and 43 percent of the variance in effective treatment. To put this in context, chronic sleep deprivation explains only around a quarter of the variance in clinical performance. You might be better off having a care team that hadn't slept for the past thirty hours than one that had just encountered an asshole.

But it isn't just nurses. Rudeness and incivility are endemic in most organizations. Research by Christine Porath, a professor at Georgetown University, finds that 98 percent of workers report being the victims of rudeness at work. Close to half of employees were the targets of incivility on a weekly basis. Our coworkers are some of our most difficult connections.

Almost everyone who experiences incivility reacts negatively one way or another. Many retaliate. Almost 95 percent of employees who were treated uncivilly say they got even with the instigator, while 88 percent say they retaliated against their employer. Oftentimes this will spiral out of control, and what are initially small acts of rudeness will eventually become more overt forms of outright aggression.

Another common response is resignation. As one manager reflected, "I was hurt and angry and a little scared. At first I wanted to get even, but there was too much at stake. I tried to respond in a calm, logical way and that set him off more. As he blew up again, I knew that he had crossed a line—things wouldn't be the same. I stayed another two years, but I never worked as hard again. I just didn't care as much."

According to Porath and Christine Pearson, who wrote "The Price of Incivility," victims of office incivility experience significant changes in behavior: 48 percent don't work as hard, 47 percent spend less time at work, 38 percent purposefully produce poorer quality work, 80 percent lose valuable time worrying about the incident, 78 percent are less committed to their organization, 66 percent experience a decline in work performance, and 12 percent eventually quit their job.

Even if boorishness doesn't lead workers to be intentionally less effective, the hot emotions insolence induces can impair performance. Anger, for instance, decreases cognitive functioning and consumes psychological resources. In one experiment, Porath and her colleague, Amir Erez, gathered participants for an experiment and had an actor who was in on the experiment arrive late. The experimenter told the actor he had to leave because he was late. Once he exited, the experimenter commented to the remaining subjects in the experiment, "What is it with you undergrads here? You always arrive late; you're not professional. I conducted this type of study at other universities, and I can tell you that students here leave a lot to be desired as participants." Porath and Erez then asked the subjects to come up with uses for a brick—a somewhat strange but common way of assessing creativity. Participants who were treated rudely came up with 25 percent fewer ideas and their ideas were less creative.

Just as psychological safety is contagious, so is negativity. Anger, anxiety, loneliness, and fear are all contagious. They propagate through networks.

"Incivility is a virus that spreads," wrote Porath, "making the lives of everyone exposed to it more difficult. Incivility might start in one office, and before you know it, it's down the hall, up three floors, and in the break room, infecting someone who may have contact with clients and customers. Left unchecked, incivility can drag down an entire organization. It makes people less kind, less patient, less energetic, and less fun. Those exposed to incivility also contribute less."

To see how the contagion unfolded, Will Felps created teams of four, composed of three college students and an actor, Nick, who would act like "a jerk, a slacker, or a depressive pessimist." The group was charged with making some fairly basic business decisions. The group that performed best would be given $100.

In some groups, Nick would hurl various insults like "Are you kidding me?" or "Have you actually taken a business course?" In others, he would act like a slacker, feet on the table, snacking, and texting a friend. As the depressive, he'd frequently lay his head down and try to conjure up memories of his cat dying.

Despite the purported power of groups, invariably when a group had Nick behaving badly in it, it performed worse. It didn't matter if the other group members were extremely smart, talented, or charismatic. In trial after trial, the groups that had a jerk, a slacker, or a pessimist performed 30 to 40 percent worse.

What was more surprising to the experimenters was how the team members acted toward one another. When Nick was acting like a jerk, people would withhold information. They would fight. "But what was sort of eerily surprising was how these team members would start to sort of take on his characteristics," according to Felps, who videotaped teams working together. When Nick would act like a jerk, other team members would start to be a little more obnoxious or insulting. When he portrayed a slacker, that behavior, too, would spill over. In one video, "All the members are sitting up straight, energized, very excited to take on this potentially interesting and challenging task. And then by the end, they are, like him, all with their heads on the desk." His depressive pessimism infected the team.

For the most part, one bad apple spoils the bunch. But there was one case that stood out as different. One team didn't get thwarted by Nick's behavior. A member of that team was a diplomat's son. He asked a lot of questions and solicited everyone's opinion, and got everyone to listen to one another. Remarking on this in his interview with Will Felps, Ira Glass of *This American Life* reflected, "If that is true, if listening is all that it takes to overcome bad behavior, if listening is more powerful than meanness, sloth, or depression, it's like a trick from a children's story, a golden-rule kind of lesson that seems way too after-school-special to possibly be true: that by listening to each other, trying to understand each other, we can get to the point where nobody can ruin things for everyone else."

If incivility is so detrimental, why does it happen so frequently? Christine Porath has found two common explanations in surveys of hundreds of employees working in more than seventeen industries. More than 50 percent of workers say they were rude because they were overwhelmed, and 40 percent said they didn't have time to be kind.

Another reason is power. Many employees—one in four—believe that if they are kind, they will be seen as less of a leader. And at times they might be right. A study that examined 4,428 employees found that kindness, cooperativeness, and sympathy were negatively, albeit somewhat weakly, related to promotion. Other work has found that disagreeableness increases the chance a group will adopt your ideas. However, research has also found the reverse to be true—civility increases perceptions of leadership. Part of the inconsistency in research may come from the fact that being a jerk is risky. It produces extreme outcomes. Companies with narcissistic CEOs, for example, either do really well or do really poorly.

Unfortunately, being nice can become harder with each promotion. Perpetrators of incivility are likely to be powerful. If someone is a jerk to you at work, it is most likely your boss or a superior. Our more powerful colleagues are three times more likely than other employees to interrupt, hurl insults, and shout.

Power makes people rude, more likely to swear, gamble, and inappropriately flirt. Even when you give people a small amount of fake power, they are more selfish and impulsive. Power also makes people more inconsiderate of others' perspectives. Adam Galinsky, a professor at Columbia University, and his colleagues creatively demonstrated how feelings of power can result in self-centeredness. After inducing feelings of high or low power, the researchers asked each participant to draw the letter *E* on his or her forehead. Those that were primed to feel more powerful were nearly three times more likely than those made to feel powerless to draw an *E* from their own perspective. They would be able to read it, but it would be backward to another person. In contrast, people in the lower power condition were more likely to write an *E* on their forehead that would be legible to others but backward from their perspective. As Dacher Keltner, who wrote *The Power Paradox*, summarized, "When you feel powerful, you kind of lose touch with other people. You stop attending carefully to what other people think."

Power can certainly be a good thing. It leads to an action orientation, encourages people to take initiative when there is risk or uncertainty, and increases the well-being of those who have it. As Keltner wrote, "My research has shown that power puts us in something like a manic state—making us feel expansive, energized, omnipotent, hungry for rewards, and immune to risk—which opens us up to rash, rude, and unethical actions."

Why Bad Beats Good

Less than 10 percent of colleagues are true adversaries. Studies typically find that somewhere between 1 percent and 8 percent of our work relationships are negative. Unlike acts of incivility, negative relationships are enduring and recurring. They are frequently characterized by conflict, jealousy, criticism, humiliation, and rejection. Despite being few in number, they have a disproportionate impact on our mood, well-being, and productivity.

"Bad emotions, bad parents, and bad feedback have more impact than good ones, and bad information is processed more thoroughly than good . . . Bad impressions and bad stereotypes are quicker to form and more resistant to disconfirmation than good ones," begins a seminal paper on the power of bad by Roy Baumeister and colleagues.

There is considerable debate about how many core emotions there are, but for the sake of example, take a look at six of the most common and essential emotions: anger, fear, sadness, joy, disgust, and surprise. Notice any commonalities? The majority of words we have for emotions are negative. In a more far-reaching study, James Averill found 558 English words to describe emotions. There were more than one and a half times as many words to convey negative emotions as there were words to describe positive emotions. There was a negative valence to 62 percent of words, while only 38 percent of emotions were considered positive.

Our lived experience is much the same. When something bad happens to us, it has a stronger impact on our mood than when we experience a happy surprise. Bad moods are significantly more likely to persist and create an emotional hangover the next day than are good moods. The same is true for people. The power of bad means that we need significantly more positive interactions with a friend or colleague in order to overcome one bad interaction. In discussing marriage, relationship guru John Gottman put this ratio at five to one. He contends that for a marriage to survive, you need five times as many positive interactions as negative ones. Fall below that number and your relationship will likely be on the rocks.

Bad's power comes from its danger. As Baumeister and his colleagues put it:

> From our perspective, it is evolutionarily adaptive for bad to be stronger than good. We believe that throughout our evolutionary history, organisms that were better attuned to bad things would have been more likely to survive threats and, consequently, would have increased probability of passing along their genes . . . A person who ignores the possibility of a positive outcome may later experience significant regret at having missed an opportunity for pleasure or advancement, but nothing directly terrible is likely to result. In contrast, a person who ignores danger (the possibility of a bad outcome) even once may end up maimed or dead.

While it is unlikely that you will end up directly maimed or dead from an office enemy, a study that tracked women for ten years did conclude that stressful jobs elevated the risk of a cardiovascular event by 38 percent. Seven percent of workers in one survey reported that workplace stress had sent them to the hospital. Of course, not all workplace stress is due to negative interactions with coworkers. But a poll found that half of respondents ranked stress at the office as the primary impact of a toxic coworker. Whether it is an enemy, an exploitative relationship, or an opponent, such negative ties aren't simply the opposite of positive relationships.

All of the basic rules that govern social networks—reciprocity, homophily, a tendency toward closure—do not generally apply in adversarial relationships. Perhaps most surprising is the relative lack of reciprocity. Just because you don't like someone doesn't mean they don't like you. Past studies have found that reciprocity of positive ties—friendship, for instance—is roughly three to six times higher than that of negative ties. Put differently, private enemies are more common than public ones.

It's Not Just About Nice

If they wanted to try to encourage civility, rather than be a source of incivility, what can companies do? "Many companies have nice sounding value statements displayed in the lobby, such as: integrity, communication, respect, excellence," begins Netflix's famous slide deck on culture. "Enron, whose leaders went to jail, and which went bankrupt from fraud, had these values displayed in their lobby . . . The actual company values, as opposed to the nice-sounding values, are shown by who gets rewarded, promoted, or let go," continued the document, which went viral and was called by Facebook COO Sheryl Sandberg one of "the most important documents ever to come out of Silicon Valley."

At the core of Netflix's hiring and promotion policies are two core values: the company doesn't tolerate anything less than stellar performance and there is no pass for "brilliant jerks." As CEO Reed Hastings said, "Some companies tolerate them. For us, the cost to effective teamwork is too high."

Netflix has what Stanford University professor Robert Sutton calls "the no asshole rule." In his excellent book, named after the rule, Sutton offers critical advice, including:

1. It takes only one or two schmucks to ruin an otherwise healthy and congenial workplace.
2. The rule works only if it is followed and enforced. "Say the rule, write it down, and act on it. But if you can't or won't follow the rule, it is better to say nothing at all."
3. One of the best tests for identifying an asshole is observing how they treat people who have less power than they do.

Hiring is one of the places where managers have the greatest impact. But it can be difficult to discern what someone is really like in an interview. As Weebly CEO David Rusenko said, "Assholes can hide it in interviews, but for whatever reason, they cannot hide it for a whole week. I don't know why, but it all comes out within a week." To suss out potential jerks, Weebly invites job candidates to come work for a week to see how things go.

If it isn't possible to do a full-on tryout, get as much information as possible. When checking references, ask for feedback from subordinates as well as superiors. Take the potential coworker out to lunch with a couple of people from the office. How do they treat the waitstaff? Do they dominate the conversation talking about themselves, or do they take genuine interest in other people at the table? Are they dismissive of women or minorities? Finally, if you hear anything approaching a red flag from an administrator or someone who would be their subordinate, it's over. No matter how good they seem on paper, they probably aren't worth it.

It's worth pointing out that you may not find Netflix a particularly "nice" place to work. People don't sit around eating chocolate chip cookies and drinking warm milk. Just as psychological safety isn't about being nice, civility isn't, either. Netflix is arguably one of the most competitive and cutthroat companies around. The company has something known as a "keeper test"—they fire anyone that their manager "would not fight to keep." Even Patty McCord, who helped write Netflix's culture deck, was fired by the CEO.

Netflix may be taking it too far. Fear often comes up in discussions of its company culture. But the point is that keeping out assholes doesn't mean everyone needs to be nice.

Beyond hiring, there is a crucial moment of opportunity when a team is first formed to get the team's culture right. Psychological safety is the highest it will be for years. Each year, I see dozens and dozens of teams come together just after MBA orientation. You can usually tell within thirty minutes of observing them how they are likely going to fare months later. Giving teams the opportunity to see for themselves how they behave toward one another by recording them and asking them to honestly reflect on their individual behavior, as well as establishing early group norms, can help put teams on the right trajectory.

A powerful technique for dealing with jerks is to show them their own behavior and let them arrive at their own conclusions. Direct confrontation isn't always the most effective approach. If you are planning on confronting someone, providing feedback on specific behaviors they engage in that aren't well received is better than generalizing or making broad characterizations. The more examples and people you have to back up your assertions, the better.

Before attacking, try to suspend judgment. The truth of the matter is that much of the time people do not realize they are spreading negativity. You never really know what else might be going on in someone's life that could make them more temperamental than usual. If they are in the middle of a divorce, they may be a little more distracted than usual or quicker to escalate a problem. Hurt people hurt people. Simply bringing it to their attention may do wonders.

The truth is that we've all probably acted like an asshole at some point. Take an extreme case of workplace bullying. According to a 2017 survey of 11,000 Americans, close to 20 percent reported being the target of abusive conduct by others, but less than 0.5 percent said they had bullied someone else. Employees were almost 60 times more likely to call someone else out than to see they had been at fault. As the saying goes, before pointing the finger at someone else, realize that there are three pointing back at you.

Sutton offers some diagnostics that might help you realize if jerk-like tendencies are emerging: Do you think of your coworkers as competition? Feel like you are surrounded by imbeciles and feel like it is your responsibility to occasionally let them know? Have a penchant for teasing and making digs? Do you find yourself in email flame wars? Does the room empty when you walk in?

Power, stress, and exhaustion can often make otherwise sweet, kindhearted souls act like tyrants and tormentors. If you are guilty of occasionally acting in ways you regret, try not to beat yourself up. We are all human. Take a look at the circumstances that led you to act out. Did you feel threatened? Afraid? Intoxicated by power? Addressing behavioral triggers can be a useful starting point for personal change. If you are feeling particularly brave, you might even consider apologizing. It is far easier to change one's own behavior and perspective than try to fix everyone else at the office.

Respect and candor aren't just nice to have at the office. In some teams and workplaces, civility may actually lead to better performance and enhance promotion prospects. In one biotech company's R&D department, employees who were seen as civil—people felt these employees treated them with respect and were polite—were asked for advice more frequently and "were twice as likely to be viewed as leaders" compared to uncivil employees.

There are two reasons why being respectful may ultimately pay off. The first is retribution. Close to a third of victims of incivility retaliated by spreading rumors or withholding information from the perpetrator. The second is that civility allows you to overcome what Susan Fiske and her colleagues identified as the warmth-competence trade-off. The combination of warmth and competence explains close to 90 percent of the variance in how you will be perceived and received. The problem is that if you are seen as warm, you are often perceived to be incompetent. The opposite is true if people think you are competent. However, Porath found that small acts of civility—a smile and thank-you—increased perceptions of warmth and competence by 27 percent and 13 percent, respectively. The opposite is also true. One employee who was quitting a "toxic, horrible, and depressing company" vented: "I have never once had my supervisor say 'Good Morning' to me. When I said 'Good Morning,' my supervisor did not respond at all."

Good mornings, thank-yous, and small acts are where civility takes root. "We dramatically underestimate how powerful appreciation is," according to Adam Grant. "For instance, just getting a simple thank-you after you give somebody feedback on a job application cover letter. Would you have guessed that just the words *thank you* would be enough to not only lead to a fifty percent increase that they're willing to help you again, but also then make them more likely to help somebody else who reaches out?" Respect doesn't require a radical personality change.

Much of this book has focused on the multitude of benefits that social relationships can provide. But the health of our relationships ultimately depends on the balance between positivity and negativity. Outside of our family, we are most likely to have difficult relationships at work. Relationships at work are often fragile. Much of the time, they do not have the same depth and resiliency as our relationships with friends. Relationships with family and friends are often strong enough and multiplex enough to hold both positivity and negativity. This isn't as true at work. Our work relationships need protection against negativity.

It is a whole lot easier to build a happy, healthy, well-functioning team than to fix one that has gone toxic. There is a moment of opportunity during the birth of every team to develop the candor necessary to thrive—to create a culture of respect and civility.

Sometimes cultures become so toxic, though, that it is better to just go. As Sutton writes, "I believe in quitting." Some provoked employees make more dramatic exits than others. When Steven Slater, who had been a flight attendant for twenty years, asked a passenger to remain seated since the plane wasn't yet parked, she refused. The luggage she was messing with fell from the overhead compartment and hit Slater. The woman then began cursing at him. Slater couldn't take the hostility anymore. He called out the passenger over the PA system, announced "It's been great," grabbed two beers from a service cart, activated the emergency exit chute, and joyfully fled.

"Slater is our icon. He has done what I could only think of," admitted one flight attendant. Some organizations manage to create a community of cordial respect even though they are built on transactional footings, like buying a plane ticket. Some don't. But as individuals we can choose to look for and contribute to the joy or the positivity. If all else fails, it may be time to head for the emergency exit.

WORK ⟶

⟵ FRIENDS

9. WORK/LIFE

Two days before my fortieth birthday, my husband, our three kids, and I piled into a van headed to the airport at four thirty in the morning. We didn't come home for more than three months and 31,000 miles. My eldest daughter, Sydney, surfed in her name-sake city. The baby, Julian, began to crawl in Costa Rica. Grace, our three-year-old, fell in love with a stuffed monkey given to her by a friend in Indonesia. It was my own *Eat, Pray, Love*, with all the privilege that entails. But rather than seeking spiritual enlightenment, I was on a search for work/life balance.

For the hundred and five days we were away, I was a full-time mom. On Mother's Day, Sydney made a video for me in which she interviewed Grace. One of the interview questions was "What is Mom's job?" With a puzzled look on her face, Grace responded after a pause, "*Umm* . . . To keep me safe?" The fact that she knew about only one aspect of my identity filled me with unexpected joy.

The trip was possible because I wasn't able to take a traditional maternity leave. My leave came six months after Julian was born. Both Julian and I were incredibly lucky that the birth went smoothly and he took a bottle. No one told me I had to go back to work so soon after he was born. But I didn't really feel like I had another option. I teach as part of a team. They are my friends. I felt obligated to them.

Our "big trip," as we called it, was also a backlash against previous bouts of burnout. I had realized after my last maternity leave that if we didn't physically remove ourselves from anywhere close to the office, I wouldn't have any time with the baby. I was also more spent than I knew. In my case, I was a big part of the problem.

For many parents, taking time off to be with their newborns isn't financially feasible. I was lucky I could take time away from work at all. One in four women in the United States return to work two weeks after giving birth. Three weeks after her son Jayden was born, Natasha Long was pumping breast milk in her truck outside the ACCO Office Supplies factory where she worked, tears running down her face. "I felt like I was alone," she said. "I wanted to fall off the face of the earth."

For many men and women, relationship entanglements with work aren't created solely out of financial necessity. In her parting words to her "PepsiCo family," former CEO Indra Nooyi shared one of her greatest regrets: "Think hard about time. We have so little of it on this earth. Make the most of your days, and make space for the loved ones who matter most. Take it from me. I've been blessed with an amazing career, but if I'm being honest, there have been moments I wish I'd spent more time with my children and family. So, I encourage you: be mindful of your choices on the road ahead." As a painful reminder to herself of the stakes, she keeps a letter her daughter wrote to her when she was young. It reads, "Dear mom, Please, please, please, please please come home. I love you, but I'd love you more if you came home."

I once heard that balance is something you know when you are passing it by. I've given up on the idea of balance. It reminds me of a coin standing precariously on edge. Within a week of returning to the office from our trip, I was once again checking emails in the lead-up to dinnertime. The next morning, Grace grumpily told me to "just go" when it was time to leave for work. It was time for yet another adjustment. But a tweak, rather than a trip.

Work isn't just about the work we do, it is about relationships. The relationships we have and the ones work leads us to forsake. Indra thinks of her colleagues as family. Some people recoil at the notion of a work family. I didn't return to work because I was told to or was afraid of losing my job but because I felt obligated to my colleagues.

As we have seen, arguably no place is harder to manage relationships than the workplace. But certain networks are more adept at managing the complexities that arise when our relationships have multiple dimensions. Brokers have more work/life balance. According to my research, extreme brokers, whose networks place them in the top ten percent of the broker-convener continuum, are roughly 30 percent more likely than conveners to report having work/life balance. Why?

Segmenters and Integrators

Speaking of his relationship with the office, one cardiologist reflected, "I try to leave this place behind when I go home at night. That's one of the therapeutic things about having a long drive home. If I needed only five minutes to get home, I might spend a good deal more time thinking about things. You have to try to have some life other than here." I would not be surprised to find out that the cardiologist is a broker.

Everyone has a different tolerance for how comfortable they are with their personal lives and work lives overlapping. Segmenters, like the cardiologist, prefer to keep work and family life separate. They erect "mental fences." They often use spatial distance and time to demarcate the realms. Segmenters prefer to live a drive away from work, rather than within walking distance. They keep separate calendars, maybe even separate phones, for home and work.

Integrators are more comfortable with the lines between friendship, family, and work being fuzzy. They have an easier time transitioning between the world of work and the world of home. Changing a diaper in the morning and leading a meeting in the afternoon doesn't require as much of a mental and physical pivot. Pictures of their family adorn the walls in their office. They answer emails in bed on Saturday.

Segmenters tend to agree with statements like "I prefer to keep work life at work" and "I don't like to have to think about work while I'm at home." Integration and segmentation lie on a continuum. In their influential work on the subject, Blake Ashforth and his colleagues give two extreme examples. An exotic dancer who conceals his work from his friends and family is an extreme segmenter, while a nun living in a convent is an extreme integrator. But most of us live somewhere between these extremes.

There are a lot of dimensions to the segmentation/integration continuum: how we deal with time, interruptions, spatial boundaries, and, critically, the boundaries of our relationships. These get reflected in our networks.

When my collaborator Nicholas Caplan (who is also my husband) and I surveyed more than 500 individuals, we found that most people were closer to the segmenting end of the scale. If someone was a complete integrator, they would have scored a 1 on our scale. If they were a complete segmenter, they would have scored a 5. If they were completely indifferent, they would be a 3. On average, the people we surveyed scored around a 3.8. They tended to prefer segmentation. But close to a quarter of people were at the very high end of the scale, scoring over a 4.5. They were truly segmenters.

Other studies have found similar numbers. An ambitious study by Google, which tracked more than 4,000 Googlers over time, found that 31 percent were segmenters. But what was particularly interesting is that more than half of integrators in their study wanted to get better at segmenting.

One isn't necessarily better than the other, though. Integrators expend less time and energy transitioning between domains. As Sheryl Sandberg, the chief operating officer of Facebook, told graduates during a keynote speech at Harvard Business School, "I don't believe we have a professional self from Mondays through Fridays and a real self for the rest of the time." Seeing work in this way probably makes Mondays a little easier. Integrators' ability to bring multiple parts of their identity to work—for example, mom, engineer, and painter—also reduces the tension of trying to keep the roles separate. It can also enhance integrators' experiences at home and work. For instance, if someone truly loves his or her job and is energized by it, that can create positive emotional spillovers at home. On the other hand, as Nancy Rothbard, a professor at Wharton and expert in work/life balance, summarized, "One of the benefits of segmentation is that people who are segmenters actually report higher levels of well-being than integrators."

Some of the well-being benefits that befall segmenters might arise from how they handle relationships. Segmenters don't just want to leave work at work. A "classic segmentist"—according to Christena Nippert-Eng, who coined the term—also eschews work friendships. For segmenters, relationships that cross over from home to work or vice versa are "threats to the integrity and purpose of each realm and the selves associated with them."

Jimmy, a thirty-year-old machinist in a lab and a father of three, described his uneasiness with the "personal" encroaching on his work life to Nippert-Eng: "If they needed something from me, I would do it. No matter what it is. If it's not personal . . . People having problems with their marriage or something like that. I just feel uncomfortable because I'm very personal about it. First of all, I feel like I can't be very much of a help. But then people say, well, just lending the ear is help. But I just, I feel uncomfortable just— Like I said, especially if I'm not that friendly with him, I don't relate to him *on the outside*."

For Rob, a research coordinator at a university, there is comparatively little distinction between work and the "outside." He's an integrator and a convener. On a random Tuesday, he has plans to play volleyball with Kayla, whom he's been friends with for twelve years. She moved four doors down from him. Later, there are birthday drinks with Ashley and six other coworkers. Rob is the guy everyone in the office loves. They come to him when they need help figuring out how to work through bureaucratic red tape. They also come to him when they are trying to figure out where to host a party. They tell him things they wouldn't disclose to anyone else in the office. He makes other people comfortable, lowering their boundaries.

When planning a big fortieth birthday, Rob was trying to figure out whom to invite. When a friend asked Rob whom he would like to invite, rather than whom he felt obligated to invite, Rob responded, "Well, if I could, I would invite my therapist, my hairdresser, and my massage therapist." Recounting his friend's disbelief, Rob recalled that his response was, "You're the only person I know who hangs out and has drinks with their massage therapist and hangs out and has drinks with their hairdresser, and that would invite them to your birthday party with your inner core group of friends."

Why are some people more comfortable blurring the boundaries between work friends and "real" friends? Between transactional and affective relationships? "Well, I don't know how much of it is nature versus nurture, right?" Rob reflected. "Growing up in Turkey, not having very many Americans around on the high school campus that I grew up on . . . almost all of the ex-pats regardless of age were my aunts and uncles . . . I've got very used to having nonblood relatives." Due to the itinerant nature of his parent's work, he attended nine schools in five years. In his view, "Home's not a physical place. Relatives aren't blood related."

Preferences for segmentation and integration are shaped by the way we grew up, our personalities, caregiving responsibilities, and gender. But the demands and nature of work—whether a boss expects an email response within an hour, if the job offers a flexible schedule, whether company social events are obligatory—determine what's really possible.

We are all being nudged to varying degrees toward more integration. Email, smartphones, and online meetings make it possible to be more available than ever. Social media makes parts of our lives that historically wouldn't have been visible to colleagues accessible. As work becomes more global, nine-to-five isn't really an option for a lot of workers. Companies have on-site gyms and day care, and allow people to bring their pets to work. They are embracing community service days, offer free dinners, and have kegs in their kitchens. Increasingly, people are encouraged by the popular press and CEOs to "bring their whole selves to work." There is a rampant rhetoric of authenticity. For instance, a recent article in *Forbes* opened, "How well do you know your coworkers? Really know them. Do you know their highest aspirations? What did they want to be when they were kids? What keeps them up at night? Chances are we keep even our personal conversations at work at a surface level."

Work Friends

Most of us don't have many close friends at work. We consider most of the people we work with coworkers or strangers. On average, people have five friends at work, but we usually don't count them among our nearest and dearest. Only 15 percent meet the criteria of a "real friend." Put differently, most people only have one real friend at work.

Why is it so hard to have friends at work? And if it is so hard, is it even worth it?

Employees often don't have a whole lot of choice about whom they interact with at the office. Our teammates, office neighbors, and bosses are frequently assigned. The quasi-voluntary nature of our work relationships is one of the reasons making friends at work can be more difficult than making friends "in the wild."

Another reason the workplace is inhospitable to friendship is its transactional nature. For a salary, you agree to work a certain amount of hours or produce a given amount of a good. But in friendship, you help your friends out because they need it, not because you expect something in return. Work life is primarily a pursuit of instrumental goals, often making money. Our friendships are about affect—love, joy, shared sorrow.

Money and social connection are conflicting values, according to a study by Fred Grouzet, a psychologist at the University of Victoria, and his colleagues. The researchers asked 1,854 university students living in Australia, Egypt, China, the United States, and South Korea among other places to rate how important fifty-seven different goals were to them. The goals covered multiple domains, including hedonism, safety, spirituality, popularity, conformity, self-acceptance, and community. Based on the respondents' answers, the researchers created a map. Goals that people rated similarly—for instance, physical health and safety—were close together. Values that were rated differently—if one was very important, the other tended to be less important, and vice versa—were farther apart in the map. Financial success was the polar opposite of community and affiliation.

Dozens of psychology experiments have found that thinking about or touching money makes people less generous, less helpful, and less likely to socialize. People are happiest when they are either socializing or having sex. But simply mentioning money can make people change their priorities, according to Cassie Mogilner Holmes, a professor at UCLA.

Holmes gave 318 adults the task of creating as many three-word sentences as possible from four words in three minutes. Some of the participants in the study were given words that had to do with money, for instance, *the, change, price*. Others were given words that had to do with time (e.g., *the, change, clock*). A third control group was given neutral words. The group who thought about money were more likely to report that they planned on working in the coming twenty-four hours. They were also less likely than groups who thought about time or random things like socks to report that they planned to socialize or have sex over the next twenty-four hours. Beyond what people planned to do, people in a separate study in which they were asked to think about money were more likely to work and less likely to socialize than people asked to reflect on other topics.

The increasingly transactional nature of work may partly explain the decline in workplace friendships, according to Adam Grant. Historically, it was far more common for our work and personal lives to overlap. In 1985, close to half of Americans had a "close confidant" at the office. By 2004, only 30 percent reported having a cubicle confidant. If we look across generations, 54 percent of baby boomers graduating from high school in 1976 placed value on finding a job where they could make friends. Among generation Xers, who graduated when the first Bush was president, it was 48 percent. Among millennials, it dropped to 41 percent.

At the same time, the value placed on leisure time has consistently increased—almost doubling from 1976 to 2006. As Grant wrote, "When we see our jobs primarily as a *means to leisure*, it's easy to convince ourselves that efficiency should reign supreme at work so we have time for friendships outside work." Increasingly, we work to get a break from work.

The tension between instrumentality and affect can lead people to avoid work friends altogether or to worry that a friendly hello in the hallway has ulterior motives, or can make it difficult to manage and sustain office friendships.

Consider the following situation, which has likely been enacted with variations in hundreds of offices: John and Mario immediately hit it off when a mutual friend introduces them. They both work in sales, have kids in seventh grade, and are avid Manchester United fans. They chat about Premier League scores but also vent when sales are slow. When a position opened up at Mario's firm, he helped John secure the job. Things move along swimmingly for a while. Their families occasionally get together for dinner and they trade sales tips over coffee a couple of times a month. When Mario gets asked to spend six weeks at a training in Germany, he doesn't think twice before asking John to cover his accounts. When he returns, John keeps calling on some of the customers that were formerly Mario's. But John is his friend. Despite the lost commissions, Mario doesn't say anything. Maybe John misunderstood and thought Mario was permanently giving him the accounts? Mario tries to forget it. Resentment builds. Weekend invitations get declined. Mario becomes a little more guarded when they discuss tactics or office politics. Eventually all that is left of the former friendship is an awkward brief man hug when they meet and empty talk about how they should get together soon.

Present Company Excluded

Regardless of what they would prefer, women and minorities have a harder time developing close relationships with colleagues. They often face different demands at home and role expectations at work. But they are also frequently excluded.

One of the first studies to examine gender differences in workplace networks was conducted by Herminia Ibarra, who is now a professor at London Business School. She compared men's and women's communication, advice, social support, influence, and friendship networks in an advertising firm in New England during the 1990s. She asked both men and women to make a list of those they were friends with and the ones they turned to for advice. Men went to friends for work advice. This wasn't the case for women. Women's networks were more segmented. They were more likely than men to have separate spheres for home and work. This difference was most conspicuous for working moms, whose life outside of work is often dominated by family, school, and their kids' activities.

"Maintaining separate spheres can put women at a disadvantage for two reasons," Ibarra explained. "First, it's more time-consuming to manage two separate networks; you can kill two birds with one stone when you are talking shop over a drink, and you'll be better informed about what is going on. Second, participating in conversations about important work matters outside formal meetings creates camaraderie and increases trust. Because women are consistently excluded from informal gatherings such as golf games and private dinners, it takes longer to achieve influence."

More than half of women and 45 percent of men think it is inappropriate to have dinner with someone of the opposite sex who isn't your spouse. According to a *New York Times* poll of 5,282 registered voters, about 40 percent of people think it is inappropriate for men and women to have lunch together. A third don't think it is okay to ride in a car. Roughly one in four thought it was inappropriate to have a work meeting alone with members of the opposite sex.

Underlying this tension is a question about whether it's even possible for women and men to be just friends. To see if *platonic* means different things to men and women, researchers brought eighty-eight mixed-gender pairs of friends into the lab. The experimenters wanted to see if one or both of the friends secretly hoped "romance" was in the cards. The research team from the

University of Wisconsin, Eau Claire, carefully ensured that the participants' answers were anonymous and confidential to avoid relationship fallout after the study. They also required both friends to verbally agree not to talk about the study after it ended. After being sworn to secrecy, the friends were separated and asked about their romantic feelings toward each other.

Even among young adults, where boundaries are likely less rigid, there was far from overwhelming evidence of attraction to opposite-sex friends. On a scale of 1 to 9, with a 1 equal to definitely not attracted to your friend and a 9 equivalent to "extremely attracted," college students averaged around a 4.5—fairly agnostic. Both men and women saw the clear downsides of being attracted to a friend—they were five times more likely to list it as a cost than a benefit. It is the threat, not the reality, that creates the problem.

As Rob said, "Most of my work friends tend to be women who are between the ages of twenty-nine and thirty-five right now. And most of them are in relationships, but not all of them. And I think one of the reasons I can be friends with them is because there is clarity that this is not something that's romantic or sexual . . . There's nothing going on."

It isn't just on the golf course that women and men aren't hanging out. It is in everyday interactions. This exclusion potentially has huge implications for careers. Summarizing the problem, Shannon Healy, a property manager in Michigan, said, "If I couldn't meet with my boss one-on-one, I don't get that face time to show what I can do to get that next promotion."

It isn't just women. All demographic minorities face similar obstacles. Two factors we've seen again and again as key determinants of friendship explain the persistence of the problem: likes attract and self-disclosure.

Company parties and picnics won't help solve this problem. It isn't simply about individuals having the opportunity to get to know one another. Developing close relationships that cross cultural, racial, gender, or sexual orientation lines can be difficult even when there are opportunities to interact outside of work. Another part of the problem, according to a study by Tracy Dumas, Katherine Phillips, and Nancy Rothbard, is that opening up about elements from your personal life is easier within your own group. The researchers surveyed 228 MBA students, 40 percent of whom were working full-time, and asked them about the types of work-related social engagements they participated in.

Just over half of the people they surveyed went to holiday parties, picnics, sporting events, and other get-togethers their companies sponsored. Forty-one percent went to employee-organized social events like happy hours and lunches. Out of the assortment of activities, drinks and happy hours were the most common (35 percent), followed by holiday parties (25 percent) and outings to the theater or sporting events (13 percent). The researchers also looked at whether employees brought friends or family along with them to company gatherings and social events with colleagues, as well as how much they talked about their life outside of work. They dubbed these *integration behaviors.*

Showing up at company parties and other integration behaviors were associated with feeling closer to colleagues—but only for employees who were in the demographic majority.

It wasn't that minorities didn't show up. They were more likely to attend. But they were also more likely to tell the researchers that they participated because they felt obligated to or were afraid of the career consequences of not showing up. Any time anyone shows up to an event out of a sense of obligation, their chances of making a new connection are about as good as if they had never walked in the door.

Finding Boundaries

Despite the barriers to having work friends—the lack of choice over whom we interact with, the instrumentality of work, tendencies of likes to attract, preferences for segmentation in a time of increasing integration—some people have and keep friends at work, even close friends.

Companies are founded by them. High school friends Bill Gates and Paul Allen brought us Microsoft. Ben and Jerry met circling the school track in middle school gym class. William Harley and Arthur Davidson, founders of Harley-Davidson, were childhood friends fascinated by how to develop a small engine that could power a bike.

Work spouses are a thing. These surrogate spouses provide support in the same way real husbands and wives do. You'd turn to them if you needed an aspirin or a phone charger or wanted to vent about a coworker down the hall. Work spouses know how you take your coffee and what you like for lunch. Estimates of how common work marriages are very widely, but Vault.com estimates that around 30 percent of people have a work spouse. Jack Donaghy and Liz Lemon from *30 Rock* are a quintessential example. In their words, Jack is Liz's "work-husband-slash-uncle," while she's his "coworker-slash-little-brother." When they try to confine their relationship to strictly work, they are at a loss. Floundering for words, Liz asks, "Hey, Jack. How's . . . business things?"

And the evidence is incontrovertible: having work friends has benefits. A meta-analysis that brought together the results from twenty-six studies incorporating more than a thousand teams found that teams composed of friends perform better than teams made up of acquaintances. Social support from coworkers reduces job stress, helps people cope with work and time pressures, reduces work/family conflict, and helps people guard against burnout. In his book *Vital Friends*, Tom Rath explores the relationship between friendship at work and performance. Utilizing a large database of respondents, he finds that employee engagement increases sevenfold when someone has a "best friend at work." Employees who report having close friends at work are more efficient, more satisfied with their job, and even less likely to get in accidents at work. The select few who have more than three close friends at work have a 96 percent greater chance of being extremely satisfied with life.

But their inherent contradictions make work friends a mixed blessing. Work friendships are difficult to maintain, can create a sense of felt obligation, and are emotionally exhausting. These downsides, according to a study of restaurant, insurance, and retail employees by Jessica Methot of Rutgers University and colleagues, can impair productivity as well as employees' emotional well-being.

While relationships with colleagues can be energizing, at

some point they become taxing. Expansionists in particular are often overloaded, which puts them at risk for burnout. When coworkers are looking for advice or help, they disproportionately turn to expansionists. Research by Rob Cross and coauthors Reb Rebele and Adam Grant found that in collaborative work as much as a third of the value added comes from no more than 5 percent of the employees. As Cross and his collaborators wrote, "What starts as a virtuous cycle soon turns vicious. Soon helpful employees become institutional bottlenecks: Work doesn't progress until they've weighed in. Worse, they are so overtaxed that they're no longer personally effective."

How can you reap the benefits of having friends at work while minimizing the downsides? Brokers are particularly adept at this.

To better understand how to balance the competing tensions that workplace relationships present, Nick and I surveyed around 500 employees and students about work/life balance and burnout; we ascertained whether they were segmenters or integrators, and we looked at their networks. They ranged in age from seventeen to sixty-four. A little more than half were female, 65 percent were white, most were employed, and around 30 percent were married.

Brokers were more likely than conveners and expansionists to report that they have work/life balance. On a scale where a 1 indicated that someone strongly disagreed with the notion that they had work/life balance and a 5 indicated they strongly agreed, conveners and expansionists were the worst off. Both groups averaged close to a 3. On the other hand, people at the top of the brokerage scale averaged a 3.7. The difference equates to moving from being ambivalent about whether you have work/life balance to pretty much agreeing that you do.

The benefits to brokerage remained statistically different once we controlled for other factors that one would suspect would influence perceptions of work/life balance, including the number of hours respondents worked, the length of time they had been in the work force, their age, their gender, their race, whether they were married, and their position along the segmentation scale. (People who were younger and worked fewer hours also felt that they had more work/life balance. There wasn't a difference between segmenters and integrators in our study.)

The same was true when we looked at work/life conflict. When asked questions about how strongly they felt that their "job produces strain that makes it difficult to fulfill outside obligations" and that the demands of their work interfere with their home and personal life, once again brokers had significantly less work/life conflict.

Like other researchers, we found that people with more colleagues they felt close or very close to were less lonely, felt more connected, and were less likely to feel personally burned out.

Brokers do not completely avoid developing close relationships at work. But they manage those relationships differently. Their worlds do not overlap. They may be close to their colleagues, family, and club friends. But they don't invite their work friends to hang out with their family. The structure of brokers' networks allows them to benefit from these upsides, while minimizing the downsides.

Courage to Change the Things You Can

As the world pushes toward greater and greater integration, brokers are holdouts. Their networks are frequently segmented. Sigmund Freud purportedly said, "Love and work are the cornerstones of our humanness." Brokers don't try to build bridges between the two.

Separating work and family is associated with less work/family conflict. Regardless of whether one wants their life to be segmented, there is often less choice about how to manage these boundaries than one would hope. As we have seen, half of integrators want more separation between their home and work lives. Much of the time, where we work and when we work is determined by our employers. One might prefer to work from home in the comfort of one's pj's, but for many people that is simply not an option. Neither is not responding to an urgent email from a boss on a scheduled day off.

One solution—according to organizational psychologists Nancy Rothbard, Katherine Phillips, and Tracy Dumas—is finding a work environment that matches your preferences. Segmenters probably won't be happy somewhere that expects employees to "bring their whole selves to work." But they would be thrilled with Google's "Dublin Goes Dark" initiative where employees left their devices at work each night. German automaker Daimler's Mail on Holiday policy would make vacation even better. The policy lets employees switch on an autodelete option that informs senders that their email will be deleted since the recipient is on vacation. It's easy to imagine, though, that either of these policies would just create anxiety for integrators. Integrators, on the other hand, would likely be happier with on-site child care and gyms in the office. When integrators work in environments that allow the boundaries of work and home to blur, they are more satisfied with their jobs and more committed to their workplace. The opposite is true for segmenters.

But what if it isn't possible to find a match? Some companies and managers have tried to create policies that give employees greater control over how they manage work/life boundaries—for instance, by allowing them to schedule "predictable time off." Summarizing one such policy, Nancy Rothbard and Ariane Ollier-Malaterre wrote, "It was the degree of control that individuals experienced when working that was associated with significantly lower family-work conflict and depression," as opposed to the policy itself.

One of the key differences between relationships at work and other aspects of our job is that we have greater control over the relationships. You don't control whom you work with but you do control the nature of your relationship with them. Will you use that power to segment or integrate? People who prefer segmentation tend to be brokers. In fact, we found that segmenters are more than twice as likely as integrators to be brokers. And while segmentation doesn't completely explain brokers' better work/life balance, relationships are one arena in which we actually have the ability to choose how much work and life collide. Many people might be expected to show up to office social events, but they probably aren't required to invite coworkers to their birthday party. No matter how privileged your position is at work, whether at a coffee shop or Goldman Sachs, you do control the nature of your relationships.

Surviving the Company Party

For people who prefer to keep home and work separate, company social events can be challenging. What may seem warm and inclusive to an integrator, like inviting families to company parties, is downright nauseating to a segmenter. An invitation may feel like an obligation. Being mindful that these differences exist when organizing company events and parties can go a long way toward helping everyone feel included.

As we have seen, for women and racial minorities these challenges can be daunting. Minorities are often reluctant to open up at work because they fear that they may not be understood, according to Sylvia Ann Hewlett, Carolyn Buck Luce, and Cornel West. "When I do try and open up personally, people just don't get it . . . So you stop trying," explained Latisha, an African American consumer goods executive. Describing his reticence to talk with colleagues about his experience working on the board of a prominent charity that supports faith-based groups and focuses on minorities, Michael, an Asian American energy firm executive, said he doesn't mention it because it involves "the big taboo subjects of the workplace: religion and ethnicity." He worries that this will lead his colleagues to conclude, "You're *differ-*

ent. I have always suspected that—and now you're confirming it."
A fear of seeming different can lead anyone to feel excluded.

The fear of difference is primarily a problem when we are
searching for similarity. One solution Katherine Phillips and her
colleagues offer is to adopt a learning mindset. It is advice that is
widely applicable for those looking to create closer relationships
at work. Instead of asking, "Did you see the Patriots game last
night?" inquire, "Have you watched anything good lately?" As the
trio wrote, "This legitimizes everyone's choices and reduces the
feeling that people may be judged on their answers, or that certain parts of the culture should be universal." Not only will it
avoid offending someone who hates the Patriots, you also won't
create a conversation stopper and potential relationship killer for
non–football fans. You also might discover something new to
keep you entertained, as well as deeper and less obvious commonalities.

Similarities lead to greater feelings of closeness if they are rare.
When people in an experiment were told they had similar fingerprints, feelings of closeness increased a bit. When participants were
informed that they shared extremely rare "type E" fingerprints—
occurring in just 2 percent of the population—their connection
was stronger. If you want to build trust and connection, Adam
Grant suggests, "don't just look for commonalities. Look for uncommon commonalities."

Ben Friberg, a photographer, was waiting with his colleague
for an interview. While waiting, the pair began talking about the
film *Troy*. (Hopefully, he didn't ask her if she had seen *Troy*, but
had asked what movies she had recently seen.) "We were still in

the 'getting to know you' phase," recalled Friberg, who had just joined the television station. When his colleague began pointing out differences between the *Iliad* and the film, they discovered a mutual love of Greek mythology. "I can remember thinking, 'This is going to be a different type of relationship,'" recalled Friberg.

As Phillips, Dumas, and Rothbard wrote, "Bonding around the work itself is powerful, especially for those who are collaborating across racial boundaries. But over time, deeper relationships depend on people's opening up about their personal lives. For that to happen, colleagues must be intentional about getting out of their comfort zones and connecting with people who are different. That may feel like a risk, but it's one worth taking."

And while companies can't force people to be friends, it is possible for them to design events that harness the diversity of the workplace and allow trust to develop. The lack of choice and need to overcome preferences for similarity, which can make developing close relationships at the office so difficult, turn out to have potentially radically positive benefits for companies and society— if companies can get it right.

We encounter people who don't look like us at the office—this is true irrespective of race. While workplace racial segregation remains significant in the United States, offices are far more racially and ethnically diverse than schools, voluntary organizations, and churches. Martin Luther King Jr. once said, "It is appalling that the most segregated hour of Christian America is eleven o'clock on Sunday morning." More than sixty years later, churches and other voluntary organizations are the second most segregated domains of life. Schools are even more racially and ethnically divided than churches. Friendships created at school have a 13 percent chance of being interracial, according to a representative survey of more than 1,000 adults by University of New Mexico professor Reuben Thomas. At the office it's almost twice as likely that we will have friendships that cross racial lines. Close to one in four work friends are racially dissimilar.

If we are going to have a society where people understand people who are different from them, work is where that is most likely to take root.

The Career-Making Relationship

Consider for a moment the person who has most profoundly impacted your career. Take a moment to thank them. Whether you'd call that person a mentor, sponsor, or something else entirely, the more significant a presence he or she has had in your life, the more successful you are likely to be. To succeed at work, you need someone to advocate for you, put your name in the hat for stretch assignments, and make introductions. Sometimes the person is a friend, but sometimes he or she isn't.

The vast majority of men and women—76 percent and 83 percent, respectively—report having at least one mentor during their careers. The relationship between mentors and protégés differs from other types of relationships, such as friendships, supervisor/employee, or therapist/patient, though it combines elements of all of them. Mentors are role models with more experience than protégés. They provide guidance, emotional support, and an opportunity for self-reflection and development. As Simmons College professor Stacy Blake-Beard put it, mentorship is a "dynamic, reciprocal relationship that is mutually beneficial, empowering and enabling."

Like most social relationships, mentor/protégé relationships usually form along lines of surface-level similarities. Mentors and protégés look alike. This disadvantages women and people of color, since post-MBA protégés make roughly $28,000 more if they are mentored by a white man. As Sylvia Ann Hewlett and her collaborators wrote in the *Harvard Business Review*, because cross-gender relationships "can be misconstrued as sexual interest, highly qualified women and highly placed men avoid" them. In the wake of recent waves of sexual harassment charges, the number of men who report being uncomfortable mentoring or sponsoring women has tripled.

But research consistently finds that the best mentoring, like many of the best relationships, occurs when there is some similarity and some difference. A study of more than 220 pairs of doctoral students and their advisers found that approximately two-thirds of protégés had a mentor of the same sex. In the short term, when a doctoral student had a same-sex adviser, they received more emotional support, assistance, visibility, and sponsorship. However, as time went on, the relationships stagnated. They didn't get better or worse, just stayed the same. But for opposite sex mentorships, there was a marked improvement over time. Once mentors and mentees got past the difficulties of working with someone who was different, those differences actually made for a better relationship.

Mentoring relationships based on deeper similarities—beliefs, values, and experience—have better outcomes. For instance, a study that examined how much psychological support and satisfaction was provided by mentors found that relationships based on deeper similarities provided far more emotional and instrumental support than relationships in which partners were simply of the same sex or race.

We gravitate toward people who are similar to us, though we are most likely to benefit from difference.

Mentorship can help create more productive and advantageous relationships at work by providing access to people with power and influence, developing the social skills of the protégé, creating opportunities to form new ties, and acting as an endorsement and signal of respect. It is one of the most effective relationship interventions companies have at their disposal. While trying to force workplace friendships isn't advisable, even if it is possible, assigning mentors is. Yet many companies still insist on assigning mentors along demographic lines. Recruiters often tout mentorship programs for women and other minorities in which people are paired with a mentor of the same sex, same race, or same sexual preference.

A formal program could help obviate some of the endemic problems of networks built on self-similarity. However, despite the potential benefits of formal network interventions, 82 percent of women and 84 percent of men found their work mentors informally through their own networks.

A study by Sameer Srivastava, a professor at the University of California, Berkeley, compared the career outcomes of employees with high potential in a software development laboratory who were randomly assigned a mentor to the careers of similar employees in a matched control group. Employees who were randomly assigned a mentor gained greater access to people in power and developed a broader network as a result of participating in the mentorship program. Similarly, Forrest Briscoe at Penn State and Katherine Kellogg at MIT found that lawyers who were randomly assigned to a powerful supervisor when entering a firm had bonuses that were on average $30,000 higher and were 18 percent less likely to quit than associates who spent no time with powerful supervisors when they joined the organization.

In a separate study of MBA alumni from across the globe, Herminia Ibarra and her colleagues compared the effect of formal and informal mentors on career success. Women who connected with a mentor through a formal program received 50 percent more promotions than women who found their mentor informally. The same isn't true for men. They are more likely than women to find powerful mentors who can advance their careers through their informal ties, so they may be less likely to benefit from formal assignment.

"Intentionality on both sides really matters," according to W. Brad Johnson, a professor at the U.S. Naval Academy and author of several books on mentoring. "If there is one variable that shows if mentorship relationships are likely to take off or not, it's frequency of interaction during the first several months of the relationship."

While many people can fondly recall a mentor who provided guidance and emotional support, there is a relationship that is far rarer but much more important for career advancement: sponsorship. One in five men have a sponsor. One in eight women do.

Sponsors differ from mentors in that they advocate for the sponsee, make social connections, and use their own social capital on behalf of the sponsee. The former Chief Diversity Officer at GE, Deborah Elam, said the distinction between sponsors and mentors lies in the fact that a sponsor will "put their name next to your performance." While both mentors and sponsors often provide emotional and instrumental support, mentors are closer to friends. Sponsors are advocates and investors. Their support is public and they use their reputation to support yours.

Sponsorship is one of the strongest predictors of promotions and salaries—roughly equivalent to the number of hours someone works—according to a study that examined the careers of tens of thousands of employees and dozens of predictors of job success. For promotion prospects, sponsorship matters more than someone's gender, personality, education, and experience. The same was true for career satisfaction. Career success is as much a game of getting a sponsor as it is one of performing well.

Unlike mentors, sponsors are difficult (if not impossible) to assign. Given the nature of the relationship, sponsorship has to be earned. When asked what it took to build relationships with three great sponsors, Sian McIntyre, the Managing Director of Advocacy and Customer Experience at Barclays, put it succinctly: "I've delivered."

Stretch assignments in which you have the opportunity to showcase your skills can be helpful if you are looking for a sponsor. Other options are volunteering to take on roles and tasks that give you exposure to people you might not otherwise come across—organizing panels, writing special reports, or participating in programs to onboard new employees. However, performance and loyalty may not be enough to earn sponsorship, according to Hewlett. You need to be able to differentiate yourself from peers.

We need sponsors at work and we often need mentors in life. Work isn't all there is to life, and in life—just as at work—we often need help to get by and realize our full human potential.

You Are Not Crazy

Work friends have many benefits, but those friendships often come with a lot of baggage. This is particularly true when friends from work become "real" friends—when our work relationships overlap with family, neighbors, and confidants. Brokers have found a way to have friends at work while mitigating some of the potential downsides.

Brokering is one personal strategy for overcoming some of the work/life conflicts that arise at the office. The personal nature of the approach is part of what allows brokers to achieve work/life balance even when their employers are pushing for more and more integration. Yet the benefits of work/life balance must also be weighed against other upsides. Some expansionists thrive both personally and professionally by meeting other people. Feeling disconnected may be the real threat for them. Convening provides psychological support. A desire to feel supported may be more important to conveners than balance.

When we walk into the office, we all have different needs. We also bring with us different roles—parent, son, daughter, wife, husband, artist, advocate. No matter what approach we take, it is always a struggle to meet competing demands and negotiate different roles. As Indra Nooyi put it, "I think it's very important that we all understand that if you struggle with these choices, you're not crazy. You are human."

Thirty-three days after we returned from our trip, my mother died. In the immediate aftermath, I burrowed deep in the cocoon of my immediate family. My mentor, Lisa, who had reminded my mom and others gathered at my wedding that "Love is the only path," and who had brought me Hershey's Kisses in the delivery room, was the only person outside my family I could let in. Once I could open up a tiny bit more, I emailed my sponsor. He's never seen me cry and we don't get together outside work. His position isn't official, but he has been instrumental in my career. I knew he would help manage what needed to be taken care of at work so I could grieve. After expressing his sympathies, he said of the help I needed, "Consider it done."

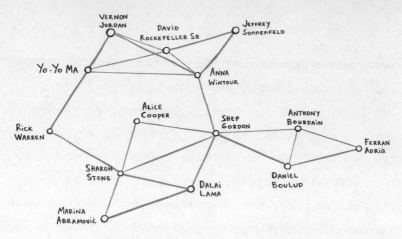

10. Everyone's Connected

Anna Wintour is among the New York City elite who frequented the Grill Room at the old Four Seasons. She is a huge fan of red meat. At the Four Seasons, it seems likely that she crossed paths with fellow regular Vernon Jordan. Vernon Jordan was a pall bearer at *The Washington Post* publisher Katharine Graham's funeral, where Yo-Yo Ma performed the Allemande from Bach's Cello Suite no. 6. The cellist also performed at Barack Obama's 2009 inauguration, where Rick Warren delivered the invocation. A few years prior, the pastor sat near Sharon Stone at the L.A. premiere of *An Inconvenient Truth*. The actress has described herself as a friend of the Dalai Lama. She introduced her onetime boyfriend Shep Gordon, whom she met at a Cannes Film Festival party, to His Holiness. The talent manager once served the Dalai Lama yak tea.

The notion that all 7.7 billion people on the planet are closely connected was popularized in the John Guare play *Six Degrees of Separation*. As his character recounts:

> I read somewhere that everyone on this planet is separated by only six other people. Six degrees of separation. Between us and everybody else on this planet. The president of the United States. A gondolier in Venice. Fill in the names. I find that A) tremendously comforting that we're so close and B) like Chinese water torture that we're so close. Because you have to find the right six people to make the connection. It's not just big names. It's anyone.

The idea is often attributed to a clever experiment conducted in 1967 by famed psychologist Stanley Milgram. During his travels to locales as far-flung as Madagascar and American Samoa, Milgram would engage locals and fellow travelers in a game. Approaching someone, perhaps at a bar overlooking a beach, he would ask if they would humor him and see if they could find friends or acquaintances that would connect them to him. It was a shortcut to the common cocktail party phenomenon of discovering a common acquaintance and proclaiming, "What a small world!" Eventually Milgram decided to formally test the proposition. The experiment and the paper that reported his findings were aptly titled "The Small-World Problem."

Milgram and Jeffrey Travers sent packets describing the experiment to close to three hundred people in Nebraska and Boston. The goal was to pass the packet through the shortest possible chain to a target. The target was a stockbroker who worked in Boston and lived in Sharon, Massachusetts.

A third of the people at the beginning of the chain were people who lived near Boston but didn't have any other known connections to the stockbroker. A third were Nebraskans who were "blue chip stockholders." And the final third were randomly chosen Nebraskans. The idea was to see if being geographically closer or loosely professionally connected to the target would produce shorter chains.

The experiment had a critical rule: messages were to be passed along only to someone the sender knew on a first-name basis. If the sender happened to know the target personally, which was unlikely at the start, they could send him the letter directly. If not, they were asked to send it to someone they knew who they thought would be closer to the target.

The average chain length or number of intermediaries required to link the initial sender to the target was 5.2. Of the initial 296 letters, 217 were passed on at least once. Of those, 29 percent eventually made it to the stockbroker in Massachusetts. Chains beginning in Boston were a bit shorter than those originating in Nebraska. Boston-based letters required 4.4 intermediaries, compared to 5.7 for randomly selected people in Nebraska. Stock owners didn't have any real advantage. The length of their chains was indistinguishable from others. Rounding the average number to the nearest whole to avoid partial people, there were six degrees of separation.

Of letters that reached the stockbroker, close to half reached him through the same three people. One of which was Mr. G., a clothing merchant in Sharon. He was responsible for completing 25 percent of the chains. Packets weren't passed at random. They funneled through key channels.

Three questions remained for decades after the small world experiment: Was the world getting smaller? Why was the world small? And could Milgram's experiment be replicated? Duncan Watts, a sociologist and pioneering network scientist, set out to tackle these questions more than thirty years after Milgram's original experiment.

Watts, along with collaborators Peter Dodds and Roby Muhamad, who were then all at Columbia University, set out to once again see how small the world was. In their version of the experiment, more than 60,000 participants in 166 countries tried to reach one of eighteen targets in thirteen countries, including a Norwegian army veterinarian, an Australian police officer, an Estonian archival inspector, and an Indian technology consultant. Despite the enormous geographic and social distances, the researchers reached a familiar conclusion. After accounting for chains that were never completed, it took roughly six steps for the messages to reach their targets.

This time, however, they didn't find a Mr. G. or a Kevin Bacon. Chains didn't funnel. As Watts wrote: "Ordinary individuals . . . are just as capable of spanning critical divides between social and professional circles, between different nations, or between different neighborhoods, as exceptional people."

Successful searches disproportionately relied on professional relationships. It is at work where diversity is most likely to take root, where we are most likely to interact with people who don't look like us or think like us, where brokers are likely to thrive. Without weak ties or professional relationships, the world wouldn't be quite so small. The wonder and awe that comes with connection across cultures would be diminished. Whether it is

Facebook friends, a stockbroker in Massachusetts, or Rick Warren and Yo-Yo Ma, we are all closely connected. But how?

Perfect Order or Perfect Disorder?

Neural networks, food chains, power grids, corporate board interlocks, movie stars, the internet, and your neighbors all share a set of network properties. They are all small worlds. But as Watts wrote, rather than asking, "'How small is our world?,' one could ask, 'What would it take for any world, not just ours, but any world at all, to be small?'"

Rather than going out into the world and measuring different networks and comparing their properties, he took a different approach. Watts and his dissertation adviser, Steven Strogatz, decided to approach the problem by relying on mathematical models. The problem seemed answerable by graph theory, the mathematical domain for studying and representing social networks. Watts and Strogatz began by creating two extreme forms of a network.

One is what they called a "regular" network. Its name derived from its consistent pattern, not its ordinariness. Visualize a network as twenty dots on the perimeter of a circle, with each dot representing a person with connections to four others. In a regular network, everyone is connected to the person directly to the right and the person to the right of their neighbor. The same is true on the left side. If your neighborhood worked like this, you would be friends with your next-door neighbors and the person two doors down on either side. A regular network is perfectly ordered, there is nothing random about it.

At the other extreme is a perfectly random network. There isn't a pattern to who is likely to be friends. You could drop four marbles and whichever dot they were closest to on the circle would be your friends. Random networks that were the same size as regular networks didn't have clusters. There weren't neighborhoods. But there were very short chains between everyone in the circle.

Small world networks, of which human networks are just one example, lie in the middle of the continuum. They have enough order to make them searchable and enough randomness to provide the shortcuts necessary to create a small world. They strike a perfect balance of chaos and order.

To illustrate how small worlds work, let's go back to the circle imagery. Imagine you are sitting in a circle of twenty people trying to pass a message to the other side of the circle. Each person can talk only to the people on their immediate right or left. To pass a message to the other side of the circle with these rules, it would have to go through nine other people. Now imagine even one person can send a message to a random person in the circle who isn't their neighbor. The number of needed intermediaries to pass the message drops, possibly precipitously. If a few people have this power, it almost certainly declines dramatically. All it takes is a few shortcuts and the world quickly becomes smaller.

In their pathbreaking work, Watts and Strogatz found that small world networks have two properties: they have dense connected clusters or cliques and a few random ties connecting the clusters that create short chains between everyone in the network. Small worlds also tend to have a few nodes that have a very large number of connections. It is the same property we saw in human networks—most people have hundreds of connections, but expansionists have many times more.

Put differently, to create a small world you need the dense cliques of conveners. Within their dense networks, everyone is easily reachable. Within convener-heavy neighborhoods, schools, and communities, information can quickly spread. For simply passing a letter, this doesn't mean much. But, when living, procreating, building a life, and taking risks to plan for the future, these deep redundant networks help us find trust and support.

Small world networks also need brokers and expansionists to bridge the gap between these groups. In a simple note-passing experiment, these roles may seem similar. However, in society, their roles diverge. Brokers have an extraordinary ability to have differentiated relationships with people spanning different social worlds that provide benefits from creativity to organizational influence. While expansionists, with more plentiful but shallower contacts, have an incredible ability to mobilize large groups quickly and inspire.

In combination, brokers, expansionists, and conveners make the world small. They strike a beautiful balance between order and randomness. This is how brains and ecosystems and ant colonies work. Despite the differences in personality and preferences of brokers, expansionists, and conveners, they all contribute to creating a brilliant, vibrant human order.

Notes

1. Making Connections

1 **how Jordan describes what happened:** Vernon E. Jordan Jr., "American Odyssey." *Newsweek,* October 29, 2001. https://www.newsweek.com /american-odyssey-154197.

2 **"more corporate executives than anyone":** Jeff Gerth, "The First Friend—A Special Report. Being Intimate with Power, Vernon Jordan Can Wield It." *New York Times,* July 14, 1996. https://www.nytimes.com/1996 /07/14/us/first-friend-special-report-being-intimate-with-power-vernon -jordan-can-wield-it.html.

3 **His rebuttal is:** Sujeet Indap, "Vernon Jordan: 'It's Not a Crime to Be Close to Wall St.'" *Financial Times,* August 17, 2018. https://www.ft.com/content /429c9540-9fd0-11e8-85da-eeb7a9ce36e4.

3 **center of the *inner circle*:** Michael Useem, *The Inner Circle: Large Corporations and the Rise of Business Political Activity in the U.S. and U.K.* New York: Oxford University Press, 1986.

3 **"network remained highly connected":** Johan S. G. Chu and Gerald F. Davis, "Who Killed the Inner Circle? The Decline of the American Corporate Interlock Network." *American Journal of Sociology* 122, no. 3 (November 2016): 714–54. https://doi.org/10.1086/688650.

3 **unparalleled ability to network:** Indap, "Vernon Jordan: 'It's Not a Crime to Be Close to Wall St.'"

3 **"Rosa Parks of Wall Street":** Ibid.

3 **commencement address:** Patricia Sellers, "A Boss's Advice to Young Grads." *Fortune,* June 7, 2012. https://fortune.com/2012/06/07/a-bosss-advice-to-young-grads/.

4 *social capital* **makes "possible":** James S. Coleman, *Foundations of Social Theory.* Cambridge, MA: Harvard University Press, 1990.

5 **different network structures:** Nicholas A. Christakis, "Making Friends in New Places." *New York Times,* August 1, 2015. https://www.nytimes.com/2015/08/02/education/edlife/making-friends-in-new-places.html.

7 **which type is Vernon Jordan:** Throughout this book I frequently draw on the stories of individuals to exemplify different network structures. While I wish I were able to analyze their actual networks, I unfortunately do not have access to the data to do a formal analysis. Unless otherwise noted, they should only be taken as illustrative examples of many of the characteristics of brokers, conveners, and expansionists.

7 **a seeming contradiction:** Vernon E. Jordan Jr., "Vernon Jordan, Living Self-Portrait." Interview by Marc Pachter. National Portrait Gallery, Smithsonian Institution, April 6, 2012. Video, 1:16:17. https://www.youtube.com/watch?v=chxO0gYrW4U.

7 **his brokering role:** Gerth, "The First Friend—A Special Report."

8 **personality and networks:** Ruolian Fang et al., "Integrating Personality and Social Networks: A Meta-Analysis of Personality, Network Position, and Work Outcomes in Organizations." *Organizational Science* 26, no. 4 (July–August 2015): 1243–60. https://doi.org/10.1287/orsc.2015.0972.

8 **track individuals' social interactions:** Marissa King and Ingrid Nembhard, "Networks and Nonverbal Behavior." Academy of Management, 2015. Slides available at socialchemistry.com.

9 **Jordan is an extreme case:** Jordan, "Vernon Jordan, Living Self-Portrait."

9 **found their jobs:** Stanford Center on Poverty and Inequality, "Social Networks and Getting a Job: Mark Granovetter." Video, 5:51. https://www.youtube.com/watch?v=g3bBajcR5fE.

10 **"not a friend, just an *acquaintance*":** Ibid.

10 **how social networks function:** Mark S. Granovetter, "The Strength of Weak Ties." *American Journal of Sociology* 78, no. 6 (May 1973): 1360–80. https://doi.org/10.1086/225469.

10 **changes in the professional landscape:** Peter V. Marsden and Elizabeth E. Gorman, "Social Networks, Job Changes, and Recruitment." In *Sourcebook of Labor Markets,* eds. Ivar Berg and Arne L. Kalleberg, 467–502. New York: Springer, 2001; Emilio J. Castilla, George J. Lan, and Ben A. Rissing, "Social Networks and Employment: Outcomes (Part 2)." *Sociology Compass* 7, no. 12 (December 2013): 1013–26. https://doi.org/10.1111/soc4.12095.

10 **less time searching:** Federico Cingano and Alfonso Rosolia, "People I Know: Job Search and Social Networks." *Journal of Labor Economics* 30, no. 2 (2012): 291–332.

10 **end up in higher paying:** Marsden and Gorman, "Social Networks, Job Changes, and Recruitment."

10 **more prestigious occupations:** Nan Lin, "Social Networks and Status Attainment." *Annual Review of Sociology* 25, no. 1 (August 1999): 467–87. https://doi.org/10.1146/annurev.soc.25.1.467.

10 **get buy-in:** Joel M. Podolny and James N. Baron, "Resources and Relationships: Social Networks and Mobility in the Workplace." *American Sociological Review* 62, no. 5 (October 1997): 673–93.

10 **have better ideas:** Ronald S. Burt, *Brokerage and Closure: An Introduction to Social Capital.* New York: Oxford University Press, 2005.

11 **attend conferences and large meetings:** PricewaterhouseCoopers LLP, *The Economic Significance of Meetings to the U.S. Economy.* Tampa: PricewaterhouseCoopers, 2014.

11 **the *structure* of your contacts:** Ronald S. Burt, *Structural Holes: The Social Structure of Competition.* Cambridge, MA: Harvard University Press, 1992.

11 **chance of premature death:** Julianne Holt-Lunstad et al., "Loneliness and Social Isolation as Risk Factors for Mortality: A Meta-Analytic Review." *Perspectives on Psychological Science* 10, no. 2 (2015): 227–37. https://doi .org/10.1177/1745691614568352.

11 **"epidemic of loneliness":** Vivek H. Murthy, "Emotional Well-Being Is the Missing Key to Better Health." TEDMED, October 4, 2016. Accessed September 19, 2017. http://blog.tedmed.com/emotional-well-missing-key -better-health/.

12 **loneliness can lead to:** Louise C. Hawkley and John T. Cacioppo, "Loneliness Matters: A Theoretical and Empirical Review of Consequences and Mechanisms." *Annals of Behavioral Medicine* 40, no. 2 (October 2010): 218–27. https://doi.org/10.1007/s12160-010-9210-8.

12 **because they are lonely:** Stephen Marche, "Is Facebook Making Us Lonely?" *The Atlantic,* May 2012. https://www.theatlantic.com/magazine /archive/2012/05/is-facebook-making-us-lonely/308930/.

12 **users per month:** Evan Asano, "How Much Time Do People Spend On Social Media?" Social Media Today, January 4, 2017. http://www .socialmediatoday.com/marketing/how-much-time-do-people-spend -social-media-infographic.

12 **[Facebook] market capitalization:** "Facebook Market Cap 2009–2019," Macrotrends, 2019. https://www.macrotrends.net/stocks/charts/FB /facebook/market-cap.

12 **GDP of Norway:** "Norway GDP," Trading Economics, 2019. https:// tradingeconomics.com/norway/gdp.

12 **four hours a day:** Hacker Noon, "How Much Time Do People Spend on Their Mobile Phones in 2017?" Hacker Noon, May 9, 2017. https:// hackernoon.com/how-much-time-do-people-spend-on-their-mobile -phones-in-2017-e5f90a0b10a6.

12 **teens who see their friends:** Jean M. Twenge, "Have Smartphones Destroyed a Generation?" *The Atlantic,* September 2017. https://www .theatlantic.com/magazine/archive/2017/09/has-the-smartphone -destroyed-a-generation/534198/.

12   **Positive social interactions:** Emily D. Heaphy and Jane E. Dutton, "Positive Social Interactions and the Human Body at Work: Linking Organizations and Physiology." *Academy of Management Review* 33, no. 1 (2008): 137–62. https://doi.org/10.5465/amr.2008.27749365.

12   **depression, anxiety, and suicide:** Sally C. Curtin, Margaret Warner, and Holly Hedegaard, "Increase in Suicide in the United States, 1999–2014." NCHS Data Brief 241 (April 2016): 1–8; Kevin Eagan et al., *The American Freshman: Fifty-Year Trends: 1966–2015.* Los Angeles: Higher Education Research Institute, 2016; Ramin Mojtabai, Mark Olfson, and Beth Han, "National Trends in the Prevalence and Treatment of Depression in Adolescents and Young Adults." *Pediatrics* 138, no. 6 (2016): e20161878.

13   **predict loneliness:** Joseph P. Stokes, "The Relation of Social Network and Individual Difference Variables to Loneliness." *Journal of Personality and Social Psychology* 48, no. 4 (1985): 981–90. http://dx.doi.org/10.1037/0022 -3514.48.4.981.

13   **happier and more satisfied:** Xi Zou, Paul Ingram, and E. Tory Higgins, "Social Networks and Life Satisfaction: The Interplay of Network Density and Regulatory Focus." *Motivation and Emotion* 39, no. 5 (October 2015): 693–713. https://doi:10.1007/s11031-015-9490-1.

13   **Brokers are more satisfied with:** Henk Flap and Beate Völker, "Goal Specific Social Capital and Job Satisfaction: Effects of Different Types of Networks on Instrumental and Social Aspects of Work." *Social Networks* 23, no. 4 (October 2001): 297–320. https://doi.org/10.1016/S0378 -8733(01)00044-2.

14   **"The answer is one word":** Adam Ruben, "Nothing but Networking." *Science,* October 23, 2014. https://www.sciencemag.org/careers/2014/10 /nothing-networking.

14   **strategically thinking about social relationships:** Ben M. Bensaou, Charles Galunic, and Claudia Jonczyk-Sédès, "Players and Purists: Networking Strategies and Agency of Service Professionals." *Organization Science* 25, no. 1 (January–February 2014): 29–56. https://doi.org/10.1287 /orsc.2013.0826.

14   **"He's an associate partner":** Ibid.

16   **instrumental professional networking:** Tiziana Casciaro, Francesca Gino, and Maryam Kouchaki, "The Contaminating Effects of Building Instrumental Ties: How Networking Can Make Us Feel Dirty." *Administrative Science Quarterly* 59, no. 4 (October 2014): 705–35. https:// doi.org/10.1177/0001839214554990.

17   **a key change:** Francesca Gino, Maryam Kouchaki, and Adam D. Galinsky, "The Moral Virtue of Authenticity: How Inauthenticity Produces Feelings of Immorality and Impurity." *Psychological Science* 26, no. 7 (May 2015): 983–96. https://doi.org/10.1177/0956797615575277.

18   **impression management can lead to:** Kathleen D. Vohs, Roy F. Baumeister, and Natalie J. Ciarocco, "Self-Regulation and Self-Presentation: Regulatory Resource Depletion Impairs Impression

Management and Effortful Self-Presentation Depletes Regulatory Resources." *Journal of Personality and Social Psychology* 88, no. 4 (2005): 632–57. http://dx.doi.org/10.1037/0022-3514.88.4.632; Roy F. Baumeister, "Motives and Costs of Self-Presentation in Organizations." In *Impression Management in the Organization,* eds. Robert A. Giacalone and Paul Rosenfeld, 57–72. Hillsdale, NJ: Lawrence Erlbaum Associates, 1989.

19 **the heart of authenticity:** Bruce J. Avolio and Ketan H. Mhatre, "Advances in Theory and Research on Authentic Leadership." In *The Oxford Handbook of Positive Organizational Scholarship,* eds. Kim S. Cameron and Gretchen M. Spreitzer, 773–83. New York: Oxford University Press, 2012.

19 **"When we view authenticity":** Herminia Ibarra, "The Authenticity Paradox." In *HBR's 10 Must Reads of 2016: The Definitive Management Ideas of the Year from Harvard Business Review.* Cambridge, MA: Harvard Business Review, 2016.

20 **People with a fixed mindset:** Jennifer S. Beer, "Implicit Self-Theories of Shyness." *Journal of Personality and Social Psychology* 83, no. 4 (October 2002): 1009–24. http://dx.doi.org/10.1037/0022-3514.83.4.1009.

20 **the fixed mindset defined:** Carol S. Dweck, *Mindset: The New Psychology of Success.* New York: Ballantine Books, 2016.

21 **behaviors of shy people:** Beer, "Implicit Self-Theories of Shyness."

21 **"The ingredients of social intelligence":** Daniel Goleman, *Social Intelligence: The New Science of Human Relationships.* New York: Bantam Books, 2006, 84.

21 **less likely to socially engage:** Ko Kuwabara, Claudius A. Hildebrand, and Xi Zou, "Lay Theories of Networking: How Laypeople's Beliefs About Networks Affect Their Attitudes and Engagement Toward Instrumental Networking." *Academy of Management Review* 43, no. 1 (April 2016): 50–64. https://doi.org/10.5465/amr.2015.0076.

22 **"others like us more than we know":** Erica Boothby et al., "The Liking Gap in Conversations: Do People Like Us More Than We Think?" *Psychological Science* 29, no. 11 (2018): 1742–56. https://doi.org/10.1177 /0956797618783714.

22 **"Conversation appears to be a domain":** Ibid.

22 **in the most positive light:** Yechiel Klar and Eilath E. Giladi, "Are Most People Happier Than Their Peers, or Are They Just Happy?" *Personality and Social Psychology Bulletin* 25, no. 5 (1999): 586–95. https://doi.org /10.1177/0146167299025005004; Vera Hoorens and Peter Harris, "Distortions in Reports of Health Behaviors: The Time Span Effect and Illusory Superiority." *Psychology and Health* 13, no. 3 (1998): 451–66. https://doi.org/10.1080/08870449808407303; Jonathon D. Brown, "Understanding the Better Than Average Effect: Motives (Still) Matter." *Personality and Social Psychology Bulletin* 38, no. 2 (2012): 209–19. https:// doi.org/10.1177/0146167211432763; Sebastian Deri, Shai Davidai, and Thomas Gilovich, "Home Alone: Why People Believe Others' Social Lives

Are Richer Than Their Own." *Journal of Personality and Social Psychology* 113, no. 6 (2017): 858–77. http://dx.doi.org/10.1037/pspa0000105; Mark D. Alicke, "Global Self-Evaluation as Determined by the Desirability and Controllability of Trait Adjectives." *Journal of Personality and Social Psychology* 49, no. 6 (1985): 1621–30. http://dx.doi.org/10.1037/0022 -3514.49.6.1621.

23 **their social lives stacked up:** Deri, Davidai, and Gilovich, "Home Alone: Why People Believe Others' Social Lives Are Richer Than Their Own."

23 **"because extroverts and socialites":** Ibid.

23 **feelings lead to:** Kuwabara, Hildebrand, and Xi Zou, "Lay Theories of Networking: How Laypeople's Beliefs About Networks Affect Their Attitudes and Engagement Toward Instrumental Networking."

24 **made people feel more powerful:** Tiziana Casciaro, Francesca Gino, and Maryam Kouchaki, "Learn to Love Networking." *Harvard Business Review,* May 2016. https://hbr.org/2016/05/learn-to-love-networking.

24 **our species should be renamed:** Howard Becker, *Man in Reciprocity: Introductory Lectures on Culture, Society, and Personality.* Oxford, England: Frederick A. Praeger, 1956.

25 **"givers are able to":** Adam M. Grant, *Give and Take: A Revolutionary Approach to Success.* New York: Penguin Books, 2013, 59.

25 **MRI scans show:** William T. Harbaugh, Ulrich Mayr, and Daniel R. Burghart, "Neural Responses to Taxation and Voluntary Giving Reveal Motives for Charitable Donations." *Science* 316, no. 5831 (June 2007): 1622–25. https:// doi.org/10.1126/science.1140738.

25 **"everyone has something to give":** Heidi Roizen, "Interview with Heidi Roizen (Heroes)." Interview by Lucy Sanders, Larry Nelson, and Lee Kennedy, 2007. Entrepreneurial Heroes, National Center for Women & Information Technology. Audio, 34:33. https://www.ncwit.org/audio /interview-heidi-roizen-heroes.

25 **different types of resources:** Allan R. Cohen and David L. Bradford, *Influence Without Authority,* 2nd ed. Hoboken, NJ: John Wiley & Sons, 2005.

26 **"we cannot live for ourselves":** Sellers, "A Boss's Advice to Young Grads."

27 *cocktail party effect*: Barry Arons, "A Review of the Cocktail Party Effect." Cambridge, MA: MIT Media Lab, 1992.

28 **"know" someone:** Christopher McCarty et al., "Comparing Two Methods for Estimating Network Size." *Human Organization* 60, no. 1 (2001): 28–39. https://doi.org/10.17730/humo.60.1.efx5t9gjtgmga73y.

28 **610 people in their network:** Tian Zheng, Matthew J. Salganik, and Andrew Gelman, "How Many People Do You Know in Prison? Using Overdispersion in Count Data to Estimate Social Structure in Networks." *Journal of the American Statistical Association* 101, no. 474 (June 2006): 409–23. https://doi.org/10.1198/016214505000001168.

28 **four names:** Tyler McCormick, Matthew Salganik, and Tian Zheng, "How Many People Do You Know? Efficiently Estimating Personal Network Size." *Journal of the American Statistical Association* 105 (2010): 59–70.

29 **average person has five lines:** Author's calculations based on own survey
of 513 respondents; see also Miller McPherson, Lynn Smith-Lovin, and
James M. Cook, "Birds of a Feather: Homophily in Social Networks."
Annual Review of Sociology 27 (August 2001): 415–44. https://doi.org
/10.1146/annurev.soc.27.1.415.

30 **brokerage using a scale:** David Obstfeld, "Social Networks, the Tertius
Iungens Orientation, and Involvement in Innovation." *Administrative
Science Quarterly* 50, no. 1 (March 2005): 100–30. https://doi.org/10.2189
/asqu.2005.50.1.100.

31 **"invisible threads":** Sellers, "A Boss's Advice to Young Grads."

32 **way of drawing social networks:** "Emotions Mapped by New Geography."
New York Times, April 3, 1933. https://www.nytimes.com/1933/04/03
/archives/emotions-mapped-by-new-geography-charts-seek-to-portray
-the.html.

2. The Nature of Networks

33 **David Rockefeller's Rolodex:** David Rockefeller, *Memoirs*. New York:
Random House, 2003.

33 **cards containing details:** Joann S. Lublin, "David Rockefeller's Rolodex
Was the Stuff of Legend. Here's a First Peek." *Wall Street Journal,*
December 5, 2017. https://www.wsj.com/articles/david-rockefellers
-famous-rolodex-is-astonishing-heres-a-first-peek-1512494592.

34 **"interactions were always transformational":** Alan Fleischmann, "What
David Rockefeller Taught Me About Life and Leadership." *Fortune,* March
21, 2017. https://fortune.com/2017/03/21/david-rockefeller-died-heart/.

34 **"opportunities to form lasting friendships":** David Rockefeller, *Memoirs*.

35 **"misfit with few social skills":** James R. Hagerty, "David Rockefeller
Overcame Youthful Shyness and Insecurities." *Wall Street Journal,* March
24, 2017. https://www.wsj.com/articles/david-rockefeller-overcame
-youthful-shyness-and-insecurities-1490347811.

35 **stark contrast to his brother:** David Rockefeller, *Memoirs*.

35 **"develop a network of people":** Ibid.

36 **stable contacts we can maintain:** Robin Dunbar, *Grooming, Gossip, and the
Evolution of Language*. Cambridge, MA: Harvard University Press, 1996.

36 **size of our social group:** Robin I. M. Dunbar, "Coevolution of Neocortical
Size, Group Size and Language in Humans." *Behavioral and Brain Sciences*
16, no. 4 (December 1993): 681–94.

37 **historical and contemporary significance:** Ibid.

37 **less than 5 percent:** Robin I. M. Dunbar et al., "The Structure of Online
Social Networks Mirrors Those in the Offline World." *Social Networks* 43
(October 2015): 39–47. https://doi.org/10.1016/j.socnet.2015.04.005.

37 **users maintain between:** Bruno Gonçalves, Nicola Perra, and Alessandro
Vespignani, "Modeling Users' Activity on Twitter Networks: Validation of

Dunbar's Number." *PLoS One* 6, no. 8 (August 2011): e22656. https://doi
.org/10.1371/journal.pone.0022656.

37 **offline networks:** Thomas V. Pollet, Sam G. B. Roberts, and Robin I. M.
Dunbar, "Use of Social Network Sites and Instant Messaging Does Not
Lead to Increased Offline Social Network Size, or to Emotionally Closer
Relationships with Offline Network Members." *Cyberpsychology, Behavior,
and Social Networking* 14, no. 4 (April 2011): 253–58. https://doi.org
/10.1089/cyber.2010.0161.

37 **series of concentric circles:** James Stiller and Robin I. M. Dunbar,
"Perspective-Taking and Memory Capacity Predict Social Network Size."
Social Networks 29, no. 1 (January 2007): 93–104. https://doi.org/10.1016/j
.socnet.2006.04.001.

37 **roughly multiples of three:** Wei-Xing Zhou et al., "Discrete Hierarchical
Organization of Social Group Sizes." *Proceedings of the Royal Society B:
Biological Sciences* 272, no. 1561 (February 22, 2005): 439–44. https://doi
.org/10.1098/rspb.2004.2970.

39 **"fixed amount of social capital":** Maria Konnikova, "The Limits of
Friendship." *The New Yorker,* October 7, 2014. https://www.newyorker
.com/science/maria-konnikova/social-media-affect-math-dunbar-number
-friendships.

39 **minutes a day:** Bureau of Labor Statistics, "American Time Use Survey,"
2017. Accessed July 24, 2019. https://www.bls.gov/tus/database.htm.

40 **The strength of a tie:** Peter V. Marsden and Karen E. Campbell,
"Measuring Tie Strength." *Social Forces* 63, no. 2 (December 1984):
482–501. https://doi.org/10.1093/sf/63.2.482; Peter V. Marsden and Karen
E. Campbell, "Reflections on Conceptualizing and Measuring Tie
Strength." *Social Forces* 91, no. 1 (September 2012): 17–23. https://doi.org
/10.1093/sf/sos112.

40 **from acquaintances to casual friends:** Jeffrey A. Hall, "How Many Hours
Does It Take to Make a Friend?" *Journal of Social and Personal
Relationships* 36, no. 4 (April 2010): 1278–96. https://doi.org/10.1177
/0265407518761225.

41 **tie strength was likely:** Mark S. Granovetter, "The Strength of Weak Ties."
American Journal of Sociology 78, no. 6 (May 1973): 1360–80. https://doi
.org/10.1086/225469.

41 **"difference between acquaintances and friends":** Marcia Ann Gillespie,
"Maya Angelou on the Difference Between Acquaintances and Friends."
Interview by Marcia Ann Gillespie, 2011. *Essence,* May 28, 2014. http://
people.com/celebrity/maya-angelou-dies-read-her-thoughts-on
-friendship/.

41 **closeness and intimacy:** Catherine L. Bagwell and Michelle E. Schmidt,
Friendships in Childhood and Adolescence. New York: Guilford Press, 2011.

41 **evolution of the relationship:** Ronit Kark, "Workplace Intimacy in
Leader-Follower Relationships." In *The Oxford Handbook of Positive*

Organizational Scholarship, eds. Kim S. Cameron and Gretchen M. Spreitzer, 423–38. New York: Oxford University Press, 2012.

42 **provide emotional support, help guard against depression:** Nan Lin, Alfred Dean, and Walter M. Ensel, eds., *Social Support, Life Events, and Depression.* London: Academic Press, 1986.

42 **receive financial support from:** Barry Wellman and Scot Wortley, "Different Strokes from Different Folks: Community Ties and Social Support." *American Journal of Sociology* 96, no. 3 (November 1990): 558–88. https://doi.org/10.1086/229572.

43 **a long shared history:** Mario L. Small and Christopher Sukhu, "Because They Were There: Access, Deliberation, and the Mobilization of Networks for Support." *Social Networks* 47 (October 2016): 73–84. https://doi.org /10.1016/j.socnet.2016.05.002; Alejandro Portes, "Social Capital: Its Origins and Applications in Modern Sociology." *Annual Review of Sociology* 24 (August 1998):1–24. https://doi.org/10.1146/annurev.soc.24.1.1.

43 **difficulty of saying no:** Ester Villalonga-Olives and Ichiro Kawachi, "The Dark Side of Social Capital: A Systematic Review of the Negative Health Effects of Social Capital." *Social Science and Medicine* 194 (December 2017): 105–27. https://doi.org/10.1016/j.socscimed.2017.10.020.

43 **advice from people with experience:** Mario Luis Small, "Weak Ties and the Core Discussion Network: Why People Regularly Discuss Important Matters with Unimportant Alters." *Social Networks* 35, no. 3 (July 2013): 470–83.

44 **because they crossed paths:** Mario Luis Small, *Unanticipated Gains: Origins of Networks Inequality in Everyday Life.* New York: Oxford University Press, 2009.

44 **because they were available:** Small and Sukhu, "Because They Were There: Access, Deliberation, and the Mobilization of Networks for Support."

45 **has two confidants:** Matthew E. Brashears, "Small Networks and High Isolation? A Reexamination of American Discussion Networks." *Social Networks* 33, no. 4 (October 2011): 331–41.

45 **40 percent of phone calls:** Jari Saramäki et al., "Persistence of Social Signatures in Human Communication." *Proceedings of the National Academy of Sciences of the USA* 111, no. 3 (January 21, 2014): 942–47. https://doi.org/10.1073/pnas.1308540110.

45 **five close friends:** David Nield, "Humans Can Really Only Maintain Five Close Friends, According to this Equation," May 5, 2016. https://www .sciencealert.com/the-latest-data-suggests-you-can-only-keep-five-close -friends.

46 **primary caregiver influenced:** John Bowlby, *Attachment and Loss.* New York: Basic Books, 1969.

46 **expectations determine how we behave:** R. Chris Fraley et al., "Patterns of Stability in Adult Attachment: An Empirical Test of Two Models of

Continuity and Change." *Journal of Personality and Social Psychology* 101, no. 5 (November 2011): 974–92. http://dx.doi.org/10.1037/a0024150.

46 **your attachment style:** Bethany Saltman, "Can Attachment Theory Explain All Our Relationships?" The Cut, *New York*, July 5, 2016. https://www.thecut.com/2016/06/attachment-theory-motherhood-c-v-r .html.

46 **three attachment styles:** Omri Gillath, Gery C. Karantzas, and Emre Selcuk, "A Net of Friends: Investigating Friendship by Integrating Attachment Theory and Social Network Analysis." *Personality and Social Psychology Bulletin* 43, no. 11 (November 2017): 1546–65. https://doi.org /10.1177/0146167217719731.

46 **statements like:** O. Gillath et al., "Development and Validation of a State Adult Attachment Measure (SAAM)." *Journal of Research in Personality* 43, no. 3 (2009): 362–73. http://dx.doi.org/10.1016/j.jrp.2008.12.009.

46 **the anxiously attached:** Elizabeth Laura Nelson, "What Your Relationship Attachment Style Says About You." SHE'SAID', August 4, 2019. https:// shesaid.com/relationship-attachment-style/.

47 **associated with weaker ties:** Gillath, Karantzas, and Selcuk, "A Net of Friends: Investigating Friendship by Integrating Attachment Theory and Social Network Analysis."

48 **Take Brittany Wright as an example:** Brittany Wright, "What It's Like to Have No Real Friends." *Cosmopolitan,* February 23, 2016. https://www .cosmopolitan.com/lifestyle/a53943/i-have-no-real-friends.

49 **people are insecurely attached:** Amir Levine and Rachel S. F. Heller, *Attached: The New Science of Adult Attachment and How It Can Help You Find—and Keep—Love.* New York: TarcherPerigee, 2012.

49 **when they aren't securely attached:** Elaine Scharfe, "Sex Differences in Attachment." In *Encyclopedia of Evolutionary Psychological Science*, eds. Todd K. Shackelford and Viviana A. Weekes-Shackelford. New York: Springer, 2017.

49 **poverty during childhood:** Marian J. Bakermans-Kranenburg, Marinus H. van IJzendoorn, and Pieter M. Kroonenberg, "Differences in Attachment Security Between African-American and White Children: Ethnicity or Socio-Economic Status?" *Infant Behavior and Development* 27, no. 3 (October 2004): 417–33. https://doi.org/10.1016/j .infbeh.2004.02.002.

49 **less likely to dissolve ties:** Gillath, Karantzas, and Selcuk, "A Net of Friends: Investigating Friendship by Integrating Attachment Theory and Social Network Analysis."

50 **predict where you will be:** Chaoming Song et al., "Limits of Predictability in Human Mobility." *Science* 327, no. 5968 (February 19, 2010): 1018–21. https://doi.org/10.1126/science.1177170.

50 **"Spontaneous individuals are largely absent":** News@Northeastern, "Human Behavior Is 93 Percent Predictable, Research Says," February 19, 2010. https://news.northeastern.edu/2010/02/19/network_science-2/.

51 **"Cupid may have wings":** James H. S. Bossard, "Residential Propinquity as a Factor in Marriage Selection." *American Journal of Sociology* 38, no. 2 (September 1932): 219–24.

51 **among next-door neighbors:** Leon Festinger, Stanley Schachter, and Kurt Back, *Social Pressures in Informal Groups: A Study of Human Factors in Housing.* New York: Harper, 1950.

51 **proximity was a stronger predictor:** Mady W. Segal, "Alphabet and Attraction: An Unobtrusive Measure of the Effect of Propinquity in a Field Setting." *Journal of Personality and Social Psychology* 30, no. 5 (1974): 654–57.

52 **the effect of propinquity remains:** Ben Waber, *People Analytics: How Social Sensing Technology Will Transform Business and What It Tells Us About the New World of Work.* Upper Saddle River, NJ: FT Press, 2013.

52 **Merely being exposed:** Robert Zajonc, "Attitudinal Effects of Mere Exposure." *Journal of Personality and Social Psychology* 9, no. 9, pt. 2 (1968): 1–27. http://dx.doi.org/10.1037/h0025848.

52 **increase in perceptions of likability:** Robert F. Bornstein, "Exposure and Affect: Overview and Meta-Analysis of Research, 1968–1987." *Psychological Bulletin* 106, no. 2 (1989): 265–89. http://dx.doi.org/10.1037 /0033-2909.106.2.265.

53 **their chance co-location:** Peter Dizikes, "The Office Next Door." *MIT Technology Review,* October 25, 2011. https://www.technologyreview.com /s/425881/the-office-next-door/.

53 **adopt an open layout:** Maria Konnikova, "The Open-Office Trap." *The New Yorker,* January 7, 2014. https://www.newyorker.com/business /currency/the-open-office-trap.

53 **2,800 employees:** Todd C. Frankel, "What These Photos of Facebook's New Headquarters Say About the Future of Work." *Washington Post,* November 30, 2015. https://www.washingtonpost.com/news/the-switch /wp/2015/11/30/what-these-photos-of-facebooks-new-headquarters-say -about-the-future-of-work/.

54 **greater stress and unhappiness:** Matthew C. Davis, Desmond J. Leach, and Chris W. Clegg, "The Physical Environment of the Office: Contemporary and Emerging Issues." In *International Review of Industrial and Organizational Psychology*, vol. 26, eds. Gerard P. Hodgkinson and J. Kevin Ford, 193–237. Hoboken, NJ: John Wiley & Sons, 2011.

54 **social cohesion among residents:** Thomas R. Hochschild Jr., "The Cul-de-sac Effect: Relationship Between Street Design and Residential Social Cohesion." *Journal of Urban Planning and Development* 141, no. 2 (March 2015): 05014006. https://doi.org/10.1061/(ASCE)UP.1943 -5444.0000192 .

55 **idyllic cul-de-sac life:** Thomas R. Hochschild Jr., "Cul-de-sac Kids." *Childhood* 20, no. 2 (May 2013): 229–43. https://doi.org/10.1177 /0907568212458128.

55 **"a domed and steepled solitude":** Mark Twain, *Mark Twain's Notebooks & Journals,* vol. I: 1855–1873. Berkeley: University of California Press, 1975.

55 **two years after her death:** Audrey Gillan, "Body of Woman, 40, Lay Unmissed in Flat for More Than Two Years." *The Guardian*, April 13, 2006. https://www.theguardian.com/uk/2006/apr/14/audreygillan.uknews2.

55 **more socially connected:** Edward L. Glaeser and Bruce Sacerdote, "The Social Consequences of Housing." *Journal of Housing Economics* 9, no. 1/2 (2000): 1–23.

56 **"ordinary, everyday social behavior":** G. C. Homans, *Social Behavior: Its Elementary Forms.* Oxford, England: Harcourt, Brace, 1961.

57 **largest when we are twenty-five:** Kunal Bhattacharya et al., "Sex Differences in Social Focus Across the Life Cycle in Humans." *Royal Society Open Science* 3, no. 4 (2016): https://doi.org/10.1098/rsos.160097.

57 **network tends to get smaller:** Ibid.

57 **central in your work world:** Ronald S. Burt, "Decay Functions." *Social Networks* 22, no. 1 (2000): 1–28. http://dx.doi.org/10.1016/S0378 -8733(99)00015-5.

58 **Adolescents experience even greater turnover:** Robert Faris and Diane H. Felmlee, "Best Friends for Now: Friendship Network Stability and Adolescents' Life Course Goals." In *Social Networks and the Life Course: Integrating the Development of Human Lives and Social Relational Networks*, eds. Duane F. Alwin, Diane H. Felmlee, and Derek A. Kreager, 185–203. Cham, Switzerland: Springer, 2018.

58 **understand what predicted career success:** H. G. Wolff and K. Moser, "Effects of Networking on Career Success: A Longitudinal Study." *Journal of Applied Psychology* 94, no. 1 (2009): 196–206. http://dx.doi.org/10.1037 /a0013350.

58 **a greater sense of well-being:** Xiumei Zhu et al., "Pathways to Happiness: From Personality to Social Networks and Perceived Support." *Social Networks* 35, no. 5 (July 2013): 382–93. https://doi.org/10.1016/j .socnet.2013.04.005.

59 **deteriorating relationships can induce:** Hyo Jung Lee and Maximiliane E. Szinovacz, "Positive, Negative, and Ambivalent Interactions with Family and Friends: Associations with Well-Being." *Journal of Marriage and Family* 78, no. 3 (June 2016): 660–79.

60 **as likely to interact with:** Paul Ingram and Michael W. Morris, "Do People Mix at Mixers? Structure, Homophily, and the 'Life of the Party.'" *Administrative Science Quarterly* 52, no. 4 (December 2007): 558–85. https://doi.org/10.2189/asqu.52.4.558.

60 **clinically diagnosable social anxiety:** Ronald C. Kessler et al., "Lifetime Prevalence and Age-of-Onset Distributions of DSM-IV Disorders in the National Comorbidity Survey Replication." *Archives of General Psychiatry* 62, no. 6 (2005): 593–602.

60 **exposure to difficult social situations:** Olga Khazan, "The Strange, Surprisingly Effective Cure for Social Anxiety." *The Atlantic*, October 22, 2015. https://www.theatlantic.com/health/archive/2015/10/what-is-social -anxiety/411556/.

60 **Some exposure ideas:** Melissa Dahl, "The Best Way to Get Over Social Anxiety Is by Embarrassing Yourself in Public." The Cut, *New York,* November 14, 2016. https://www.thecut.com/2016/11/how-to-get-over -social-anxiety.html.

61 **acts of kindness or exposure:** Jennifer L. Trew and Lynn E. Alden, "Kindness Reduces Avoidance Goals in Socially Anxious Individuals." *Motivation and Emotion* 39, no. 6 (December 2015): 892–907.

62 **access to resources and knowledge:** Nan Lin, "Social Networks and Status Attainment." *Annual Review of Sociology* 25, no. 1 (1999): 467–87.

62 **described this difficulty:** Alex Williams, "Why Is It Hard to Make Friends Over 30?" *New York Times,* July 13, 2012. https://www.nytimes.com/2012 /07/15/fashion/the-challenge-of-making-friends-as-an-adult.html.

63 **feelings of closeness:** Sam G. B. Roberts and Robin I. M. Dunbar, "Communication in Social Networks: Effects of Kinship, Network Size, and Emotional Closeness." *Personal Relationships* 18, no. 3 (September 2011): 439–52. https://doi.org/10.1111/j.1475-6811.2010.01310.x.

63 **investments required to maintain friendships:** Giovanna Miritello et al., "Limited Communication Capacity Unveils Strategies for Human Interaction." *Scientific Reports* 3, no. 1950 (January 2013). https://doi.org /10.1038/srep01950.

64 **men start off more social:** K. Bhattacharya et al., "Sex Differences in Social Focus Across the Life Cycle in Humans." *Royal Society Open Science* 3, no. 4 (2016). https://doi.org/10.1098/rsos.160097.

64 **the transition to parenthood:** Cornelia Wrzus et al., "Social Network Changes and Life Events Across the Life Span: A Meta-Analysis." *Psychological Bulletin* 139, no. 1 (January 2013): 53–80. https://doi.org /10.1037/a0028601.

65 **relationships end because of:** Gerald Mollenhorst, Beate Volker, and Henk Flap, "Changes in Personal Relationships: How Social Contexts Affect the Emergence and Discontinuation of Relationships." *Social Networks* 37 (May 2014): 65–80. https://doi.org/10.1016/j.socnet.2013.12.003.

66 **listed as difficult ties:** Shira Offer and Claude S. Fischer, "Difficult People: Who Is Perceived to Be Demanding in Personal Networks and Why Are They There?" *American Sociological Review* 83, no. 1 (February 2018): 111–42. https://doi.org/10.1177/0003122417737951.

3. Conveners

69 **"undisputed party of the year":** Vanessa Friedman, "It's Called the Met Gala, but It's Definitely Anna Wintour's Party." *New York Times,* May 2, 2015. https://www.nytimes.com/2015/05/03/style/its-called-the-met-gala -but-its-definitely-anna-wintours-party.html.

69 **"here today because of Anna":** Krissah Thompson, "Michelle Obama and Anna Wintour's Mutual Admiration Society." *Washington Post,* May 5,

2014. https://www.washingtonpost.com/news/arts-and-entertainment/wp
/2014/05/05/michelle-obama-and-anna-wintours-mutual-admiration
-society.

70   **More is spent on fashion:** See https://www.commonobjective.co/article
/the-size-of-the-global-fashion-retail-market.

70   **economy of Brazil:** "GDP-Brazil." The World Bank, 2019. https://data
.worldbank.org/indicator/NY.GDP.MKTP.CD?locations=BR.

70   **named her the most powerful woman:** Natalie Robehmed, "From
Beyonce to Shonda Rhimes, the Most Powerful Women in Entertainment
2018." *Forbes,* December 4, 2018. https://www.forbes.com/sites
/natalierobehmed/2018/12/04/from-beyonce-to-shonda-rhimes-the-most
-powerful-women-in-entertainment-2018/#557bfa0b1110.

70   **Nuclear Wintour:** Madeline Stone and Rachel Askinasi, "Vogue's
Editor-in-Chief Anna Wintour Is Worth an Estimated $35 Million."
Business Insider, May 6, 2019. https://www.businessinsider.com/the
-fabulous-life-of-anna-wintour-2016-9.

70   **lose twenty pounds:** Stephen M. Silverman, "The Day Anna Wintour Told
Oprah Winfrey to Lose Weight." *People,* May 19, 2009. https://people.com
/bodies/the-day-anna-wintour-told-oprah-winfrey-to-lose-weight/.

70   **"picking people very astutely":** Joshua Levine, "Brand Anna." *Wall
Street Journal,* March 24, 2011. https://www.wsj.com/articles
/SB10001424052748704893604576200722939264658.

70   **"somebody in your corner":** Lydia Dishman, "I've Planned the Met Gala
for the Last 8 Years. Here's What I've Learned." *Fast Company,* May 1,
2017. https://www.fastcompany.com/40415014/ive-planned-the-met-gala
-for-the-last-8-years-heres-what-ive-learned.

71   **"I care deeply about my friends":** Levine, "Brand Anna."

71   **importance of these friendships:** Amy Larocca, "In Conversation with
Anna Wintour." The Cut, *New York,* May 4, 2015. https://www.thecut.com
/2015/05/anna-wintour-amy-larocca-in-conversation.html.

71   **"Behind the publicly cold facade":** Sophia Money-Coutts, "Vogue
Documentary Tries to Get a Read on the Chilly Wintour." The National,
August 3, 2009. https://www.thenational.ae/arts-culture/vogue
-documentary-tries-to-get-a-read-on-the-chilly-wintour-1.549892.

72   **"a tight and densely connected social network":** Elizabeth Currid-
Halkett, *Starstruck: The Business of Celebrity.* New York: Farrar, Straus,
and Giroux, 2011.

72   **"a stronger element of trust":** Levine, "Brand Anna."

72   **strangers can be trusted:** World Values Survey, 2019. http://www
.worldvaluessurvey.org/.

72   **most people can be trusted:** General Social Survey, 2019. https://
gssdataexplorer.norc.org.

72   **In Sweden:** World Values Survey, 2019. http://www.worldvaluessurvey.org/.

73   **trust their neighbors:** George Gao, "Americans Divided on How Much
They Trust Their Neighbors." April 13, 2016. Washington, DC: Pew

Research Center. http://www.pewresearch.org/fact-tank/2016/04/13 /americans-divided-on-how-much-they-trust-their-neighbors/.

73 **high level of trust in their employer:** Karyn Twaronite, "A Global Survey on the Ambiguous State of Employee Trust." *Harvard Business Review*, July 22, 2016. https://hbr.org/2016/07/a-global-survey-on-the-ambiguous-state -of-employee-trust.

73 **three years:** Ronald S. Burt, *Brokerage and Closure: An Introduction to Social Capital.* New York: Oxford University Press, 2005.

73 **stay with an employer:** Bureau of Labor Statistics, "Employee Tenure Survey." BLS Economic News Release, September 20, 2018. https://www .bls.gov/news.release/tenure.nr0.htm.

73 **"or life becomes impossible":** Anton Chekhov, *Uncle Vanya. Plays by Anton Tchekoff*, translated from the Russian by Marian Fell. New York: Charles Scribner's Sons, 1916. Translation revised and notes added 1998 by James Rusk and A. S. Man. https://www.ibiblio.org/eldritch/ac /vanya.htm.

73 **trust our husbands and wives:** Carolyn E. Cutrona, *Social Support in Couples: Marriage as a Resource in Times of Stress,* vol. 13. Thousand Oaks, CA: SAGE Publications, 1996.

73 **we are healthier:** Iris K. Schneider et al., "A Healthy Dose of Trust: The Relationship Between Interpersonal Trust and Health." *Personal Relationships* 18, no. 4 (December 2011): 668–76. https://doi.org/10.1111 /j.1475-6811.2010.01338.x.

73 **from teachers they trust:** University of Chicago, Urban Education Institute, "Fostering Student-Teacher Trust: New Knowledge," 2017. Accessed July 30, 2019. https://uei.uchicago.edu/sites/default/files /documents/UEI%202017%20New%20Knowledge%20-%20Fostering %20Student-Teacher%20Trust.pdf.

73 **In teams, trust improves performance:** Paul A. M. Van Lange, "Generalized Trust: Four Lessons from Genetics and Culture." *Current Directions in Psychological Science* 24, no. 1 (February 2015): 71–76. https:// doi.org/10.1177/0963721414552473; B. A. De Jong, K. T. Dirks, and N. Gillespie, "Trust and Team Performance: A Meta-Analysis of Main Effects, Moderators, and Covariates." *Journal of Applied Psychology* 101, no. 8 (2016), 1134–50. http://dx.doi.org/10.1037/apl0000110.

74 **"people at high-trust companies":** Paul J. Zak, "The Neuroscience of Trust: Management Behaviors That Foster Employee Engagement." *Harvard Business Review*, January–February 2017.

74 **physical signals of trustworthiness:** David DeSteno, *The Truth About Trust: How It Determines Success in Life, Love, Learning, and More.* New York: Plume, 2015.

74 **Wearing fake sunglasses:** Francesca Gino, Michael I. Norton, and Dan Ariely, "The Counterfeit Self: The Deceptive Costs of Faking It." *Psychological Science* 21, no. 5 (May 2010): 712–20. https://doi.org/10.1177 /0956797610366545.

75 **definition of *trust*:** Denise M. Rousseau et al., "Not So Different After All: A Cross-Discipline View of Trust." *Academy of Management Review* 23, no. 3 (1998): 393–404. https://doi.org/10.5465/amr.1998.926617.

75 **relationship between vulnerability and honesty:** B. von Dawans et al., "The Social Dimension of Stress Reactivity: Acute Stress Increases Prosocial Behavior in Humans." *Psychological Science* 23, no. 6 (2012): 651–60. https://doi.org/10.1177/0956797611431576.

75 **"tend to think of vulnerability":** Daniel Coyle, "How Showing Vulnerability Helps Build a Stronger Team." Ideas. Ted. Com, February 20, 2018. https://ideas.ted.com/how-showing-vulnerability-helps-build-a-stronger-team/.

76 **"witch hunt":** Jeffrey A. Sonnenfeld, "The Jamie Dimon Witch Hunt." *New York Times,* May 8, 2013. https://www.nytimes.com/2013/05/09/opinion/the-jamie-dimon-witch-hunt.html.

76 **Coca-Cola to the Chicago Bears:** Jeffrey Pfeffer, Kimberly D. Elsbach, and Victoria Chang, "Jeffrey Sonnenfeld (A): The Fall from Grace." Stanford Graduate School of Business Cases, OB-34A. Stanford: Stanford Graduate School of Business, 2000.

76 **"the scuffed halls of ivy":** "The Scuffed Halls of Ivy: Emory University," *60 Minutes.* Aired on July 23, 2000. New York: Columbia Broadcasting System.

77 **"does not hold up":** Josh Barro, "Black Mark for Fiorina Campaign in Criticizing Yale Dean." *New York Times*, September 23, 2015. https://www.nytimes.com/2015/09/24/upshot/black-mark-for-fiorina-campaign-in-criticizing-yale-dean.html.

77 **"destroyed a twenty-five-year career":** "The Scuffed Halls of Ivy: Emory University."

77 **"every night I cry":** Philip Weiss, "Is Emory Prof Jeffrey Sonnenfeld Caught in a New Dreyfus Affair?" *Observer,* May 17, 1999. https://observer.com/1999/05/is-emory-prof-jeffrey-sonnenfeld-caught-in-a-new-dreyfus-affair/.

77 **"If there's proof":** Kevin Sack, "Adviser to Chief Executives Finds Himself in Odd Swirl." *New York Times,* December 22, 1997. https//www.nytimes.com/1997/12/22/us/adviser-to-chief-executives-finds-himself-in-odd-swirl.html.

77 **"the cutthroat politics":** "The Scuffed Halls of Ivy: Emory University."

77 **"feel your pain":** Jeffrey Pfeffer, Kimberly D. Elsbach, and Victoria Chang, "Jeffrey Sonnenfeld (B): The Road to Redemption." Stanford Graduate School of Business Cases, OB-34B. Stanford: Stanford Graduate School of Business, 2000.

77 **powerful supporters to draw upon:** Jeffrey A. Sonnenfeld and Andrew J. Ward, "Firing Back: How Great Leaders Rebound After Career Disasters." *Harvard Business Review,* January 2007. https://hbr.org/2007/01/firing-back-how-great-leaders-rebound-after-career-disasters.

78 **"very depressed":** Pfeffer, "Jeffrey Sonnenfeld (B): The Road to Redemption."

79 **"trust is 60% network context":** Ronald S. Burt, Yanjie Bian, and Sonja Opper, "More or Less *Guanxi*: Trust Is 60% Network Context, 10% Individual Difference." *Social Networks* 54 (July 2018): 12–25. https://doi .org/10.1016/j.socnet.2017.12.001.

79 **network closure:** Ronald S. Burt, *Brokerage and Closure: An Introduction to Social Capital.* New York: Oxford University Press, 2005; James S. Coleman, "Social Capital in the Creation of Human Capital." In *Knowledge and Social Capital: Foundations and Applications*, ed. Eric L. Lesser, 17–41. Woburn, MA: Butterworth-Heinemann, 2000; Avner Greif, "Reputation and Coalitions in Medieval Trade: Evidence on the Maghribi Traders." *Journal of Economic History* 49, no. 4 (December 1989): 857–82.

79 **parental network closure:** Anette Eva Fasang, William Mangino, and Hannah Brückner, "Social Closure and Educational Attainment." *Sociological Forum* 29, no. 1 (March 2014): 137–64. https://doi.org/10.1111 /socf.12073.

80 **90 percent of the U.S.'s diamond imports:** Alexandra Cheney, "Changing Facets of the Diamond District." *Wall Street Journal,* July 23, 2011. https:// www.wsj.com/articles/SB10001424053111903554904576462291635801406.

80 **$24 billion:** Pratt Center for Community Development, "The Perfect Setting: Economic Impact of the Diamond and Jewelry Industry in New York City," January 21, 2009. https://prattcenter.net/research/perfect -setting-economic-impact-diamond-and-jewelry-industry-new-york-city.

80 **"the real treasure of 47th Street":** Roger Starr, "The Real Treasure of 47th Street." *New York Times,* March 26, 1984.

80 **One diamond dealer:** Tamar Skolnick, "New York's Diamond District and Jewish Tradition." The Algemeiner, May 21, 2014. https://www.algemeiner .com/2014/05/21/new-yorks/.

80 **seen as weak and unlikable:** Sally D. Farley, "Is Gossip Power? The Inverse Relationships Between Gossip, Power, and Likability." *European Journal of Social Psychology* 41, no. 5 (August 2011): 574–79. https://doi.org/10.1002 /ejsp.821.

80 **"Gossip is what makes":** Robin I. M. Dunbar, "Gossip in Evolutionary Perspective." *Review of General Psychology* 8, no. 2 (June 2004): 100–10. https://doi.org/10.1037/1089-2680.8.2.100.

81 **inordinate amount of time gossiping:** Dunbar, "Gossip in Evolutionary Perspective"; Robin I. M. Dunbar, Anna Marriott, and N. D. C. Duncan, "Human Conversational Behavior." *Human Nature* 8, no. 3 (September 1997): 231–46. https://doi.org/10.1007/BF02912493.

81 **ability to gossip:** Matthew Feinberg et al., "The Virtues of Gossip: Reputational Information Sharing as Prosocial Behavior." *Journal of Personality and Social Psychology* 102, no. 5 (May 2012): 1015–30; Matthew Feinberg, Joey T. Cheng, and Robb Willer, "Gossip as an Effective and

Low-Cost Form of Punishment." *Behavioral and Brain Sciences* 35, no. 1 (February 2012): 25. https://doi.org/10.1017/S0140525X11001233.

82 **willingness and motivation:** Ray Reagans and Bill McEvily, "Network Structure and Knowledge Transfer: The Effects of Cohesion and Range." *Administrative Science Quarterly* 48, no. 2 (June 2003): 240–67. https://doi .org/10.2307/3556658.

82 **hallmarks of convening networks:** Marco Tortoriello, Ray Reagans, and Bill McEvily, "Bridging the Knowledge Gap: The Influence of Strong Ties, Network Cohesion, and Network Range on the Transfer of Knowledge Between Organizational Units." *Organizational Science* 23, no. 4 (July–August 2012): 907–1211. https://doi.org/10.1287/orsc.1110.0688.

82 **"makes people feel uncomfortable":** Amandine Ody-Brasier and Isabel Fernandez-Mateo, "When Being in the Minority Pays Off: Relationships Among Sellers and Price Setting in the Champagne Industry." *American Sociological Review* 82, no. 1 (2017): 147–78. https://doi.org/10.1177 /0003122416683394.

82 **strong informal relationships:** Ibid.

82 **Each additional close tie:** Paul Ingram and Peter W. Roberts, "Friendships Among Competitors in the Sydney Hotel Industry." *American Journal of Sociology* 106, no. 2 (September 2000): 387–423. https://doi.org/10.1086 /316965. Figure of $390,000 in revenue arises from $268,000 given in the original paper adjusted for inflation through 2019.

83 **responsible for transmitting information:** Martin Gargiulo, Gokhan Ertug, and Charles Galunic, "The Two Faces of Control: Network Closure and Individual Performance Among Knowledge Workers." *Administrative Science Quarterly* 54, no. 2 (2009): 299–333. https://doi.org/10.2189 /asqu.2009.54.2.299.

83 **buy-in is critical:** Joel M. Podolny and James N. Baron, "Resources and Relationships: Social Networks and Mobility in the Workplace." *American Sociological Review* 62, no. 5 (October 1997): 673–93. https://doi.org /10.2307/2657354.

83 **associated with higher bonuses:** Mark S. Mizruchi, Linda Brewster Stearns, and Anne Fleischer, "Getting a Bonus: Social Networks, Performance, and Reward Among Commercial Bankers." *Organization Science* 22, no. 1 (January–February 2011): 42–59. https://doi.org/10.1287 /orsc.1090.0516.

83 **Social relationships were key:** Monique Valcour, "What We Can Learn About Resilience from Female Leaders of the UN." *Harvard Business Review,* September 28, 2017. https://hbr.org/2017/09/what-we-can-learn -about-resilience-from-female-leaders-of-the-un.

83 **networks after natural disasters:** Tuan Q. Phan and Edoardo M. Airoldi, "A Natural Experiment of Social Network Formation and Dynamics." *Proceedings of the National Academy of Sciences of the USA* 112, no. 21 (2015): 6595–600. https://doi.org/10.1073/pnas.1404770112.

84 **"like a boosting club":** Valcour, "What We Can Learn About Resilience from Female Leaders of the UN."

84 **"aren't cliques in high school":** Interview with author. October 31, 2018.

84 **social relations tend to focus on dyads:** Catherine Bagwell and Michelle Schmidt, *Friendships in Childhood and Adolescence.* New York: Guilford Press, 2011.

85 **"going back to high school":** Julie Suratt, "The Terrifyingly Nasty, Backstabbing, and Altogether Miserable World of the Suburban Mom." *Boston*, March 25, 2014. https://www.bostonmagazine.com/news/2014/03 /25/mean-moms-suburbs/.

85 **"Clique warfare in new-mommy circles":** Amy Sohn, "The Bitch on the Playground." *New York*, April 28, 2005. http://nymag.com/nymetro /nightlife/sex/columns/mating/11881/.

85 **populated by cliques:** CareerBuilder, "Forty-Three Percent of Workers Say Their Office Has Cliques, Finds CareerBuilder Survey." Press release, July 24, 2013. http://www.careerbuilder.com/share/aboutus/pressreleasesdetail .aspx?sd=7%2F24%2F2013&id=pr773&ed=12%2F31%2F2013.

86 **"to become mean old ladies":** Paula Span, "Mean Girls in Assisted Living." The New Old Age, May 31, 2011. https://newoldage.blogs.nytimes .com/2011/05/31/mean-girls-in-the-nursing-home/.

86 **senior communities experience bullying:** Eleanor Feldman Barbera, "Senior Bullying: How to Recognize It, How to Handle It." McKnight's Long-Term Care News, March 4, 2015. https://www.mcknights.com /the-world-according-to-dr-el/senior-bullying-how-to-recognize-it-how -to-handle-it/article/401679/.

86 **in high school:** Deborah Lessne and Christina Yanez, "Student Reports of Bullying: Results from the 2015 School Crime Supplement to the National Crime Victimization Survey. Web Tables. NCES 2017-015." Washington, DC: National Center for Education Statistics, 2016.

86 **in-group favoritism to form:** Henri Tajfel et al., "Social Categorization and Intergroup Behaviour." *European Journal of Social Psychology* 1, no. 2 (April–June 1971): 149–78. https://doi.org/10.1002/ejsp.2420010202.

87 **coin tosses:** Michael Billig and Henri Tajfel, "Social Categorization and Similarity in Intergroup Behavior." *European Journal of Social Psychology* 3, no. 1 (January–March 1973): 27–52. https://doi.org/10.1002/ejsp .2420030103.

87 **T-shirt colors:** Carlos David Navarrete et al., "Fear Is Readily Associated with an Out-Group Face in a Minimal Group Context." *Evolution and Human Behavior* 33, no. 5 (September 2012): 590–93.

87 **cooperative:** Lorenz Goette, David Huffman, and Stephan Meier, "The Impact of Social Ties on Group Interactions: Evidence from Minimal Groups and Randomly Assigned Real Groups." *American Economic Journal: Microeconomics* 4, no. 1 (February 2012): 101–15.

87   **words like *sunshine*:** Jing Yang et al., "The Brief Implicit Association Test Is Valid: Experimental Evidence." *Social Cognition* 32, no. 5 (2014): 449–65. https://doi.org/10.1521/soco.2014.32.5.449.

87   **Such membership boosts self-esteem:** Jolanda Jetten et al., "Having a Lot of a Good Thing: Multiple Important Group Memberships as a Source of Self-Esteem." *PLoS One* 10, no. 6 (2015): e0124609. https://doi.org/10.1371/journal.pone.0124609.

87   **likely to consider suicide:** Peter S. Bearman and James Moody, "Suicide and Friendships Among American Adolescents." *American Journal of Public Health* 94, no. 1 (January 2004): 89–95. https://doi.org/10.2105/AJPH.94.1.89.

88   **"the 'glue' that held us together":** Joseph Bonanno and Sergio Lalli, *A Man of Honor: The Autobiography of Joseph Bonanno.* New York: Simon & Schuster, 1983.

88   **a psychological need for familiarity:** John T. Jones et al., "How Do I Love Thee? Let Me Count the Js: Implicit Egotism and Interpersonal Attraction." *Journal of Personality and Social Psychology* 87, no. 5 (2004): 665–83. http://dx.doi.org/10.1037/0022-3514.87.5.665.

88   **likely to trust someone who:** Kaitlin Woolley and Ayelet Fishbach, "A Recipe for Friendship: Similar Food Consumption Promotes Trust and Cooperation." *Journal of Consumer Psychology* 27, no. 1 (January 2017): 1–10. https://doi.org/10.1016/j.jcps.2016.06.003.

88   **"birds of a feather":** Miller McPherson, Lynn Smith-Lovin, and Matthew E. Brashears, "Social Isolation in America: Changes in Core Discussion Networks over Two Decades." *American Sociological Review* 71, no. 3 (June 2006): 353–75. https://doi.org/10.1177/000312240607100301.

88   **"apparent universality":** Mark T. Rivera, Sara B. Soderstrom, and Brian Uzzi, "Dynamics of Dyads in Social Networks: Assortive, Relational, and Proximity Mechanisms." *Annual Review of Sociology* 36, no. 1 (August 11, 2010): 91–115. https://doi.org/10.1146/annurev.soc.34.040507.134743.

89   **the tendency toward homophily:** Daniel Cox, Juhem Navarro-Rivera, and Robert P. Jones, "Race, Religion, and Political Affiliation of Americans' Core Social Networks." Public Religion Research Institute, August 3, 2016. https://www.prri.org/research/poll-race-religion-politics-americans-social-networks/.

89   **Eighty percent:** Ibid.

90   **made cliques less ubiquitous:** Daniel A. McFarland et al., "Network Ecology and Adolescent Social Structure." *American Sociological Review* 79, no. 6 (December 25, 2014): 1088–121. https://doi.org/10.1177/0003122414554001.

91   **quick tool to assess:** Brian Uzzi and Shannon Dunlap, "How to Build Your Network." *Harvard Business Review,* December 2005. https://hbr.org/2005/12/how-to-build-your-network.

92   **poor predictors:** Hugh Louch, "Personal Network Integration: Transitivity and Homophily in Strong-Tie Relations." *Social Networks* 22, no. 1 (May 2000): 45–64.

92 **Consider the following:** A. W. Kruglanski, D. M. Webster, and A. Klem, "Motivated Resistance and Openness to Persuasion in the Presence or Absence of Prior Information." *Journal of Personality and Social Psychology* 65, no. 5 (1993): 861–76. http://dx.doi.org/10.1037/0022-3514.65.5.861.

92 **people who prefer certainty have:** Francis J. Flynn, Ray E. Reagans, and Lucia Guillory, "Do You Two Know Each Other? Transitivity, Homophily, and the Need for (Network) Closure." *Journal of Personality and Social Psychology* 99, no. 5 (2010): 855–69. http://dx.doi.org/10.1037/a0020961. Quote lightly edited for grammar and formal consistency.

92 **causes and consequences of convening:** Joseph B. Bayer et al., "Brain Sensitivity to Exclusion Is Associated with Core Network Closure." *Scientific Reports* 8 (2018): article ID 16037.

93 **social disconnection and social pain:** Naomi I. Eisenberger, "Social Ties and Health: A Social Neuroscience Perspective." *Current Opinion in Neurobiology* 23, no. 3 (February 8, 2013): 407–13. https://doi.org/10.1016/j.conb.2013.01.006.

93 **effective perspective taking:** James Stiller and Robin I. M. Dunbar, "Perspective-Taking and Memory Capacity Predict Social Network Size." *Social Networks* 29, no. 1 (January 2007): 93–104. https://doi.org/10.1016/j.socnet.2006.04.001.

93 **"Emma worked in":** Ibid. Quote lightly edited for grammar and formal consistency.

94 **perspective taking promotes:** Michelle Williams, "Perspective Taking: Building Positive Interpersonal Connections and Trustworthiness One Interaction at a Time." In *The Oxford Handbook of Positive Organizational Scholarship,* eds. Kim S. Cameron and Gretchen M. Spreitzer, 462–73. New York: Oxford University Press, 2013.

95 **fortifies social bonds:** Adam D. Galinsky, Gillian Ku, and Cynthia S. Wang, "Perspective-Taking and Self-Other Overlap: Fostering Social Bonds and Facilitating Social Coordination." *Group Processes & Intergroup Relations* 8, no. 2 (April 2005): 109–24. https://doi.org/10.1177/1368430205051060.

95 **Peter Boyd:** Peter Boyd. Yale School of Management Case Study.

96 *New York Times* **posted:** Mandy Len Catron, "To Fall in Love with Anyone, Do This." *New York Times,* January 9, 2015. https://www.nytimes.com/ . . . /modern-love-to-fall-in-love-with-anyone-do-this.html.

96 **thirty-six increasingly personal:** Arthur Aron et al., "The Experimental Generation of Interpersonal Closeness: A Procedure and Some Preliminary Findings." *Personality and Social Psychology Bulletin* 23, no. 4 (1997): 363–77. https://doi.org/10.1177/0146167297234003.

97 **self-disclosure leads to interpersonal closeness:** Ibid.

97 **leads to connection:** Nancy L. Collins and Lynn Carol Miller, "Self-Disclosure and Liking: A Meta-Analytic Review." *Psychological Bulletin* 116, no. 3 (1994): 457–75. http://dx.doi.org/10.1037/0033-2909.116.3.457.

97 **colleague who overshares:** Sue Shellenbarger, "How to Curb Office Oversharing: Co-Workers Who Talk Too Much Often Need Clear Feedback." *Wall Street Journal,* June 24, 2014. https://www.wsj.com /articles/how-to-stop-office-oversharing-1403650837.

98 **a more positive effect:** Collins and Miller, "Self-Disclosure and Liking: A Meta-Analytic Review."

98 **interpersonal intimacy is greatest when:** Susan Sprecher et al., "Taking Turns: Reciprocal Self-Disclosure Promotes Liking in Initial Interactions." *Journal of Experimental Social Psychology* 49, no. 5 (September 2013): 860–66. https://doi.org/10.1016/j.jesp.2013.03.017.

99 **"feel in some ways excluded":** R. J. Cutler, *The September Issue.* Documentary, September 25, 2009. Roadside Attractions. Quote lightly edited for grammar.

99 **having a louder echo chamber:** Burt, *Brokerage and Closure: An Introduction to Social Capital.*

4. Brokers

100 **"best cook on the planet":** Arthur Lubow, "A Laboratory of Taste." *New York Times,* August 10, 2003. https://www.nytimes.com/2003/08/10 /magazine/a-laboratory-of-taste.html.

100 **made surprise a hallmark taste:** "Spark Creates Gastronomic Storm." CNN.com, June 27, 2005. http://www.cnn.com/2005/TECH/06/27/spark .elbulli/index.html.

100 **best restaurant in the world:** "El Bulli, 'World's Best Restaurant,' Closes." BBC.com, July 30, 2011. https://www.bbc.com/news/world-europe-14352973.

101 **"nothing new under the sun":** Anthony Bourdain, "Decoding Ferran Adrià: Hosted by Anthony Bourdain." *No Reservations,* season 2, episode 13, March 28, 2006.

101 **Countless other innovations:** Andrew Hargadon, *How Breakthroughs Happen: The Surprising Truth About How Companies Innovate.* Cambridge, MA, Harvard University Press, 2003.

102 **"the big and great difference":** Bourdain, "Decoding Ferran Adrià: Hosted by Anthony Bourdain."

102 **delighted in bringing together:** Co.Create Staff, "Chef/Innovator Ferran Adrià on elBullifoundation and Feeding Creativity," March 19, 2014. https://www.fastcompany.com/3027889/chef-innovator-ferran-adria-on -the-elbulli-foundation-and-feeding-creativity; "Ferran Adrià Teams Up with Barack Obama Advisor." September 12, 2011. https://www.phaidon .com/agenda/food/articles/2011/september/12/ferran-adria-teams-up -with-barack-obama-advisor/.

102 **"connected to other disciplines":** Alison Beard and Sara Silver, "Life's Work: Ferran Adrià." *Harvard Business Review,* June 2011. https://hbr.org /2011/06/lifes-work-ferran-adria.

103 **a strong tie in common:** Gueorgi Kossinets and Duncan J. Watts, "Empirical Analysis of an Evolving Social Network." *Science* 311, no. 5757 (January 2006): 88–90. https://www.jstor.org/stable/3843310.

103 *triadic closure:* Georg Simmel, *Soziologie: Untersuchungen über die Formen der Vergesellschaftung.* Berlin: Duncker & Humblot, 1908.

104 **stronger with social similiarity:** Louch, "Personal Network Integration: Transitivity and Homophily in Strong-Tie Relations."

105 **high rates of triadic closure:** Jinseok Kim and Jana Diesner, "Over-Time Measurement of Triadic Closure in Coauthorship Networks." *Social Network Analysis and Mining* 7, no. 9 (December 2017). https://doi.org /10.1007/s13278-017-0428-3.

105 **triangles are closed:** James A. Davis, "Clustering and Hierarchy in Interpersonal Relations: Testing Two Graph Theoretical Models on 742 Sociomatrices." *American Sociological Review* 35, no. 5 (October 1970): 843–51. https://doi.org/10.2307/2093295; Hugh Louch, "Personal Network Integration: Transitivity and Homophily in Strong-Tie Relations." *Social Networks* 22, no. 1 (May 2000): 45–64. https://doi.org/10.1016/S0378 -8733(00)00015-0; Brandon Brooks et al., "Assessing Structural Correlates to Social Capital in Facebook Ego Networks." *Social Networks* 38 (July 2004): 1–15; Aneeq Hashmi et al., "Are All Social Networks Structurally Similar?" IEEE/ACM International Conference on Advances in Social Networks Analysis and Mining, 2012. https://doi.org/10.1109 /ASONAM.2012.59.

105 **significant homophily in research teams:** Richard B. Freeman and Wei Huang, "Collaborating with People Like Me: Ethnic Coauthorship Within the United States." *Journal of Labor Economics* 33, S1, pt. 2 (July 2015): S289—S318. https://doi.org/10.1086/678973.

106 **papers written by diverse teams:** Richard B. Freeman, "The Edge Effect." Hosted by Shankar Vedantam. *Hidden Brain*, NPR, July 2, 2018. Audio, 38:21. https://www.npr.org/2018/07/02/625426015/the-edge -effect.

106 **matter for performance:** Ray Reagans, Ezra Zuckerman, and Bill McEvily, "How to Make the Team: Social Networks vs. Demography as Criteria for Designing Effective Teams." *Administrative Science Quarterly* 49, no. 1 (March 2004): 101–33. https://doi.org/10.2307/4131457.

106 **employees who bridge structural holes:** Ronald S. Burt, *Brokerage and Closure: An Introduction to Social Capital.* New York: Oxford University Press, 2005.

107 **"creativity is an import-export game":** Michael Erard, "THINK TANK; Where to Get a Good Idea: Steal It Outside Your Group." *New York Times,* May 22, 2004. https://www.nytimes.com/2004/05/22/arts/think-tank -where-to-get-a-good-idea-steal-it-outside-your-group.html.

107 **IDEO:** IDEO, "Work." Accessed July 30, 2019. https://www.ideo.com/work.

107 **brokerage was instrumental in innovation:** Lee Fleming, Santiago Mingo, and David Chen, "Collaborative Brokerage, Generative Creativity,

and Creative Success." *Administrative Science Quarterly* 52, no. 3 (September 2007): 443–75. https://doi.org/10.2189/asqu.52.3.443.

107 **technology brokering:** Andrew Hargadon and Robert I. Sutton, "Technology Brokering and Innovation in a Product Development Firm." *Administrative Science Quarterly* 42, no. 4 (December 1997): 716–49. https://doi.org/10.2307/2393655.

107 **their own little island:** Erard, "THINK TANK; Where to Get a Good Idea: Steal It Outside Your Group."

108 **the *edge effect*:** Yo-Yo Ma, "Behind the Cello." HuffPost, January 21, 2014. https://www.huffpost.com/entry/behind-the-cello_b_4603748.

108 ***Sing Me Home*:** Recording Academy, "Silk Road Ensemble." Accessed July 30, 2019. https://www.grammy.com/grammys/artists/silk-road-ensemble.

108 **"In Silk Road, you also have to":** Cristina Pato, "The Edge Effect." Hosted by Shankar Vedantam. *Hidden Brain*, NPR, July 2, 2018. Audio, 38:21. https://www.npr.org/2018/07/02/625426015/the-edge-effect.

109 **"necessity to avoid falling into monotony":** Richard Hamilton and Ferran Adrià, "Ferran Adrià: Notes on Creativity." Drawing Center's Drawing Papers, vol. 110. New York: Drawing Center, 2014. Accessed July 30, 2019. https://issuu.com/drawingcenter/docs/drawingpapers110_adria.

109 **When careers wander:** Adam M. Kleinbaum, "Organizational Misfits and the Origins of Brokerage in Intrafirm Networks." *Administrative Science Quarterly* 57, no. 3 (2012): 407–52. https://doi.org/10.1177/0001839212461141.

111 **"Self-monitoring gets at a":** Melissa Dahl, "Can You Blend in Anywhere? Or Are You Always the Same You?" The Cut, *New York*, March 15, 2017. https://www.thecut.com/2017/03/heres-a-test-to-tell-you-if-you-are-a-high-self-monitor.html.

111 **High self-monitors find it easy:** Mark Snyder, "Self-Monitoring of Expressive Behavior." *Journal of Personality and Social Psychology* 30, no. 4 (1974): 526–37. http://dx.doi.org/10.1037/h0037039.

112 **Whom would you invite:** Dahl, "Can You Blend in Anywhere? Or Are You Always the Same You?"

112 **trying to discern:** Hongseok Oh and Martin Kilduff, "The Ripple Effect of Personality on Social Structure: Self-Monitoring Origins of Network Brokerage." *Journal of Applied Psychology* 93, no. 5 (2008): 1155–64. http://dx.doi.org/10.1037/0021-9010.93.5.1155.

112 **often speak first:** William Ickes and Richard D. Barnes, "The Role of Sex and Self-Monitoring in Unstructured Dyadic Interactions." *Journal of Personality and Social Psychology* 35, no. 5 (1977): 315–30. http://dx.doi.org/10.1037/0022-3514.35.5.315.

112 **humor to lighten the mood:** Robert G. Turner, "Self-Monitoring and Humor Production." *Journal of Personality* 48, no. 2 (1980): 163–72. http://dx.doi.org/10.1111/j.1467-6494.1980.tb00825.x.

112 **reciprocate self-disclosures:** David R. Shaffer, Jonathan E. Smith, and Michele Tomarelli, "Self-Monitoring as a Determinant of Self-Disclosure Reciprocity During the Acquaintance Process." *Journal of Personality and Social Psychology* 43, no. 1 (1982): 163–75. http://dx.doi .org/10.1037/0022-3514.43.1.163.

112 **less judgmental:** I. M. Jawahar, "Attitudes, Self-Monitors, and Appraisal Behaviors." *Journal of Applied Psychology* 86, no. 5 (2001): 875–83. http://dx.doi.org/10.1037/0021-9010.86.5.875.

112 **predictors of what position:** Ronald S. Burt, Martin Kilduff, and Stefano Tasselli, "Social Network Analysis: Foundations and Frontiers on Advantage." *Annual Review of Psychology* 64 (January 2013): 527–47. https://doi.org/10.1146/annurev-psych-113011-143828.

113 **more like a high self-monitor:** Dahl, "Can You Blend in Anywhere? Or Are You Always the Same You?"

113 **behavior comes across as contrived:** David V. Day and Deidra J. Schleicher, "Self-Monitoring at Work: A Motive-Based Perspective." *Journal of Personality* 74, no. 3 (June 2006): 685–714. https://doi.org /10.1111/j.1467-6494.2006.00389.x.

113 **another piece of advice:** Oh and Kilduff, "The Ripple Effect of Personality on Social Structure: Self-Monitoring Origins of Network Brokerage."

114 **greater control over valued resources:** Dacher Keltner, Deborah Gruenfeld, and Cameron Anderson, "Power, Approach, and Inhibition." *Psychological Review* 110, no. 2 (2003): 265–84. http://dx.doi.org/10.1037 /0033-295X.110.2.265.

114 **willingness to broker:** Blaine Landis et al., "The Paradox of Agency: Feeling Powerful Reduces Brokerage Opportunity Recognition Yet Increases Willingness to Broker." *Journal of Applied Psychology* 103, no. 8 (2018): 929–38. https://doi.org/10.1037/apl0000299.

114 **more empathic and sensitive:** Jeremy Hogeveen, Michael Inzlicht, and Sukhvinder S. Obhi, "Power Changes How the Brain Responds to Others." *Journal of Experimental Psychology: General* 143, no. 2 (April 2014): 755–62. https://doi.org/10.1037/a0033477.

114 **more removed and heuristic fashion:** Pamela K. Smith and Yaacov Trope, "You Focus on the Forest When You're in Charge of the Trees: Power Priming and Abstract Information Processing." *Journal of Personality and Social Psychology* 90, no. 4 (April 2006): 578–96. https://doi.org/10.1037 /0022-3514.90.4.578. Quote lightly edited for formal consistency.

114 **people who feel less empowered:** Brent Simpson, Barry Markovsky, and Mike Steketee, "Power and the Perception of Social Networks." *Social Networks* 33, no. 2 (May 2011): 166–71. https://doi.org/10.1016/j.socnet .2010.10.007.

115 **extraordinarily inaccurate:** Martin Kilduff et al., "Organizational Network Perceptions Versus Reality: A Small World After All?"

Organizational Behavior and Human Decision Processes 107, no. 1 (September 2008): 15–28. https://doi.org/10.1016/j.obhdp.2007.12.003.

116 **blind them to brokerage opportunities:** Landis et al., "The Paradox of Agency: Feeling Powerful Reduces Brokerage Opportunity Recognition Yet Increases Willingness to Broker."

117 **"impossible to know about everything":** Ferran Adrià, "The New Culinary Think Tank: elBulli 2.0." Science & Culture Lecture Series, Harvard University, 2011. Video, 1:50:55. https://www.youtube.com /watch?v=dr1O3xQY8VA.

117 **"blend in effortlessly":** John Hendrickson, "Anthony Bourdain's Obama Episode Was a Proud American Moment." *Rolling Stone,* June 8, 2018. https://www.rollingstone.com/culture/culture-news/anthony-bourdains -meal-with-obama-was-a-proud-american-moment-629690/.

117 **critical for political success:** Christopher Beam, "Code Black." Slate, January 11, 2010. http://www.slate.com/articles/news_and_politics /politics/2010/01/code_black.html.

118 **tailored responses were viewed:** Christian R. Grose, Neil Malhotra, and Robert Parks Van Houweling, "Explaining Explanations: How Legislators Explain Their Policy Positions and How Citizens React." *American Journal of Political Science* 59, no. 3 (July 2015): 724–43. https://doi.org/10.1111 /ajps.12164.

119 **networks among Florentine elite families:** John F. Padgett and Christopher K. Ansell, "Robust Action and the Rise of the Medici, 1400–1434." *American Journal of Sociology* 98, no. 6 (May 1993): 1259–1319. https://doi.org/10.1086/230190.

119 **Machiavelli would later write about:** Niccolo Machiavelli and Ellis Farneworth, *The Art of War.* Cambridge, MA, Da Capo Press: 2001[1521].

119 **defining trait of Machiavellianism:** Richard Christie and Florence L. Geis, *Studies in Machiavellianism.* New York: Academic Press, 1970.

120 **the school's Power Moms:** Terry Haward, "To All the Working Moms Suffering from PTA PTSD." *Working Mother,* January 11, 2017, updated January 11, 2019. https://www.workingmother.com/good-riddance-to-pta -power-moms.

120 **"much wider array of parents":** Jordan Rosenfeld, "Not a 'PTA Mom.'" *New York Times,* October 2, 2014. https://parenting.blogs.nytimes.com /2014/10/03/not-a-pta-mom/.

121 **"shocked to see high schoolers":** Correspondence with author. June 11, 2018.

122 **publicly broker a compromise:** Chris Winters, "GHS Headmaster: Consider Common Sense Compromise for School Start and End Time." *Greenwich Free Press,* Letter to the Editor, May 14, 2018. https:// greenwichfreepress.com/letter-to-the-editor/ghs-headmaster-consider -common-sense-compromise-for-school-start-and-end-time-106384/.

122 **successful at implementing disruptive changes:** Julie Battilana and Tiziana Casciaro, "The Network Secrets of Great Change Agents." *Harvard Business Review,* July–August 2013, 62–68.

123 **cooperative and arbitraging brokers:** Giuseppe Soda, Marco Tortoriello, and Alessandro Iorio, "Harvesting Value from Brokerage: Individual Strategic Orientation, Structural Holes, and Performance." *Academy of Management Journal* 61, no. 3 (2018): 896–918.

125 **"active hand in the distribution":** Ronald S. Burt, *Structural Holes: The Social Structure of Competition.* Cambridge, MA: Harvard University Press, 1995.

125 **understanding of cooperative brokering:** David Obstfeld, "Social Networks, the Tertius Iungens Orientation, and Involvement in Innovation." *Administrative Science Quarterly* 50, no. 1 (March 2005): 100–30. https://doi.org/10.2189/asqu.2005.50.1.100.

126 **difficult colleagues were disproportionately brokers:** Ronald S. Burt and Jar-Der Luo, "Angry Entrepreneurs: A Note on Networks Prone to Character Assassination." In *Social Networks at Work* (SIOP Organizational Frontiers Series), eds. Daniel J. Brass and Stephen P. Borgatti. New York: Routledge-Taylor Francis, 2020.

128 *the ties that torture:* David Krackhardt, "The Ties That Torture: Simmelian Tie Analysis in Organizations." *Research in the Sociology of Organizations* 16, no. 1 (1999): 183–210.

128 **Tortured brokers:** Stefano Tasselli and Martin Kilduff, "When Brokerage Between Friendship Cliques Endangers Trust: A Personality–Network Fit Perspective." *Academy of Management Journal* 61, no. 3 (2018): 802–25. https://doi.org/10.5465/amj.2015.0856.

129 **blirters are perceived to be:** William B. Swann Jr. and Peter J. Rentfrow, "Blirtatiousness: Cognitive, Behavioral, and Physiological Consequences of Rapid Responding." *Journal of Personality and Social Psychology* 81, no. 6 (2001): 1160–75. http://dx.doi.org/10.1037/0022 -3514.81.6.1160.

129 **trusted even more than non-brokers:** Tasselli and Kilduff, "When Brokerage Between Friendship Cliques Endangers Trust: A Personality –Network Fit Perspective."

130 **the bridging of religious traditions:** Annelisa Stephan, "The Silk Road Ensemble Interprets Dunhuang Through Spontaneous Live Music." The Iris, June 13, 2016. http://blogs.getty.edu/iris/the-silk-road-ensemble -interprets-dunhuang-through-spontaneous-live-music/.

131 **"murals and sculptures":** Yo-Yo Ma, "A Letter from Yo-Yo Ma," 2016. Accessed September 5, 2018. https://www.silkroad.org/posts/a-letter-from -yo-yo-ma.

5. Expansionists

132 **"never had a friend over":** Mike Myers and Beth Aala, directors, *Supermensch: The Legend of Shep Gordon.* A&E IndieFilms. Documentary, June 6, 2014.

132 **"luckiest moment of my life":** Shep Gordon, "Invisible 'Supermensch' Avoided the Spotlight While Making Others Famous." Interview by Terry Gross. *Fresh Air,* NPR, June 9, 2014. Audio, 44:38. https://www.npr.org /2014/06/09/320319268/invisible-supermensch-avoided-the-spotlight -while-making-others-famous.

133 **"significant moments in cultural history":** Tim O'Shei, "Celebrity-Maker Shep Gordon Mulls the Reality He's Helped Create." *Buffalo News,* September 17, 2016. https://buffalonews.com/2016/09/17/celebrity-maker -shep-gordon-mulls-reality-hes-helped-create/.

133 **"had only sold fifty tickets":** Myers and Aala, *Supermensch: The Legend of Shep Gordon.*

134 **Reflecting on his career:** Shep Gordon, *They Call Me Supermensch: A Backstage Pass to the Amazing Worlds of Film, Food, and Rock'n'Roll.* New York: HarperCollins, 2016.

134 **the nickname Supermensch:** Myers and Aala, *Supermensch: The Legend of Shep Gordon.*

134 **Despite his famous friends:** Ibid.

135 **networks that conform to:** Robin I. M. Dunbar, "Coevolution of Neocortical Size, Group Size and Language in Humans." *Behavioral and Brain Sciences* 16, no. 4 (December 1993): 681–94. https://doi.org/10.1017 /S0140525X00032325.

135 **knows approximately 600 people:** Tian Zheng, Matthew J. Salganik, and Andrew Gelman, "How Many People Do You Know in Prison? Using Overdispersion in Count Data to Estimate Social Structure in Networks." *Journal of the American Statistical Association* 101, no. 474 (2006): 409–23. https://doi.org/10.1198/016214505000001168.

135 **follow a bell-curve distribution:** Albert-László Barabási, *Linked: The New Science of Networks.* Cambridge, MA: Perseus Publishing, 2002.

136 **108 million Twitter followers:** Twitter, "Barack Obama." Accessed August 2, 2019. https://twitter.com/BarackObama.

136 **sheep even recognize his face:** Ben Guarino, "Sheep Learned to Recognize Photos of Obama and Other Celebrities, Neuroscientists Say." *Washington Post,* November 7, 2017. https://www.washingtonpost.com/news/speaking -of-science/wp/2017/11/07/sheep-learn-to-recognize-photos-of-obama -and-other-celebrities-neuroscientists-say/.

136 **more than 22,500 acquaintances:** Howard L. Rosenthal, "Acquaintances and Contacts of Franklin Roosevelt: The First 86 Days of 1934." PhD dissertation, Massachusetts Institute of Technology, 1960; Ithiel de Sola Pool, *Humane Politics and Methods of Inquiry,* ed. Lloyd S. Etheredge. New York: Routledge, 2017.

136 **more than 10,000 connections:** Statista Research Department, "Number of 1st Level Connections of LinkedIn Users as of March 2016." Accessed August 2, 2019. https://www.statista.com/statistics/264097/number-of-1st -level-connections-of-linkedin-users/.

136 **Popular teens are better paid:** Gabriella Conti et al., "Popularity." *Journal of Human Resources* 48, no. 4 (Fall 2013): 1072–94. https://doi.org/10.3368/jhr.48.4.1072.

136 **rewards they get from work:** Ruolain Fang et al., "Integrating Personality and Social Networks: A Meta-Analysis of Personality, Network Position, and Work Outcomes in Organizations." *Organizational Science* 26, no. 4 (April 2015): 1243–60. https://doi.org/10.1287/orsc.2015.0972.

137 **are more likely to get help:** Brent A. Scott and Timothy A. Judge, "The Popularity Contest at Work: Who Wins, Why, and What Do They Receive?" *Journal of Applied Psychology* 94, no. 1 (2009): 20–33. http://dx.doi.org/10.1037/a0012951.

138 **false ranking:** Matthew J. Salganik and Duncan J. Watts, "Leading the Herd Astray: An Experimental Study of Self-Fulfilling Prophecies in an Artificial Cultural Market." *Social Psychology Quarterly* 71, no. 4 (December 2008): 338–55. https://doi.org/10.1177/019027250807100404.

138 **the Matthew effect:** Robert K. Merton, "The Matthew Effect in Science." *Science* 159, no. 3810 (January 5, 1968): 56–63. 10.1126/science.159.3810.56.

138 **British statistician Udny Yule:** George Udny Yule, "A Mathematical Theory of Evolution Based on the Conclusions of Dr. J. C. Willis, F.R.S." *Philosophical Transactions of the Royal Society of London. Series B, Containing Papers of a Biological Character* 213, issue 402–410 (January 1, 1925): 21–87. https://doi.org/10.1098/rstb.1925.0002.

138 **American social scientist Herbert Simon:** Herbert A. Simon, "On a Class of Skew Distribution Functions." *Biometrika* 42, no. 3/4 (December 1955): 425–40.

138 **British scientometrician Derek Price:** Derek de Solla Price, "A General Theory of Bibliometric and Other Cumulative Advantage Processes." *Journal of the Association for Information Technology and Science* 27, no. 5 (1976): 292–306. https://doi.org/10.1002/asi.4630270505.

138 **Barabási-Albert model:** Réka Albert and Albert-László Barabási, "Statistical Mechanics of Complex Networks." *Reviews of Modern Physics* 74, no. 1 (January 2002): 47–97.

139 **process of preferential attachment:** Ibid.

139 **hindsight bias:** Baruch Fischhoff and Ruth Beyth, "I Knew It Would Happen: Remembered Probabilities of Once-Future Things." *Organizational Behavior and Human Performance* 13, no. 1 (February 1975): 1–16. https://doi.org/10.1016/0030-5073(75)90002-1.

139 **identifying influencers:** Giordano Contestabile, "Influencer Marketing in 2018: Becoming an Efficient Marketplace." *AdWeek,* January 15, 2018. Accessed September 27, 2019. https://www.adweek.com/digital/giordano-contestabile-activate-by-bloglovin-guest-post-influencer-marketing-in-2018/.

140 **accurate predictor of popularity:** Mitch Prinstein, "Popular People Live Longer." *New York Times,* June 1, 2017. https://www.nytimes.com/2017/06/01/opinion/sunday/popular-people-live-longer.html.

140 **"I was not popular"**: Lyle Lovett, "The Truck Song," from *My Baby Don't Tolerate,* September 30, 2003.

140 **weren't popular on the playground:** Diane Clehane, "15 Celebrities Who Were Nerds in High School." Best Life, July 27, 2018. Accessed August 3, 2019. https://bestlifeonline.com/celebrity-nerds/.

140 **"secret ingredient for popularity":** Jan Kornelis Dijkstra et al., "The Secret Ingredient for Social Success of Young Males: A Functional Polymorphism in the *5HT2A* Serotonin Receptor Gene." *PLoS One* 8, no. 2 (2013): e54821. https://doi.org/10.1371/journal.pone.0054821.

141 **tendencies are inherited:** James H. Fowler, Christopher T. Dawes, and Nicholas A. Christakis, "Model of Genetic Variation in Human Social Networks." *Proceedings of the National Academy of Sciences of the USA* 106, no. 6 (February 10, 2009): 1720–24. https://doi.org/10.1073 /pnas.0806746106.

141 **Children that are physically attractive:** Judith H. Langlois et al., "Maxims or Myths of Beauty? A Meta-Analytic and Theoretical Review." *Psychological Bulletin* 126, no. 3 (May 2000): 390–423. http://dx.doi.org /10.1037/0033-2909.126.3.390.

141 **mathematically "average" faces:** Judith Langlois and Lori A. Roggman, "Attractive Faces Are Only Average." *Psychological Science* 1, no. 2 (March 1990): 115–21. https://doi.org/10.1111/j.1467-9280.1990.tb00079.x.

141 **babies paid more attention:** Rebecca A. Hoss and Judith H. Langlois, "Infants Prefer Attractive Faces." In *The Development of Face Processing in Infancy and Early Childhood: Current Perspectives,* eds. Olivier Pascalis and Alan Slater, 27–38. New York: Nova Science Publishers, 2003; Judith H. Langlois et al., "Infant Preferences for Attractive Faces." *Developmental Psychology* 23, no. 3 (May 1987): 363–69; Judith, H. Langlois et al., "Infants' Differential Social Responses to Attractive and Unattractive Faces." *Developmental Psychology* 26, no. 1 (January 1990) 153–59.

142 **willing to sacrifice fruit juice:** Robert O. Deaner, Amit V. Khera, and Michael L. Platt, "Monkeys Pay Per View: Adaptive Valuation of Social Images by Rhesus Macaques." *Current Biology* 15, no. 6 (March 2005): 543–48. https://doi.org/10.1016/j.cub.2005.01.044.

142 **more likely to be watched:** Peter La Freniere and William R. Charlesworth, "Dominance, Attention, and Affiliation in a Preschool Group: A Nine-Month Longitudinal Study." *Ethology and Sociobiology* 4, no. 2 (1983): 55–67. https://doi.org/10.1016/0162-3095(83)90030-4.

142 **pictures of popular kids:** Tessa A. M. Lansu, Antonius H. N. Cillessen, and Johan C. Karremans, "Adolescents' Selective Visual Attention for High-Status Peers: The Role of Perceiver Status and Gender." *Child Development* 85, no. 2 (March/April 2014): 421–28. https://doi.org/10.1111 /cdev.12139.

143 **neural processes that track popularity:** Noam Zerubavel et al., "Neural Mechanisms Tracking Popularity in Real-World Social Networks."

Proceedings of the National Academy of Sciences of the USA 112, no. 49 (December 8, 2015): 15072–77. https://doi.org/10.1073/pnas.1511477112.

143 **rank of primates:** Jeffery Klein and Michael Platt, "Social Information Signaling by Neurons in Primate Striatum." *Current Biology,* no. 23 (April 22, 2013): 691–96.

144 **the friendship paradox:** Scott L. Feld, "Why Your Friends Have More Friends Than You Do." *American Journal of Sociology* 96, no. 6 (May 1991): 1464–77.

144 **6 million Twitter users:** Nathan O. Hodas, Farshad Kooti, and Kristina Lerman, "Friendship Paradox Redux: Your Friends Are More Interesting Than You." In *Proceedings of the Seventh International AAAI Conference on Weblogs and Social Media.* Palo Alto, CA: AAAI Press, 2013, 225–33.

144 **more sexual partners than you:** Birgitte Freiesleben de Blasio, Åke Svensson, and Fredrik Liljeros, "Preferential Attachment in Sexual Networks." *Proceedings of the National Academy of Sciences of the USA* 104, no. 26 (June 26, 2007): 10762–67. https://doi.org/10.1073/pnas .0611337104.

144 **scientific collaborators:** Young-Ho Eom and Hang-Hyun Jo, "Generalized Friendship Paradox in Complex Networks: The Case of Scientific Collaboration." *Scientific Reports* 4, article ID 4603 (2014).

145 **fewer friends than their friends:** Johan Ugander et al., "The Anatomy of the Facebook Social Graph." arXiv preprint, November 18, 2011. https:// arxiv.org/abs/1111.4503.

145 **"guilt by association":** Myers and Aala, *Supermensch: The Legend of Shep Gordon.*

145 **Anne Murray's career:** Ibid.

146 *thin slices*: Nalini Ambady, Frank J. Bernieri, and Jennifer A. Richeson, "Toward a Histology of Social Behavior: Judgmental Accuracy from Thin Slices of the Behavioral Stream." *Advances in Experimental Social Psychology* 32 (2000): 201–71. https://doi.org/10.1016/S0065 -2601(00)80006-4.

146 **follow-up date:** Dan McFarland, Dan Jurafsky, and Craig Rawlings, "Making the Connection: Social Bonding in Courtship Situations." *American Journal of Sociology* 118, no. 6 (May 2013): 1596–649. https://doi .org/10.1086/670240.

146 **tendency to mimic or mirror:** Alex (Sandy) Pentland, *Honest Signals: How They Shape Our World.* Cambridge, MA: MIT Press, 2008.

147 **expansionists speak in longer segments:** Marissa King and Ingrid Nembhard, "Networks and Nonverbal Behavior." Academy of Management, 2015. Slides available at socialchemistry.com.

148 **personality explains very little:** Fang et al., "Integrating Personality and Social Networks: A Meta-Analysis of Personality, Network Position, and Work Outcomes in Organizations."

148 **twelve more friends than extreme introverts:** Daniel C. Feiler and Adam M. Kleinbaum, "Popularity, Similarity, and the Network Extraversion

Bias." *Psychological Science* 26, no. 5 (2015): 593–603. https://doi.org /10.1177/0956797615569580.

148 **accurately guess their level of extroversion:** Dana Carney, C. Randall Colvin, and Judith Hall, "A Thin Slice Perspective on the Accuracy of First Impressions." *Journal of Research in Personality* 41, no. 5 (October 2007): 1054–72.

148 **leads to social competence:** Ville-Juhani Ilmarinen et al., "Why Are Extraverts More Popular? Oral Fluency Mediates the Effect of Extraversion on Popularity in Middle Childhood." *European Journal of Personality* 29, no. 2 (2015): 138–51. https://doi.org/10.1002/per.1982.

149 **Confidence makes people:** Cameron Anderson et al., "A Status-Enhancement Account of Overconfidence." *Journal of Personality and Social Psychology* 103, no. 4 (2012): 718–35. http://dx.doi.org/10.1037 /a0029395.

149 **epitome of brash overconfidence:** "Mad Money Host Jim Cramer: Don't Be Silly on Bear Stearns!" YouTube, 2013. Video, 0:27. https://www .youtube.com/watch?v=V9EbPxTm5_s.

150 **stock was down 90 percent:** Andrew Ross Sorkin, "JP Morgan Pays $2 a Share for Bear Stearns." *New York Times,* March 17, 2008. https://www .nytimes.com/2008/03/07/business/17bear.html.

150 **viewership increased substantially:** Wikipedia, n.d., *"Mad Money."* Accessed July 25, 2019. https://en.wikipedia.org/wiki/Mad_Money.

150 **confidence increased:** Ben Smith and Jadrian Wooten, "Pundits: The Confidence Trick: Better Confident Than Right?" *Significance* 10, no. 4 (August 2013): 15–18. https://doi.org/10.1111/j.1740 -9713.2013.00675.x.

150 **leads to higher status:** Anderson et al., "A Status-Enhancement Account of Overconfidence."

150 **groups still reward the overconfident:** Jessica A. Kennedy, Cameron Anderson, and Don A. Moore, "When Overconfidence Is Revealed to Others: Testing the Status-Enhancement Theory of Overconfidence." *Organizational Behavior and Human Decision Processes* 122, no. 2 (November 2013): 266–79. https://doi.org/10.1016/j.obhdp.2013.08.005.

151 **launch more than 2,000 start-ups:** Accessed October 3, 2019. https:// www.ycombinator.com/.

151 **a core value:** Michael Seibel, "Michael Seibel." Twitter, February 13, 2018. https://twitter.com/mwseibel/status/963600732992647168?lang=en. Lightly edited for grammar and consistency.

151 **the five-minute favor:** Adam M. Grant, *Give and Take: A Revolutionary Approach to Success.* New York: Viking Penguin, 2013. Emphasis removed.

151 **best networkers:** Jessica Shambora, "Fortune's Best Networker." *Fortune,* February 9, 2011. https://fortune.com/2011/02/09/fortunes-best -networker/.

151 *Give and Take:* Adam M. Grant, *Give and Take: A Revolutionary Approach to Success.*

151 **networking book:** Keith Ferrazzi and Tahl Raz, *Never Eat Alone: And Other Secrets to Success, One Relationship at a Time.* New York: Currency Books, 2005.

152 **"Do something nice":** Gordon, *They Call Me Supermensch: A Backstage Pass to the Amazing Worlds of Film, Food, and Rock'n'Roll.* Emphasis removed.

152 **Givers have larger networks:** Grant, *Give and Take*; A. James O'Malley et al., "Egocentric Social Network Structure, Health, and Pro-Social Behaviors in a National Panel Study of Americans." *PLoS One* 7, no. 5 (2012): e36250. https://doi.org/10.1371/journal.pone.0036250.

152 **networks and prosocial behaviors:** René Bekkers, Beate Völker, and Gerald Mollenhorst, "Social Networks and Prosocial Behavior." *Marktdag Sociologie* 2, January 5, 2006.

153 **behavior in public or private:** Jingnan Chen et al., "Beware of Popular Kids Bearing Gifts: A Framed Field Experiment." *Journal of Economic Behavior & Organization* 132, part A (December 2016): 104–20. https://doi.org/10.1016/j.jebo.2016.10.001.

153 **recruited by others:** Woods Bowman, "Confidence in Charitable Institutions and Volunteering." *Nonprofit and Voluntary Sector Quarterly* 33, no. 2 (June 2004): 247–70.

153 **response to a direct request:** Kim Klein, *Fundraising for Social Change,* 7th ed. Hoboken, NJ: John Wiley & Sons, 2016.

153 **the puzzles of generosity:** Grant, *Give and Take.*

154 **giving more of your time:** Cassie Mogilner, Zoë Chance, and Michael I. Norton, "Giving Time Gives You Time." *Psychological Science* 23, no. 10 (2012): 1233–38. https://doi.org/10.1177/0956797612442551.

155 **cards with quotes and jokes:** Ronald Reagan, *The Notes: Ronald Reagan's Private Collection of Stories and Wisdom.* New York: HarperCollins, 2011.

155 **200 emails a day:** Annabel Acton, "How to Stop Wasting 2.5 Hours on Email Every Day." *Forbes,* July 13, 2017. https://www.forbes.com/sites/annabelacton/2017/07/13/innovators-challenge-how-to-stop-wasting-time-on-emails/#77a3831b9788.

155 **142 minutes a day:** Saima Salim, "How Much Time Do You Spend on Social Media? Research Says 142 Minutes Per Day." Digital Information World, January 4, 2019. https://www.digitalinformationworld.com/2019/01/how-much-time-do-people-spend-social-media-infographic.html.

156 **"ninety percent of the value":** Interview with author. March 23, 2018.

156 **"aspirational contacts":** Tahl Raz, "The 10 Secrets of a Master Networker." Inc., January 2003. https://www.inc.com/magazine/20030101/25049.html.

156 **began the *Social Register*:** Social Register Association, "About Us," 2019. Accessed August 5, 2019. https://www.socialregisteronline.com/home2.

156 **original list of 2,000 families:** Liddie Widdicombe, "Original." *The New Yorker,* March 12, 2012. https://www.newyorker.com/magazine/2012/03/26/original.

156 **"if someone wasn't listed":** Allison Ijams Sargent, "The Social Register: Just a Circle of Friends." *New York Times,* December 21, 1997. https://www.ny times.com/1997/12/21/style/the-social-register-just-a-circle-of-friends.html.

157 **"will probably kill you":** Myers and Aala, *Supermensch: The Legend of Shep Gordon.*

157 **leads to depression and burnout:** Christina Falci and Clea McNeely, "Too Many Friends: Social Integration, Network Cohesion and Adolescent Depressive Symptoms." *Social Forces* 87, no. 4 (June 2009): 2031–61. https://doi.org/10.1353/sof.0.0189.

157 **how close they feel:** A. James O'Malley et al., "Egocentric Social Network Structure, Health, and Pro-Social Behaviors in a National Panel Study of Americans"; Sam G. B. Roberts et al., "Exploring Variation in Active Network Size: Constraints and Ego Characteristics." *Social Networks* 31, no. 2 (May 2009): 138–46. https://doi.org/10.1016/j.socnet.2008.12.002.

158 **"have no friends":** Luke Morgan Britton, "Selena Gomez on Loneliness of Fame and Social Media: 'I Know Everybody but Have No Friends.'" NME, September 11, 2017. http://www.nme.com/news/music/selena-gomez -loneliness-fame-social-media-2139499.

158 **value added in collaborations:** Rob Cross, Reb Rebele, and Adam Grant, "Collaboration Overload." *Harvard Business Review,* January–February 2016. https://hbr.org/2016/01/collaborative-overload.

158 **"visibility, power, and influence":** Mitch Prinstein, *Popular: The Power of Likability in a Status-Obsessed World.* New York: Viking, 2017.

158 **what accounts for likability:** Ibid.

159 **likable children turned into:** Ylva Almquist and Lars Brännström, "Childhood Peer Status and the Clustering of Social, Economic, and Health-Related Circumstances in Adulthood." *Social Science and Medicine* 105 (March 2014): 67–75.

159 **"my ego probably said":** Tim Ferriss, "The Tim Ferriss Show Transcripts: Shep Gordon (#184)." Accessed August 5, 2019. https://tim .blog/2018/06/06/the-tim-ferriss-show-transcripts-shep-gordon/.

160 **"change that in our lives":** Ibid.

160 **"in service to others":** Gordon, *They Call Me Supermensch: A Backstage Pass to the Amazing Worlds of Film, Food, and Rock'n'Roll.*

6. In the Mix

161 **The answer was partially sociological:** Rob Blackhurst, "Mass Appeal: The Secret to Rick Warren's Success." Slate, August 14, 2011. https://slate .com/human-interest/2011/08/how-rick-warren-made-it-big.html.

161 **where everyone could find community:** Ibid.

162 **15,000 community members:** Richard Abanes, *Rick Warren and the Purpose That Drives Him.* Eugene, OR: Harvest House, 2005.

162 **22,000 people a week:** Barbara Bradley-Hagerty, "Rick Warren: The Purpose-Driven Pastor." NPR, January 18, 2009. Audio, 5:52. https://www.npr.org/templates/story/story.php?storyId=99529977.

162 **"one church in many locations":** Saddleback Church, "Our Church." Accessed August 6, 2019. https://saddleback.com/visit/about/our-church.

162 ***The Purpose Driven Life:*** Rick Warren, *The Purpose Driven Life: What on Earth Am I Here For?* Grand Rapids: Zondervan, 2002.

162 **34 million copies:** Zondervan, "The Purpose Driven Life." Accessed August 5, 2019. https://www.zondervan.com/9780310329060/the-purpose-driven-life/.

162 **"at their core a contradiction":** Malcolm Gladwell, "The Cellular Church." *The New Yorker,* September 12, 2005. https://www.newyorker.com/magazine/2005/09/12/the-cellular-church.

163 **Small groups:** Saddleback Church, "Small Groups." Accessed August 6, 2019. https://saddleback.com/connect/smallgroups.

163 **"pastorpreneur":** Blackhurst, "Mass Appeal: The Secret to Rick Warren's Success."

163 **extraordinary network growth:** Gladwell, "The Cellular Church."

164 **"ought never be organized":** Alcoholics Anonymous, *Twelve Steps and Twelve Traditions.* New York: Alcoholics Anonymous World Services, 1981.

165 **"not a glamorous job":** Jonathan Mahler, "G.M., Detroit and the Fall of the Black Middle Class." *New York Times Magazine,* June 24, 2009. https://www.nytimes.com/2009/06/28/magazine/28detroit-t.html.

165 **"constantly torn between":** Ibid.

165 **Gorham took a different approach:** Michael Winerip, "Résumé Writing for C.E.O.'s." *New York Times,* April 10, 2009. https://www.nytimes.com/2009/04/12/fashion/12genb.html.

166 **contrasting cognitive responses:** Edward Bishop Smith, Tanya Menon, and Leigh Thompson, "Status Differences in the Cognitive Activation of Social Networks." *Organization Science* 23, no. 1 (January–February 2012): 67–82. https://doi.org/10.1287/orsc.1100.0643.

168 **networks change based on:** Catherine T. Shea et al., "The Affective Antecedents of Cognitive Social Network Activation." *Social Networks* 43 (October 2015): 91–99. https://doi.org/10.1016/j.socnet.2015.01.003.

169 **networks "turtle":** Daniel M. Romero, Brian Uzzi, and Jon Kleinberg, "Social Networks Under Stress." *Proceedings of the 25th International Conference on World Wide Web*: 9–20. arXiv:1602.00572.

169 **"power over another individual":** Tanya Menon and Edward Bishop Smith, "Identities in Flux: Cognitive Network Activation in Times of Change." *Social Science Research* 45 (May 2014): 117–30. https://doi.org/10.1016/j.ssresearch.2014.01.001.

169   **"having a confirmed identity":** Menon and Bishop Smith, "Identities in Flux: Cognitive Network Activation in Times of Change."

170   **returns over the life course:** Ronald S. Burt, "Life Course and Network Advantage: Peak Periods, Turning Points, and Transition Ages." In *Social Networks and the Life Course: Integrating the Development of Human Lives and Social Relational Networks,* eds. Duane F. Alwin, Diane Helen Felmlee, and Derek A. Kreager, 67–87. Cham, Switzerland: Springer, 2018.

171   **an expansionist becomes less valuable:** Nan Lin, "Social Networks and Status Attainment." *Annual Review of Sociology* 25, no. 1 (1999): 467–87. https://doi.org/10.1146/annurev.soc.25.1.467.

171   **common network traps:** Rob Cross and Robert J. Thomas, "Managing Yourself: A Smarter Way to Network." *Harvard Business Review,* July–August 2011. https://hbr.org/2011/07/managing-yourself-a-smarter-way -to-network.

172   **she couldn't keep up:** Kathleen L. McGinn and Nicole Tempest, "Heidi Roizen." Harvard Business School Case Study, January 18, 2000 (revised April 2010). Lightly edited for grammar and formal consistency.

173   **"build my reputation":** Ibid. Emphasis removed.

173   **"time to build that network":** Heidi Roizen, Francis Flynn, and Brian Lowery, "Best Practices for Building a Meaningful Network." Stanford Graduate School of Business, October 18, 2006. Video, 1:04:36. https:// www.youtube.com/watch?v=56C8l4klXUg&t=1s. Lightly edited for grammar and formal consistency.

174   **"nucleus of her own network":** McGinn and Tempest, "Heidi Roizen."

175   **oscillations between brokerage and convening:** Ronald S. Burt and Jennifer Merluzzi, "Network Oscillation." *Academy of Management Discoveries* 2, no. 4 (March 2016): 368–91. https://doi.org/10.5465/amd.2015.0108.

175   **"preparation for change":** Ibid.

176   *dormant ties:* Daniel Z. Levin, Jorge Walter, and J. Keith Murnighan, "Dormant Ties: The Value of Reconnecting." *Organization Science* 22, no. 4 (July–August 2011): 923–39. https://doi.org/10.1287/orsc.1100.0576.

176   **the task of reconnecting:** Daniel Z. Levin, Jorge Walter, and J. Keith Murnighan, "The Power of Reconnection—How Dormant Ties Can Surprise You." *MIT Sloan Management Review* 52, no. 3 (Spring 2011): 45–50.

176   **"When I thought about reconnecting":** Jorge Walter, Daniel Z. Levin, and J. Keith Murnighan, "Reconnection Choices: Selecting the Most Valuable (vs. Most Preferred) Dormant Ties." *Organization Science* 26, no. 5 (2015): 1447–65. https://doi.org/10.1287/orsc.2015.0996.

177   **conducted a second study:** Ibid.

178   **afraid it will be awkward:** Ibid.

178   **"give you a loan":** Robert Cialdini, "Indirect Tactics of Image Management: Beyond Basking." In *Impression Management in the Organization,* eds. Robert A. Giacalone and Paul Rosenfeld. Hillsdale, NJ: Lawrence Erlbaum Associates, 1989.

179 **perceived more favorably:** Harold Sigall and David Landy, "Radiating Beauty: Effects of Having a Physically Attractive Partner on Person Perception." *Journal of Personality and Social Psychology* 28, no. 2 (1973): 218–24. http://dx.doi.org/10.1037/h0035740.

179 **bask in the reflected glory:** Robert B. Cialdini et al., "Basking in Reflected Glory: Three (Football) Field Studies." *Journal of Personality and Social Psychology* 34, no. 3 (1976): 366–75. http://dx.doi.org/10.1037/0022 -3514.34.3.366.

179 **yard signs for winning candidates:** Paul C. Bernhardt, Samantha J. Calhoun, and Emily B. Creegan, "Resolving Divergent Findings on Basking in Reflected Glory with Political Yard Signs." *North American Journal of Psychology* 16, no. 3 (January 2014): 507–18.

179 *The Established and the Outsiders:* Norbert Elias and John L. Scotson, *The Established and the Outsiders.* Thousand Oaks, CA: SAGE Publications, 1994.

180 **an influential boss:** Raymond T. Sparrowe and Robert C. Liden, "Two Routes to Influence: Integrating Leader-Member Exchange and Social Network Perspectives." *Administrative Science Quarterly* 50, no. 4 (December 2005): 505–35. https://doi.org/10.2189/asqu.50.4.505.

181 **Perception matters:** Martin Kilduff and David Krackhardt, "Bringing the Individual Back In: A Structural Analysis of the Internal Market for Reputation in Organizations." *Academy of Management Journal* 37, no. 1 (1994): 87–108. https://doi.org/10.5465/256771.

181 **relationships with the right colleagues:** Dora C. Lau and Robert C. Liden, "Antecedents of Coworker Trust: Leaders' Blessings." *Journal of Applied Psychology* 93, no. 5 (2008): 1130–38. http://dx.doi.org/10.1037/0021 -9010.93.5.1130.

182 **The value of an advocate:** Sze-Sze Wong and Wai Fong Boh, "Leveraging the Ties of Others to Build a Reputation for Trustworthiness Among Peers." *Academy of Management Journal* 53, no. 1 (2010): 129–48. https:// doi.org/10.5465/amj.2010.48037265.

183 **dark side to being connected:** Russell James Funk, "Essays on Collaboration, Innovation, and Network Change in Organizations." PhD dissertation, University of Michigan, 2014.

183 **price to pay for brokerage:** Isabel Fernandez-Mateo, "Who Pays the Price of Brokerage? Transferring Constraint Through Price Setting in the Staffing Sector." *American Sociological Review* 72, no. 2 (April 2007): 291–317. https://doi.org/10.1177/000312240707200208.

183 **Only the broker benefits:** Ronald S. Burt, "Secondhand Brokerage: Evidence on the Importance of Local Structure for Managers, Bankers, and Analysts." *Academy of Management Journal* 50, no. 1 (2007): 119–48. https://doi.org/10.5465/amj.2007.24162082.

183 **connected to a senior broker:** Charles Galunic, Gokhan Ertug, and Martin Gargiulo, "The Positive Externalities of Social Capital: Benefiting

from Senior Brokers." *Academy of Management Journal* 55, no. 5 (2012): 1213–31. https://doi.org/10.5465/amj.2010.0827.

184 **Child translators:** Katherine Stovel, Benjamin Golub, and Eva M. Meyersson Milgrom, "Stabilizing Brokerage." *Proceedings of the National Academy of Sciences of the USA* 108, suppl. 4 (December 27, 2011): 21326–32. https://doi.org/10.1073/pnas.1100920108.

184 **parents moved from China to Australia:** Cathy Pryor, "Language Brokering: When You're the Only One in the House Who Speaks English." Life Matters, August 9, 2017. https://www.abc.net.au/news/2017-08-10 /when-kids-translate-for-their-migrant-parents/8767820. Lightly edited for grammar.

186 **"what really matters is structure":** Rob Cross and Robert J. Thomas, "Managing Yourself: A Smarter Way to Network." *Harvard Business Review,* July–August 2011. https://hbr.org/2011/07/managing-yourself-a-smarter-way-to-network.

7. In the Moment

187 **"until it is 'almost unnoticeable'":** Malia Wollan, "How to Make Soulful Eye Contact." *New York Times,* April 28, 2017. https://www.nytimes.com /2017/04/28/magazine/how-to-make-soulful-eye-contact.html.

187 **"mutual gaze":** Marina Abramović, "The Artist Is Present," 2010. Accessed August 7, 2019. https://www.moma.org/learn/moma_learning /marina-abramovic-marina-abramovic-the-artist-is-present-2010/.

187 **with a tattoo:** Elizabeth Greenwood, "Wait, Why Did That Woman Sit in the MoMA for 750 Hours?" *The Atlantic,* July 2, 2012. https://www .theatlantic.com/entertainment/archive/2012/07/wait-why-did-that -woman-sit-in-the-moma-for-750-hours/259069/.

188 **"never even say one word":** Marina Abramović, "An Art Made of Trust, Vulnerability, and Connection." TED Talks, March 2015. Video, 15:44. https://www.ted.com/talks/marina_abramovic_an_art_made_of_trust _vulnerability_and_connection?language=en#t-128356.

188 **socially crippling:** Wollan, "How to Make Soulful Eye Contact."

188 **"enormous need of humans":** Marina Abramović, "The Artist Is Present." Marina Abramović Institute, 2019. Video, 3:07. https://mai.art /about-mai.

188 **"same attention and same respect":** Matthew Akers and Jeff Dupre, directors, *Marina Abramović: The Artist Is Present.* Music Box Films. Documentary, October 16, 2012. Quote lightly edited for clarity.

188 **an emotion:** Barbara L. Fredrickson, *Love 2.0: Finding Happiness and Health in Moments of Connection.* New York: Plume, 2013.

188 *high-quality connections*: John Paul Stephens, Emily D. Heaphy, and Jane E. Dutton, "High-Quality Connections." In *The Oxford Handbook of*

Positive Organizational Scholarship, eds. Kim S. Cameron and Gretchen
M. Spreitzer, 385–99. New York: Oxford University Press, 2012.
188 **"sense of your aliveness":** Interview with author. October 8, 2018.
189 **high emotional carrying capacity:** Belle Rose Ragins, "Relational
Mentoring: A Positive Approach to Mentoring at Work." In *The Oxford
Handbook of Positive Organizational Scholarship,* eds. Kim S. Cameron
and Gretchen M. Spreitzer, 519–536. New York: Oxford University Press,
2012.
189 **bodies respond physically:** Emily D. Heaphy and Jane E. Dutton, "Positive
Social Interactions and the Human Body at Work: Linking Organizations
and Physiology." *Academy of Management Review* 33, no. 1 (2008): 137–62.
https://doi.org/10.5465/amr.2008.27749365.
189 **stronger sense of belonging:** Gillian M. Sandstrom and Elizabeth W.
Dunn, "Is Efficiency Overrated? Minimal Social Interactions Lead to
Belonging and Positive Affect." *Social Psychological and Personality
Science* 5, no. 4 (2014): 437–42. https://doi.org/10.1177/1948550613502990.
190 **sense of social connection:** Eric D. Wesselmann et al., "To Be Looked at as
Though Air: Civil Attention Matters." *Psychological Science* 23, no. 2
(2012): 166–68. https://doi.org/10.1177/0956797611427921.
190 **conversing with a stranger:** Elizabeth W. Dunn et al., "Misunderstanding
the Affective Consequences of Everyday Social Interactions: The Hidden
Benefits of Putting One's Best Face Forward." *Journal of Personality and
Social Psychology* 92, no. 6 (June 2007): 990–1005. http://dx.doi.org
/10.1037/0022-3514.92.6.990.
191 **parable about a traveler:** Luke 10: 25–37.
192 **Who stopped?:** John M. Darley and C. Daniel Batson, "From Jerusalem to
Jericho: A Study of Situational and Dispositional Variables in Helping
Behavior." *Journal of Personality and Social Psychology* 27, no. 1 (1973):
100–108. http://dx.doi.org/10.1037/h0034449.
192 **in a rush:** Pew Research Center, "Nearly a Quarter of Americans Always
Feel Rushed." November 4, 2010. https://www.pewsocialtrends.org/2006
/02/28/whos-feeling-rushed/50-3/.
192 **"transforms us as a result":** Akers and Dupre, *Marina Abramović: The
Artist Is Present.*
192 **Being hurried and harried impairs:** Silke Paulmann et al., "How
Psychological Stress Affects Emotional Prosody." *PLoS One* 11 (2016):
e0165022. https://doi.org/10.1371/journal.pone.0165022; Matt L. Herridge
et al., "Hostility and Facial Affect Recognition: Effects of a Cold Pressor
Stressor on Accuracy and Cardiovascular Reactivity." *Brain and
Cognition* 55, no. 3 (August 2004): 564–71. https://doi.org/10.1016/j
.bandc.2004.04.004.
192 **self-absorbed and egocentric:** Nicholas Epley et al., "Perspective Taking as
Egocentric Anchoring and Adjustment." *Journal of Personality and Social
Psychology* 87, no. 3 (September 2004): 327–39; Andrew R. Todd et al.,

"Anxious and Egocentric: How Specific Emotions Influence Perspective Taking." *Journal of Experimental Psychology: General* 144, no. 2 (April 2015): 374–91.

192 *inattentional blindness:* Ira E. Hyman Jr. et al., "Did You See the Unicycling Clown? Inattentional Blindness While Walking and Talking on a Cell Phone." *Applied Cognitive Psychology* 24, no. 5 (July 2009): 597–607. https://doi.org/10.1002/acp.1638.

193 **their most recent gathering:** Lee Rainie and Kathryn Zickuhr, "Americans' Views on Mobile Etiquette." August 26, 2015. Washington, DC: Pew Research Center. http://www.pewinternet.org/2015/08/26 /americans-views-on-mobile-etiquette/.

193 **check their phone during sex:** Eileen Brown, "Phone Sex: Using Our Smartphones from the Shower to the Sack." ZDNet, July 11, 2013. Accessed August 7, 2019. https://www.zdnet.com/article/phone-sex-using-our -smartphones-from-the-shower-to-the-sack/.

193 **makes us socially disconnected:** Kostadin Kushlev, Jason Proulx, and Elizabeth W. Dunn, "'Silence Your Phones': Smartphone Notifications Increase Inattention and Hyperactivity Symptoms." In *Proceedings of the 2016 CHI Conference on Human Factors in Computing Systems,* 1011–20. https://doi.org/10.1145/2858036.2858359.

193 **ability to connect:** Kostadin Kushlev and Elizabeth W. Dunn, "Smartphones Distract Parents from Cultivating Feelings of Connection When Spending Time with Their Children." *Journal of Social and Personal Relationships* 36, no. 6 (2018): 1619–39. https://doi.org/10.1177/0265407 518769387.

193 **a phone on the table:** Ryan J. Dwyer, Kostadin Kushlev, and Elizabeth W. Dunn, "Smartphone Use Undermines Enjoyment of Face-to-Face Social Interactions." *Journal of Experimental Social Psychology* 78 (September 2018): 233–39. https://doi.org/10.1016/j.jesp.2017.10.007.

194 **If a phone was present:** Andrew K. Przybylski and Netta Weinstein, "Can You Connect with Me Now? How the Presence of Mobile Communication Technology Influences Face-to-Face Conversation Quality." *Journal of Social and Personal Relationships* 30, no. 3 (2013): 237–46. https://doi.org /10.1177/0265407512453827.

194 **perceptions of overall relationship quality:** James A. Roberts and Meredith E. David, "My Life Has Become a Major Distraction from My Cell Phone: Partner Phubbing and Relationship Satisfaction Among Romantic Partners." *Computers in Human Behavior* 54 (January 2016): 134–41. https://doi.org/10.1016/j.chb.2015.07.058.

194 **impacted marital satisfaction:** Xingchao Wang et al., "Partner Phubbing and Depression Among Married Chinese Adults: The Roles of Relationship Satisfaction and Relationship Length." *Personality and Individual Differences* 110, no. 1 (May 2017): 12–17. https://doi.org/10.1016 /j.paid.2017.01.014.

195 **reduce pain:** Jamie E. Guillory et al., "Text Messaging Reduces Analgesic Requirements During Surgery." *Pain Medicine* 16, no. 4 (April 2015): 667–72. https://doi.org/10.1111/pme.12610.

195 **disconnected because they were distracted:** Kushlev and Dunn, "Smartphones Distract Parents from Cultivating Feelings of Connection When Spending Time with Their Children"; Roberts and David, "My Life Has Become a Major Distraction from My Cell Phone: Partner Phubbing and Relationship Satisfaction Among Romantic Partners."

195 **look at them and smile:** Miles L. Patterson and Mark E. Tubbs, "Through a Glass Darkly: Effects of Smiling and Visibility on Recognition and Avoidance in Passing Encounters." *Western Journal of Communication* 69, no. 3 (2005): 219–31. https://doi.org/10.1080/10570310500202389.

195 **eliciting a smile plummets:** Miles L. Patterson et al., "Passing Encounters East and West: Comparing Japanese and American Pedestrian Interactions." *Journal of Nonverbal Behavior* 31, no. 3 (September 2007): 155–66. https://doi.org/10.1007/s10919-007-0028-4.

196 **cue of attraction:** R. Matthew Montoya, Christine Kershaw, and Julie L. Prosser, "A Meta-Analytic Investigation of the Relation Between Interpersonal Attraction and Enacted Behavior." *Psychological Bulletin* 144, no. 7 (July 2018): 673–709. http://dx.doi.org/10.1037/bul0000148.

196 **three seconds of eye contact:** Michael Argyle and Janet Dean, "Eye-Contact, Distance and Affiliation." *Sociometry* 28, no. 3 (September 1965): 289–304; Nicola Binetti et al., "Pupil Dilation as an Index of Preferred Mutual Gaze Duration." *Royal Society Open Science* 3, no. 7 (July 2016): 160086. https://doi.org/10.1098/rsos.160086.

196 **more when they are cooperating:** Argyle and Dean, "Eye-Contact, Distance and Affiliation."

196 **prefer a direct mutual gaze:** Teresa Farroni et al., "Eye Contact Detection in Humans from Birth." *Proceedings of the National Academy of Sciences of the USA* 99, no. 14 (July 9, 2002): 9602–605. https://doi.org/10.1073/pnas.152159999.

196 **more time gazing:** Zick Rubin, "Measurement of Romantic Love." *Journal of Personality and Social Psychology* 16, no. 2 (1970): 265–73.

197 **induce feelings of love:** Joan Kellerman, James Lewis, and James D. Laird, "Looking and Loving: The Effects of Mutual Gaze on Feelings of Romantic Love." *Journal of Research in Personality* 23, no. 2 (1989): 145–61. https://doi.org/10.1016/0092-6566(89)90020-2.

197 **"reading the mind in the eyes":** Simon Baron-Cohen et al., "The 'Reading the Mind in the Eyes' Test Revised Version: A Study with Normal Adults, and Adults with Asperger Syndrome or High-Functioning Autism." *Journal of Child Psychology and Psychiatry* 42, no. 2 (2001): 241–251. http://dx.doi.org/10.1111/1469-7610.00715.

197 **lose their connection with reality:** Giovanni B. Caputo, "Dissociation and Hallucinations in Dyads Engaged Through Interpersonal Gazing."

Psychiatry Research 228, no. 3 (August 2015): 659–63. https://doi.org /10.1016/j.psychres.2015.04.050.

198 **"Ask questions":** Dale Carnegie, *How to Win Friends & Influence People*. New York: Simon & Schuster, 1936.

199 **Follow-up questions were the elixir:** Karen Huang et al., "It Doesn't Hurt to Ask: Question-Asking Increases Liking." *Journal of Personality and Social Psychology* 113, no. 3 (2017): 430–52. http://dx.doi.org/10.1037 /pspi0000097.

200 **shown to increase liking:** Molly E. Ireland et al., "Language Style Matching Predicts Relationship Initiation and Stability." *Psychological Science* 22, no. 1 (2011): 39–44. https://doi.org/10.1177/0956797610392928.

200 **answer questions about themselves:** Diana I. Tamir and Jason P. Mitchell, "Disclosing Information About the Self Is Intrinsically Rewarding." *Proceedings of the National Academy of Sciences of the USA* 109, no. 21 (May 22, 2012): 8038–43. https://doi.org/10.1073/pnas.1202129109.

200 **Aron's thirty-six questions:** Arthur Aron et al., "The Experimental Generation of Interpersonal Closeness: A Procedure and Some Preliminary Findings." *Personality and Social Psychology Bulletin* 23, no. 4 (April 1, 1997): 363–77. https://doi.org/10.1177/0146167297234003.

200 **four-minute stare:** Mandy Len Catron, "To Fall in Love with Anyone, Do This." *New York Times,* January 9, 2015. https://www.nytimes.com/ . . . /modern-love-to-fall-in-love-with-anyone-do-this.html.

200 **44 percent of our time listening:** Laura Janusik, "Listening Facts." International Listening Association, n.d. Accessed October 12, 2018. https://www.listen.org/Listening-Facts.

201 **commit to listening more deeply:** Carmelene Siani, "Deep Listening: A Simple Way to Make a Difference." Sivana East, n.d. Accessed October 5, 2018. https://blog.sivanaspirit.com/mf-gn-deep-listening/.

201 **listening reduces patients' physical pain:** Vinicius C. Oliveira et al., "Effectiveness of Training Clinicians' Communication Skills on Patients' Clinical Outcomes: A Systematic Review." *Journal of Manipulative and Physiological Therapeutics* 38, no. 8 (October 2015): 601–16. https://doi.org /10.1016/j.jmpt.2015.08.002.

201 **Effective listening improves:** Jan Flynn, Tuula-Riitta Valikoski, and Jennie Grau, "Listening in the Business Context: Reviewing the State of Research." *International Journal of Listening* 22, no. 2 (2008): 141–51. https://doi.org/10.1080/10904010802174800; Harry Weger Jr., Gina R. Castle, and Melissa C. Emmett, "Active Listening in Peer Interviews: The Influence of Message Paraphrasing on Perceptions of Listening Skill." *International Journal of Listening* 24, no. 1 (2010): 34–49. https://doi.org /10.1080/10904010903466311.

201 **employees feel like their boss:** Karina J. Lloyd et al., 2015. "Is My Boss Really Listening to Me? The Impact of Perceived Supervisor Listening on Emotional Exhaustion, Turnover Intention, and Organizational

Citizenship Behavior." *Journal of Business Ethics* 130, no. 3 (September 2015): 509–24. https://doi.org/10.1007/s10551-014-2242-4.

202 **When people feel listened to:** Niels Van Quaquebeke and Will Felps, "Respectful Inquiry: A Motivational Account of Leading Through Asking Questions and Listening." *Academy of Management Review* 43, no. 1 (2018): 5–27. https://doi.org/10.5465/amr.2014.0537.

202 **"fail to listen correctly":** Richard Schuster, "Empathy and Mindfulness." *Journal of Humanistic Psychology* 19, no. 1 (1979): 71–77. https://doi.org /10.1177/002216787901900107.

202 **thinks they are good at it:** Scott Williams, "Listening Effectively." Raj Soin College of Business, Wright State University, n.d. Accessed October 5, 2018. http://www.wright.edu/~scott.williams/skills/listening.htm.

202 **a good listener:** Accenture, "Accenture Research Finds Listening More Difficult in Today's Digital Workplace." Accenture Newsroom, February 26, 2015. https://newsroom.accenture.com/industries/global-media -industry-analyst-relations/accenture-research-finds-listening-more -difficult-in-todays-digital-workplace.htm.

202 **watched the evening news:** John Stauffer, Richard Frost, and William Rybolt, "The Attention Factor in Recalling Network News." *Journal of Communication* 33, no. 1 (March 1983): 29–37.

202 **average person can comprehend:** Arthur Wingfield, "Cognitive Factors in Auditory Performance: Context, Speed of Processing, and Constraints of Memory." *Journal of the American Academy of Audiology* 7, no. 3 (June 1996): 175–82; Ronald P. Carver, Raymond L. Johnson, and Herbert L. Friedman, "Factor Analysis of the Ability to Comprehend Time Compressed Speech." *Journal of Reading Behavior* 4, no. 1 (March 1971): 40–49. https://doi.org/10.1080/10862967109546974.

202 **how frequently their minds wandered:** Matthew A. Killingsworth and Daniel T. Gilbert, "A Wandering Mind Is an Unhappy Mind." *Science* 330, no. 6006 (November 12, 2010): 932. https://doi.org/10.1126/science.1192439.

203 **"the best listeners":** Ralph G. Nichols and Leonard A. Stevens, *Are You Listening?* New York: McGraw-Hill, 1957.

203 **increase throughout the school years:** Carol K. Sigelman and Elizabeth A. Rider, *Life-Span Human Development,* 9th ed. Boston: Cengage Learning, 2018.

203 **"father of the field of listening":** Interview by Rick Bommelje, Listening Post, Summer 2003, vol. 84. Reproduced at International Listening Association, "Listening Legend Interview, Dr. Ralph Nichols. https:// listen.org/Legend-Interview).

203 **self-perceptions of listening:** Carolyn Coakley, Kelby Halone, and Andrew Wolvin, "Perceptions of Listening Ability Across the Life-Span: Implications for Understanding Listening Competence." *International Journal of Listening* 10, no. 1 (1996): 21–48. https://doi.org /10.1207/s1932586xijl1001_2.

323

203 **Younger minds are more open:** Alison Gopnik, Thomas L. Griffiths, and Christopher G. Lucas, "When Younger Learners Can Be Better (Or at Least More Open-Minded) Than Older Ones." *Current Directions in Psychological Science* 24, no. 2 (April 2015): 87–92. https://doi.org/10.1177 /0963721414556653.

204 **biggest impediments to effective listening:** Ralph G. Nichols and Leonard A. Stevens, "Listening to People." *Harvard Business Review*, September 1957.

204 **different ways of measuring listening:** Debra L. Worthington and Graham D. Bodie, *The Sourcebook of Listening Research: Methodology and Measures.* Hoboken, NJ: John Wiley & Sons, 2017.

204 **boiled down to a few essential dimensions:** Andrew D. Wolvin and Steven D. Cohen, "An Inventory of Listening Competency Dimensions." *International Journal of Listening* 26, no. 2 (2012): 64–66. https://doi.org /10.1080/10904018.2012.677665.

204 **organized listening training:** Kathleen S. Verderber, Deanna D. Sellnow, and Rudolph F. Verderber, *Communicate!,* 15th ed. Boston: Cengage Learning, 2013.

205 **"process of listening to learn":** Earl E. Bakken Center for Spirituality and Healing at the University of Minnesota, "Deep Listening," n.d. Accessed October 14, 2018. https://www.csh.umn.edu/education/focus-areas/whole -systems-healing/leadership/deep-listening.

205 **insightful revelations about their behavior:** Iris W. Johnson et al., "Self-Imposed Silence and Perceived Listening Effectiveness." *Business and Professional Communication Quarterly* 66, no. 2 (June 2003): 23–38. https://doi.org/10.1177/108056990306600203.

206 **"listen with only one purpose":** Thích Nhất Hanh, "Thích Nhất Hanh on Compassionate Listening." Oprah Winfrey Network, May 6, 2012. Video, 3:21. https://www.youtube.com/watch?v=lyUxYflkhzo&feature=youtu.be.

207 **neural coordination:** Greg J. Stephens, Lauren J. Silbert, and Uri Hasson, "Speaker–Listener Neural Coupling Underlies Successful Communication." *Proceedings of the National Academy of Sciences of the USA* 107, no. 32 (August 10, 2010): 14425–30. https://doi.org/10.1073 /pnas.1008662107.

207 **"hundred papers about vision":** Adam Gopnik, "Feel Me: What the Science of Touch Says About Us." *The New Yorker,* May 16, 2016. https:// www.newyorker.com/magazine/2016/05/16/what-the-science-of-touch -says-about-us.

208 **All of the other senses have a devoted art:** Ibid.

208 **way of conveying touch:** Ibid.

208 **twenty-two square feet:** "Skin." *National Geographic,* January 17, 2017. https://www.nationalgeographic.com/science/health-and-human-body /human-body/skin/.

208 **"primary moral experience":** Gopnik, "Feel Me: What the Science of Touch Says About Us."

208 **differentiated through touch:** Matthew J. Hertenstein et al., "Touch Communicates Distinct Emotions." *Emotion* 6, no. 3 (August 2006): 528–33. https://doi.org/10.1037/1528-3542.6.3.528; Matthew J. Hertenstein et al., "The Communication of Emotion via Touch." *Emotion* 9, no. 4 (August 2009): 566–73. https://doi.org/10.1037/a0016108.

209 **dance at a nightclub:** Nicolas Guéguen, "Courtship Compliance: The Effect of Touch on Women's Behavior." *Social Influence* 2, no. 2 (2007): 81–97. https://doi.org/10.1080/15534510701316177.

209 **lend you some change:** Chris L. Kleinke, "Compliance to Requests Made by Gazing and Touching Experimenters in Field Settings." *Journal of Experimental Social Psychology* 13, no 3 (May 1977): 218–23. https://doi .org/10.1016/0022-1031(77)90044-0.

209 **sign a survey:** Nicolas Guéguen, "Status, Apparel and Touch: Their Joint Effects on Compliance to a Request." *North American Journal of Psychology* 4, no. 2 (2002): 279–86.

209 **give a good tip:** Nicolas Guéguen and Céline Jacob, "The Effect of Touch on Tipping: An Evaluation in a French Bar." *International Journal of Hospitality Management* 24, no. 2 (2005): 295–99. https://doi.org/10.1016/j .ijhm.2004.06.004.

209 **sample pizza:** David E. Smith, Joseph A. Gier, and Frank N. Willis, "Interpersonal Touch and Compliance with a Marketing Request." *Basic and Applied Social Psychology* 3, no. 1 (1982): 35–38. https://doi.org /10.1207/s15324834basp0301_3.

209 **Touchers are seen as:** Damien Erceau and Nicolas Guéguen, "Tactile Contact and Evaluation of the Toucher." *Journal of Social Psychology* 147, no. 4 (2007): 441–44. https://doi.org/10.3200 /SOCP.147.4.441-444.

209 **Prior to stressful events:** Tiffany Field, "Touch for Socioemotional and Physical Well-Being: A Review." *Developmental Review* 30, no. 4 (December 2010): 367–83. https://doi.org/10.1016/j.dr.2011.01.001.

210 **surprisingly good at preventing them:** Sheldon Cohen et al., "Does Hugging Provide Stress-Buffering Social Support? A Study of Susceptibility to Upper Respiratory Infection and Illness." *Psychological Science* 26, no. 2 (2015): 135–47. https://doi.org/10.1177 /0956797614559284.

210 **holding his wife's hand:** Lisa Marshall, "Just the Two of Us: Holding Hands Can Ease Pain, Sync Brainwaves." CU Boulder Today, February 28, 2018. https://www.colorado.edu/today/2018/02/28/just-two-us-holding -hands-can-ease-pain-sync-brainwaves.

211 **synchronization of the alpha mu band:** Pavel Goldstein, Irit Weissman-Fogel, and Simone G. Shamay-Tsoory, "The Role of Touch in Regulating Inter-Partner Physiological Coupling During Empathy for Pain." *Scientific Reports* 7 (June 12, 2017): 3252. https://doi.org/10.1038/s41598-017-03627-7; Pavel Goldstein et al., "Brain-to-Brain Coupling During Handholding Is Associated with Pain Reduction." *Proceedings of the National Academy of*

Sciences of the USA 115, no. 11 (March 13, 2018): e2528—e2537. https://doi
.org/10.1073/pnas.1703643115.

211 **"I would describe myself as":** Mark H. Davis, "A Multidimensional
Approach to Individual Differences in Empathy." JSAS *Catalog of Selected
Documents in Psychology* 10 (1980): 85.

211 **"touch enhances coupling":** Pavel Goldstein et al., "Brain-to-Brain
Coupling During Handholding Is Associated with Pain Reduction.";
Goldstein, Weissman-Fogel, and Shamay-Tsoory, "The Role of Touch in
Regulating Inter-Partner Physiological Coupling During Empathy for
Pain."

211 **"without touch":** Lisa Marshall, "Just the Two of Us: Holding Hands Can
Ease Pain, Sync Brainwaves." CU Boulder Today, February 28, 2018.
https://www.colorado.edu/today/2018/02/28/just-two-us-holding-hands
-can-ease-pain-sync-brainwaves.

212 **The perfect touch:** David J. Linden, "A Loving Touch: Neurobiology
Recommends Warm Skin and Moderate Pressure, Moving at 1 Inch per
Second." Slate, February 12, 2015. http://www.slate.com/articles/health
_and_science/science/2015/02/touch_research_how_to_perform_the
_ideal_caress_for_valentine_s_day.html.

212 **caress-sensing fibers:** Sabrina Richards, "Pleasant to the Touch." *The
Scientist*, September 1, 2012. https://www.the-scientist.com/features
/pleasant-to-the-touch-40534.

213 **the contextual nature of touch:** David J. Linden, *Touch: The Science of
Hand, Heart, and Mind.* New York: Penguin Books, 2016; India Morrison,
Line S. Löken, and Håkan Olausson, "The Skin as a Social Organ."
Experimental Brain Research 204, no. 3 (July 2010): 305–14. https://doi.org
/10.1007/s00221-009-2007-y.

213 **pairs in coffee shops:** Sidney Jourard, "An Exploratory Study of
Body-Accessibility." *British Journal of Social & Clinical Psychology* 5,
no. 3 (1966): 221–31. http://dx.doi.org/10.1111/j.2044-8260.1966
.tb00978.x.

213 **feel comfortable being touched:** Juulia T. Suvilehto et al., "Topography
of Social Touching Depends on Emotional Bonds Between Humans."
Proceedings of the National Academy of Sciences of the USA 112,
no. 45 (November 10, 2015): 13811–816. https://doi.org/10.1073
/pnas.1519231112.

213 **awkward hug versus handshake dilemma:** Shane Snow, "Hug vs.
Handshake." Medium, May 15, 2013. https://medium.com/@shanesnow
/hug-vs-handshake-1c4f35dec45b.

214 **"Touch is ten times stronger":** Tiffany Field, *Touch*. Cambridge, MA:
MIT Press, 2014.

215 **close to nothing:** Matthew Akers and Jeff Dupre, directors. *Marina
Abramović: The Artist Is Present.*

8. Human Design

217 **didn't speak up:** Ben Truslove, "Kegworth Air Disaster: Plane Crash Survivors' Stories." BBC News, January 8, 2014. https://www.bbc.com /news/uk-england-leicestershire-25548016.

217 **"accident could have been prevented":** Air Accidents Investigation Branch, "Aircraft Accident Report 4/90. Report on the Accident to Boeing 737-400, G-OBME, near Kegworth, Leicestershire on 8 January 1989." Accessed August 9, 2019. https://assets.publishing.service.gov.uk/media /5422fefeed915d13710009ed/4-1990_G-OBME.pdf.

217 **reason planes crash:** National Research Council, *Improving the Continued Airworthiness of Civil Aircraft: A Strategy for the FAA's Aircraft Certification Service.* Washington, DC: National Academies Press, 1998. https://doi.org/10.17226/6265.

218 **National Transportation Safety Board:** "Safety Study: A Review of Flightcrew-Involved Major Accidents of U.S. Air Carriers 1978 Through 1990." Washington, DC: National Transportation Safety Board, 1994.

218 **didn't say anything:** Nadine Bienefeld and Gudela Grote, "Silence That May Kill: When Aircrew Members Don't Speak up and Why." *Aviation Psychology and Applied Human Factors* 2, no. 1 (2012): 1–10. http://dx.doi .org/10.1027/2192-0923/a000021.

218 **do not speak up because:** "Safety Study: A Review of Flightcrew-Involved Major Accidents of U.S. Air Carriers 1978 Through 1990."

218 **fear of speaking up:** Frances J. Milliken, Elizabeth W. Morrison, and Patricia F. Hewlin, "An Exploratory Study of Employee Silence: Issues that Employees Don't Communicate Upward and Why." *Journal of Management Studies* 40, no. 6 (September 2003): 1453–76. https://doi.org /10.1111/1467-6486.00387.

219 **code-named Project Aristotle:** re:Work, "Introduction." withgoogle.com, 2013. Accessed August 12, 2019. https://rework.withgoogle.com/print /guides/5721312655835136/. Emphasis added.

220 **"necessary for a stellar team":** Julia Rozovsky, "The Five Keys to a Successful Google Team." re:Work, November 17, 2015. https://rework .withgoogle.com/blog/five-keys-to-a-successful-google-team/. Emphasis removed.

220 **Others were less hierarchical:** Charles Duhigg, "What Google Learned from Its Quest to Build the Perfect Team." *New York Times Magazine,* February 25, 2016.

220 **keys to a great team:** Julia Rozovsky, "The Five Keys to a Successful Google Team."

221 **shared feeling that exists:** Amy Edmondson, "Psychological Safety and Learning Behavior in Work Teams." *Administrative Science Quarterly* 44, no. 2 (June 1999): 350–83. https://doi.org/10.2307/2666999; Amy Edmondson, "Learning from Mistakes Is Easier Said Than Done: Group

and Organizational Influences on the Detection and Correction of Human Error." *Journal of Applied Behavioral Science* 32, no. 1 (1996): 5–20.

221 **"being direct, taking risks":** Amy Edmondson, "Creating Psychological Safety in the Workplace." Interview by Curt Nickisch. HBR Ideacast, January 22, 2019. Audio, 26:48. https://hbr.org/ideacast/2019/01/creating -psychological-safety-in-the-workplace.

222 **ambiguity, volatility, complexity, or uncertainty:** Amy C. Edmondson, *The Fearless Organization: Creating Psychological Safety in the Workplace for Learning, Innovation, and Growth.* Hoboken, NJ: John Wiley & Sons, 2018.

222 **opinion is valued:** Jake Herway, "How to Create a Culture of Psychological Safety." Gallup Workplace, December 7, 2017. https://www.gallup.com /workplace/236198/create-culture-psychological-safety.aspx.

222 **facilitates innovation and learning:** Edmondson, *The Fearless Organization.*

223 **the "second victim":** JoNel Aleccia, "Nurse's Suicide Highlights Twin Tragedies of Medical Errors." NBC News, June 27, 2011. http://www .nbcnews.com/id/43529641/ns/health-health_care/t/nurses-suicide -highlights-twin-tragedies-medical-errors/#.XVGzn-hKjb0.

223 **how to create psychological safety:** Ingrid M. Nembhard and Amy C. Edmondson, "Making It Safe: The Effects of Leader Inclusiveness and Professional Status on Psychological Safety and Improvement Efforts in Health Care Teams." *Journal of Organizational Behavior* 27, no. 7 (November 2006): 941–66. http://dx.doi.org/10.1002/job.413.

224 **invited participation:** Amy C. Edmonson, "The Three Pillars of a Teaming Culture." *Harvard Business Review,* December 17, 2013. https:// hbr.org/2013/12/the-three-pillars-of-a-teaming-culture.

224 **replaced blame with curiosity:** Edmondson, *The Fearless Organization.*

225 **"many failures go unreported":** Amy C. Edmondson, "Strategies for Learning from Failure." *Harvard Business Review,* April 2011. https://hbr .org/2011/04/strategies-for-learning-from-failure.

225 **higher levels of psychological safety:** Mathis Schulte, N. Andrew Cohen, and Katherine J. Klein, "The Coevolution of Network Ties and Perceptions of Team Psychological Safety." *Organization Science* 23, no. 2 (2012): 564–81. http://dx.doi.org/10.1287/orsc.1100.0582.

225 **an immediate experience:** Edmondson, *The Fearless Organization.*

226 **perceptions of psychological safety:** Schulte, "The Coevolution of Network Ties and Perceptions of Team Psychological Safety."

226 **highest in new and old teams:** Jaclyn Koopmann et al., "Nonlinear Effects of Team Tenure on Team Psychological Safety Climate and Climate Strength: Implications for Average Team Member Performance." *Journal of Applied Psychology* 101, no. 7 (2016): 940–57. http://dx.doi.org/10.1037 /apl0000097.

228 **consequences of toxic collaborators:** Arieh Riskin et al., "The Impact of

Rudeness on Medical Team Performance: A Randomized Trial." *Pediatrics* 136, no. 3 (2015): 487–95.

228 **chronic sleep deprivation:** Ingrid Philibert, "Sleep Loss and Performance in Residents and Nonphysicians: A Meta-Analytic Examination." *Sleep* 28, no. 11 (2005): 1392–1402.

228 **98 percent of workers report:** Christine L. Porath, "Make Civility the Norm on Your Team." *Harvard Business Review,* January 2, 2018. https://hbr.org/2018/01/make-civility-the-norm-on-your-team.

229 **say they got even:** Christine L. Porath and Amir Erez, "How Rudeness Takes Its Toll." *Psychologist* 24, no. 7 (2011): 508–11; Christine Pearson and Christine Porath, *The Cost of Bad Behavior: How Incivility Is Damaging Your Business and What to Do About It.* New York: Portfolio, 2009.

229 **"never worked as hard again":** Christine L. Porath and Christine M. Pearson, "Emotional and Behavioral Responses to Workplace Incivility and the Impact of Hierarchical Status." *Journal of Applied Social Psychology* 42, suppl. 1 (December 2012): e326–e357. https://doi.org/10.1111/j.1559-1816.2012.01020.x.

229 **victims of office incivility:** Christine L. Porath and Christine M. Pearson, "The Price of Incivility." *Harvard Business Review,* February 2013: 114. https://hbr.org/2013/01/the-price-of-incivility.

230 **ideas were less creative:** Christine L. Porath and Amir Erez, "Does Rudeness Really Matter? The Effects of Rudeness on Task Performance and Helpfulness." *Academy of Management Journal* 50, no. 5 (2007): 1181–97. https://doi.org/10.5465/amj.2007.20159919. Quote lightly edited for readability.

230 **propagate through networks:** Sigal G. Barsade, Constantinos G. V. Coutifaris, and Julianna Pillemer, "Emotional Contagion in Organizational Life." *Research in Organizational Behavior* 38 (2018): 137–51.

230 **"Incivility is a virus":** Christine L. Porath, "The Incivility Bug." *Psychology Today,* September 27, 2017. https://www.psychologytoday.com/us/blog/thriving-work/201709/the-incivility-bug.

231 **one bad apple:** Ira Glass, "Ruining It for the Rest of Us." *This American Life,* December 19, 2008. https://www.thisamericanlife.org/370/ruining-it-for-the-rest-of-us. Lightly edited for grammar and formal consistency.

232 **two common explanations:** Christine L. Porath, "No Time to Be Nice at Work." *New York Times,* June 19, 2015. https://www.nytimes.com/2015/06/21/opinion/sunday/is-your-boss-mean.html.

232 **seen as less of a leader:** Ibid.

232 **related to promotion:** Thomas W. H. Ng et al., "Predictors of Objective and Subjective Career Success: A Meta-Analysis." *Personnel Psychology* 58, no. 2 (June 2005): 367–408. https://doi.org/10.1111/j.1744-6570.2005.00515.x.

232 **disagreeableness increases the chance:** Samuel T. Hunter and Lily Cushenbery, "Is Being a Jerk Necessary for Originality? Examining the

Role of Disagreeableness in the Sharing and Utilization of Original Ideas."
Journal of Business and Psychology 30, no. 4 (December 2015): 621–39.
http://dx.doi.org/10.1007/s10869-014-9386-1.

232 **civility increases perceptions of leadership:** Christine L. Porath,
Alexandra Gerbasi, and Sebastian L. Schorch, "The Effects of Civility on
Advice, Leadership, and Performance." *Journal of Applied Psychology* 100,
no. 5 (2015): 1527–41. http://dx.doi.org/10.1037/apl0000016.

232 **produces extreme outcomes:** Arijit Chatterjee and Donald C. Hambrick,
"It's All About Me: Narcissistic Chief Executive Officers and Their Effects
on Company Strategy and Performance." *Administrative Science Quarterly*
52, no. 3 (December 2007): 351–86. https://doi.org/10.2189/asqu.52.3.351.

233 **more powerful colleagues:** Dacher Keltner, *The Power Paradox: How We
Gain and Lose Influence.* New York: Penguin Books, 2017.

233 **power can result in self-centeredness:** Adam D. Galinsky et al., "Power
and Perspectives Not Taken." *Psychological Science* 17, no. 12 (2006):
1068–74. https://doi.org/10.1111/j.1467-9280.2006.01824.x.

233 **"When you feel powerful":** Dacher Keltner, "How Power Makes People
Selfish." University of California, January 13, 2015. Video, 2:03. https://
www.youtube.com/watch?v=0vvl46PmCfE#t=13.

233 **"like a manic state":** Dacher Keltner, "Don't Let Power Corrupt You."
Harvard Business Review, October 2016. https://hbr.org/2016/10/dont-let
-power-corrupt-you.

234 **work relationships are negative:** Giuseppe Labianca and Daniel Brass,
"Exploring the Social Ledger: Negative Relationships and Negative
Asymmetry in Social Networks in Organizations." *Academy of
Management Review* 31, no. 3 (July 2006): 596–614.

234 **the power of bad:** Roy F. Baumeister et al., "Bad Is Stronger Than Good."
Review of General Psychology 5, no. 4 (2001): 323–70. https://doi.org
/10.1037/1089-2680.5.4.323.

234 **words we have for emotions:** James R. Averill, "On the Paucity of Positive
Emotions." In *Assessment and Modification of Emotional Behavior.
Advances in the Study of Communication and Affect,* ed. Kirk R.
Blankstein, 7–45. New York: Springer, 1980.

235 **for a marriage to survive:** John Gottman, *Why Marriages Succeed or Fail.*
New York: Simon & Schuster, 1994.

235 **"evolutionarily adaptive for bad":** Baumeister et al., "Bad Is Stronger
Than Good."

235 **risk of a cardiovascular event:** Natalie Slopen et al., 2012. "Job Strain, Job
Insecurity, and Incident Cardiovascular Disease in the Women's Health
Study: Results from a 10-Year Prospective Study." *PLoS One* 7, no. 7 (2012):
e40512. https://doi.org/10.1371/journal.pone.0040512.

235 **sent them to the hospital:** Kathryn Dill, "Survey: 42% of Employees Have
Changed Jobs Due to Stress." *Forbes,* April 18, 2014. https://www.forbes
.com/sites/kathryndill/2014/04/18/survey-42-of-employees-have-changed
-jobs-due-to-stress/#223792263380.

236 **toxic coworker:** Zameena Mejia, "4 Steps to Productively Talk to Your Boss About a Toxic Co-Worker." CNBC, August 24, 2017. Available at https://www.cnbc.com/2017/08/24/4-steps-to-speak-with-your-boss-about-a-toxic-co-worker.html.

236 **reciprocity of positive ties:** Michael Szell and Stefan Thurner, "Measuring Social Dynamics in a Massive Multiplayer Online Game." *Social Networks* 32, no. 4 (October 2010): 313–29. https://doi.org/10.1016/j.socnet.2010.06.001; Nicholas Harrigan and Janice Yap, "Avoidance in Negative Ties: Inhibiting Closure, Reciprocity, and Homophily." *Social Networks* 48 (January 2017): 126–41. https://doi.org/10.1016/j.socnet.2016.07.003.

236 **"The actual company values":** Reed Hastings and Patty McCord, "Netflix Culture: Freedom and Responsibility," 2009. Accessed August 13, 2019. https://www.slideshare.net/reed2001/culture-1798664/2-Netflix_CultureFreedom_Responsibility2. Emphasis removed.

237 **"the most important documents":** Patty McCord, "How Netflix Reinvented HR." *Harvard Business Review,* January–February 2014. https://hbr.org/2014/01/how-netflix-reinvented-hr.

237 **"brilliant jerks":** Jim Schleckser, "Why Netflix Doesn't Tolerate Brilliant Jerks," Inc., February 2, 2016. https://www.inc.com/jim-schleckser/why-netflix-doesn-t-tolerate-brilliant-jerks.html.

237 **"no asshole rule":** Robert I. Sutton, *The No Asshole Rule: Building a Civilized Workplace and Surviving One That Isn't.* New York: Hachette, 2007.

237 **"comes out within a week":** Cameron Sepah, "Your Company Culture Is Who You Hire, Fire, and Promote." Medium, March 3, 2017. https://medium.com/s/company-culture/your-companys-culture-is-who-you-hire-fire-and-promote-c69f84902983.

238 **"keeper test":** Netflix Jobs, "Netflix Culture." Accessed August 13, 2019. https://jobs.netflix.com/culture.

238 **fired by the CEO:** Patty McCord, "How the Architect of Netflix's Innovative Culture Lost Her Job to the System." Interview by Steve Henn. *All Things Considered,* NPR, September 3, 2015. Audio, 5:15. https://www.npr.org/2015/09/03/437291792/how-the-architect-of-netflixs-innovative-culture-lost-her-job-to-the-system.

239 **people do not realize:** Porath and Pearson, "The Price of Incivility."

239 **60 times more likely:** Sutton, *The No Asshole Rule.* Updated from Workplace Bullying Institute, "2017 WBI U.S. Workplace Bullying Survey." June 2017.

239 **some diagnostics that might help:** Sutton, *The No Asshole Rule.*

240 **seen as civil:** Porath, Gerbasi, and Schorch, "The Effects of Civility on Advice, Leadership, and Performance."

240 **victims of incivility retaliated:** Christine Pearson and Christine Porath, "On the Nature, Consequences, and Remedies of Workplace Incivility: No Time for 'Nice'? Think Again." *Academy of Management Perspectives* 19, no. 1 (2005): 7–18.

240 **warmth-competence trade-off:** Susan T. Fiske, Amy J. C. Cuddy, and Peter Glick, "Universal Dimensions of Social Cognition: Warmth and Competence." *Trends in Cognitive Sciences* 11, no. 7 (February 2007): 77–83.

241 **small acts of civility:** Porath, "No Time to Be Nice at Work."

241 **"toxic, horrible, and depressing company":** Current Employee, "Viking Cruises: Employee Review." Glassdoor, May 16, 2016. https://www.glassdoor .com/Reviews/Employee-Review-Viking-Cruises-RVW10617717.htm.

241 **"underestimate how powerful appreciation is":** Adam Grant, "Adam Grant: Don't Underestimate the Power of Appreciation." Interview by Jocelyn K. Glei. Hurry Slowly, October 9, 2018. Audio, 48:20. https:// hurryslowly.co/adam-grant/. Quote lightly edited for grammar and clarity.

242 **"I believe in quitting":** Robert I. Sutton, *The Asshole Survival Guide: How to Deal with People Who Treat You Like Dirt.* New York: Houghton Mifflin Harcourt, 2017.

242 **couldn't take the hostility anymore:** Andy Newman and Ray Rivera, "Fed-Up Flight Attendant Makes Sliding Exit." *New York Times*, August 9, 2010.

242 **Slater is our icon:** "US Steward's 'Exit' Inspires Harassed Desi Counterparts." *The Times of India*, August 11, 2010.

9. Work/Life

243 *Eat, Pray, Love:* Elizabeth Gilbert, *Eat, Pray, Love: One Woman's Search for Everything Across Italy, India and Indonesia.* New York: Viking, 2006.

244 **two weeks after giving birth:** Sharon Lerner, "The Real War on Families: Why the U.S. Needs Paid Leave Now." *In These Times,* August 18, 2015. http://inthesetimes.com/article/18151/the-real-war-on-families.

244 **"Think hard about time":** Indra Nooyi, "Parting Words as I Step Down as CEO." LinkedIn, 2018. https://www.linkedin.com/pulse/parting-words-i -step-down-ceo-indra-nooyi/.

245 **"please please come home":** Marilyn Haigh, "Indra Nooyi Shared a Work Regret on Her Last Day as PepsiCo CEO." CNBC, October 3, 2018. https:// www.cnbc.com/2018/10/03/indra-nooyi-shares-a-work-regret-on-her-last -day-as-pepsico-ceo.html.

246 **"some life other than here":** Ina Yalof, *Life and Death: The Story of a Hospital.* New York: Fawcett Crest, 1988.

246 **easier time transitioning between:** Christena E. Nippert-Eng, *Home and Work: Negotiating Boundaries Through Everyday Life.* Chicago: University of Chicago Press, 1996.

246 **"keep work life at work":** Glen E. Kreiner, "Consequences of Work-Home Segmentation or Integration: A Person-Environment Fit Perspective." *Journal of Organizational Behavior* 27, no. 4 (June 2006): 485–507. https:// doi.org/10.1002/job.386.

247 **two extreme examples:** Blake E. Ashforth et al., "All in a Day's Work: Boundaries and Micro Role Transitions." *Academy of Management Review* 25, no. 3 (2000): 472–91.

247 **get better at segmenting:** Laszlo Bock, "Google's Scientific Approach to Work-Life Balance (and Much More)." *Harvard Business Review,* March 27, 2014. https://hbr.org/2014/03/googles-scientific-approach-to-work-life -balance-and-much-more.

247 **isn't necessarily better than the other:** Nancy P. Rothbard and Ariane Ollier-Malaterre, "Boundary Management." In *The Oxford Handbook of Work and Family,* eds. Tammy D. Allen and Lillian T. Eby, 109–22. New York: Oxford University Press, 2016.

247 **"a professional self":** Sheryl Sandberg, "Sheryl Sandberg Addresses the Class of 2012." Harvard Business School, May 24, 2012. Video, 22:25. https://www.youtube.com/watch?v=2Db0_RafutM.

248 **positive emotional spillovers:** Nancy P. Rothbard, "Enriching or Depleting? The Dynamics of Engagement in Work and Family Roles." *Administrative Science Quarterly* 46, no. 4 (December 2001): 655–84. https://doi.org/10.2307/3094827.

248 **"higher levels of well-being":** Adam Grant, "WorkLife with Adam Grant: When Work Takes Over Your Life." Ted Original Podcast, April 26, 2018. Audio, 37:40. https://www.ted.com/talks/worklife_with_adam_grant _when_work_takes_over_your_life?language=enhttps://www.ted.com /talks/worklife_with_adam_grant_when_work_takes_over_your_life? language=en.

248 **eschews work friendships:** Nippert-Eng, *Home and Work.*

250 **Preferences for segmentation and integration:** Ellen Ernst Kossek, Raymond A. Noe, and Beverly J. DeMarr, "Work-Family Role Synthesis: Individual and Organizational Determinants." *International Journal of Conflict Management* 10, no. 2 (1999): 102–29. https://doi.org/10.1108 /eb022820.

250 **"How well do you know":** Henna Inam, "Bring Your Whole Self to Work." *Forbes,* May 10, 2018. https://www.forbes.com/sites/hennainam/2018/05 /10/bring-your-whole-self-to-work/#d2c27ce6291a.

251 **criteria of a "real friend":** Olivet Nazarene University, "Research on Friends at Work." 2018. Accessed December 11, 2018. https://graduate .olivet.edu/news-events/news/research-friends-work.

251 **pursuit of instrumental goals:** Julianna Pillemer and Nancy P. Rothbard, "Friends Without Benefits: Understanding the Dark Sides of Workplace Friendship." *Academy of Management Review* 43, no. 4 (2018): 635–60. https://doi.org/10.5465/amr.2016.0309.

251 **Money and social connection are:** Frederick M. E. Grouzet et al., "The Structure of Goal Contents Across 15 Cultures." *Journal of Personality and Social Psychology* 89, no. 5 (2005): 800–16. http://dx.doi.org/10.1037/0022 -3514.89.5.800.

252 **thinking about or touching money:** K. D. Vohs, "Money Priming Can Change People's Thoughts, Feelings, Motivations, and Behaviors: An Update on 10 Years of Experiments." *Journal of Experimental Psychology: General* 144, no. 4 (2015): e86–e93.

252 **happiest when:** Daniel Kahneman et al., "A Survey Method for Characterizing Daily Life Experience: The Day Reconstruction Method." *Science* 306, no. 5702 (December 2004) : 1776–1780.

252 **make people change their priorities:** Cassie Mogilner, "The Pursuit of Happiness: Time, Money, and Social Connection." *Psychological Science* 21, no. 9 (2010): 1348–54. https://doi.org/10.1177/09567976103 80696.

252 **transactional nature of work:** Adam Grant, "Friends at Work? Not So Much." *New York Times,* September 4, 2015. https://www.nytimes.com /2015/09/06/opinion/sunday/adam-grant-friends-at-work-not-so-much .html.

253 **"close confidant":** Bernie DeGroat, "Do Co-Workers Engage or Estrange After Hours?" *Michigan News,* February 11, 2008. https://news.umich.edu /do-co-workers-engage-or-estrange-after-hours/.

253 **look across generations:** Jean M. Twenge et al., "Generational Differences in Work Values: Leisure and Extrinsic Values Increasing, Social and Intrinsic Values Decreasing." *Journal of Management* 36, no. 5 (2010): 1117–42. https://doi.org/10.1177/0149206309352246.

253 **"as a *means to leisure*":** Grant, "Friends at Work? Not So Much." Emphasis added.

254 **gender differences in workplace networks:** Herminia Ibarra, "Homophily and Differential Returns: Sex Differences in Network Structure and Access in an Advertising Firm." *Administrative Science Quarterly* 37, no. 3 (September 1992): 422–47. https://doi.org/10.2307/2393451.

255 **Women's networks were more segmented:** Herminia Ibarra, "Why Strategic Networks Are Important for Women and How to Build Them." September 27, 2017. Accessed December 12, 2018. https://herminiaibarra .com/why-strategic-networks-are-important-for-women-and-how-to -build-them/.

255 **"put women at a disadvantage":** Ibid. Lightly edited for formal consistency.

255 **inappropriate for men and women:** Claire Cain Miller, "It's Not Just Mike Pence. Americans Are Wary of Being Alone with the Opposite Sex." *New York Times,* July 1, 2017. https://www.nytimes.com/2017/07/01/upshot /members-of-the-opposite-sex-at-work-gender-study.html.

256 **attraction to opposite-sex friends:** April Bleske-Rechek et al., "Benefit or Burden? Attraction in Cross-Sex Friendship." *Journal of Social and Personal Relationships* 29, no. 5 (2012): 569–96. https://doi.org/10.1177 /0265407512443611.

256 **"couldn't meet with my boss":** Miller, "It's Not Just Mike Pence. Americans Are Wary of Being Alone With the Opposite Sex." Lightly edited for formal consistency.

257 *integration behaviors:* Tracy L. Dumas, Katherine W. Phillips, and Nancy P. Rothbard, "Getting Closer at the Company Party: Integration Experiences, Racial Dissimilarity, and Workplace Relationships." *Organization Science* 24, no. 5 (September–October 2013): 1377–1401. https://doi.org/10.1287/orsc.1120.0808.

258 **work spouse:** Renuka Rayasam, "Having a 'Work Spouse' Makes You Happier." BBC Worklife, November 7, 2016. https://www.bbc.com /worklife/article/20161106-having-a-work-spouse-makes-you-happier.

258 **quintessential example:** "Gentlemen's Intermission." *30 Rock,* season 5, episode 6, November 4, 2010.

259 **friends perform better:** Seunghoo Chung et al., "Friends with Performance Benefits: A Meta-Analysis on the Relationship Between Friendship and Group Performance." *Personality and Social Psychology Bulletin* 44, no. 1 (2018): 63–79. https://doi.org/10.1177/0146167217733069.

259 **Social support from coworkers:** Oliver Hämmig, "Health and Well-Being at Work: The Key Role of Supervisor Support." *SSM—Population Health* 3 (April 9, 2017): 393–402. https://doi.org/10.1016/j.ssmph.2017.04.002; T. T. Selvarajan, Peggy A. Cloninger, and Barjinder Singh, "Social Support and Work–Family Conflict: A Test of an Indirect Effects Model." *Journal of Vocational Behavior* 83, no. 3 (December 2013): 486–99. https://doi.org /10.1016/j.jvb.2013.07.004; Terry A. Beehr et al., "The Enigma of Social Support and Occupational Stress: Source Congruence and Gender Role Effects." *Journal of Occupational Health Psychology* 8, no. 3 (2003): 220–31. http://dx.doi.org/10.1037/1076-8998.8.3.220.

259 **friends at work:** Tom Rath, *Vital Friends: The People You Can't Afford to Live Without.* New York: Gallup Press, 2005.

259 **can impair productivity:** Jessica R. Methot et al., "Are Workplace Friendships a Mixed Blessing? Exploring Tradeoffs of Multiplex Relationships and Their Associations with Job Performance." *Personnel Psychology* 69, no. 2 (Spring 2016): 311–55. https://doi.org/10.1111 /peps.12109.

260 **"helpful employees become institutional bottlenecks":** Rob Cross, Reb Rebele, and Adam Grant, "Collaborative Overload." *Harvard Business Review,* January–February 2016. https://hbr.org/2016/01/collaborative -overload.

262 **environment that matches your preferences:** Nancy P. Rothbard, Katherine W. Phillips, and Tracy L. Dumas, "Managing Multiple Roles: Work-Family Policies and Individuals' Desires for Segmentation." *Organization Science* 16, no. 3 (May–June 2005): 243–58. https://doi.org /10.1287/orsc.1050.0124.

262 **"Dublin Goes Dark":** Bock, "Google's Scientific Approach to Work-Life Balance (and Much More)."

262 **Mail on Holiday policy:** Megan Gibson, "Here's a Radical Way to End Vacation Email Overload." *Time,* August 15, 2014. https://time.com /3116424/daimler-vacation-email-out-of-office/.

263 **"predictable time off":** Leslie Perlow, *Sleeping with Your Smartphone: How to Break the 24/7 Habit and Change the Way You Work*. Boston: Harvard Business Review Press, 2012.

263 **"degree of control":** Nancy P. Rothbard and Ariane Ollier-Malaterre, "Boundary Management." In *The Oxford Handbook of Work and Family*, eds. Tammy D. Allen and Lillian T. Eby, 109–22. New York: Oxford University Press, 2015.

264 **often reluctant to open up:** Sylvia Ann Hewlett, Carolyn Buck Luce, and Cornel West, "Leadership in Your Midst: Tapping the Hidden Strengths of Minority Executives." *Harvard Business Review,* November 2005.

265 **adopt a learning mindset:** Katherine W. Phillips, Tracy L. Dumas, and Nancy P. Rothbard, "Diversity and Authenticity: Why Black Employees Hesitate to Open Up About Themselves." *Harvard Business Review,* March–April 2018. https://hbr.org/2018/03/diversity-and-authenticity.

265 **"Look for uncommon commonalities":** Adam Grant, "How to Trust People You Don't Like." A Ted Original Podcast, 2018. Video, 34:19. https://www.ted.com/talks/worklife_with_adam_grant_how_astronauts _build_trust?language=en#t-5691.

266 **discovered a mutual love of:** Rayasam, "Having a 'Work Spouse' Makes You Happier."

266 **deeper relationships depend on:** Phillips, Dumas, and Rothbard, "Diversity and Authenticity: Why Black Employees Hesitate to Open Up About Themselves."

266 **racially and ethnically diverse:** Reuben J. Thomas, "Sources of Friendship and Structurally Induced Homophily Across the Life Course." *Sociological Perspectives,* February 11, 2019. https://doi.org/10.1177/0731121419828399.

267 **at least one mentor:** Herminia Ibarra, Nancy M. Carter, and Christine Silva, "Why Men Still Get More Promotions Than Women." *Harvard Business Review*, September 2010.

268 **"dynamic, reciprocal relationship":** Stacy Blake-Beard, "Mentoring: Creating Mutually Empowering Relationships." VMware Women's Leadership Innovation Lab. Video. https://womensleadership.stanford .edu/mentoring-creating-mutually-empowering-relationships.

268 **make roughly $28,000 more:** George F. Dreher and Taylor H. Cox Jr., "Race, Gender, and Opportunity: A Study of Compensation Attainment and the Establishment of Mentoring Relationships." *Journal of Applied Psychology* 81, no. 3 (1996): 297–308. http://dx.doi.org/10.1037/0021 -9010.81.3.297. Dollar amount is inflation adjusted to 2019.

268 **"misconstrued as sexual interest":** Sylvia Ann Hewlett et al., "The Sponsor Effect: Breaking Through the Last Glass Ceiling." Harvard Business Review Research Report, December 2010. https://30percentclub .org/wp-content/uploads/2014/08/The-Sponsor-Effect.pdf.

268 **uncomfortable mentoring or sponsoring women:** Lean In, "Men, Commit to Mentor Women." Accessed July 27, 2019. https://leanin .org/mentor-her.

268 **opposite sex mentorships:** Daniel B. Turban, Thomas W. Dougherty, and Felissa K. Lee, "Gender, Race, and Perceived Similarity Effects in Developmental Relationships: The Moderating Role of Relationship Duration." *Journal of Vocational Behavior* 61, no. 2 (October 2002): 240–62. https://doi.org/10.1006/jvbe.2001.1855.

269 **found their work mentors informally:** Ibarra, Carter, and Silva, "Why Men Still Get More Promotions Than Women."

270 **gained greater access to people:** Sameer B. Srivastava, "Network Intervention: Assessing the Effects of Formal Mentoring on Workplace Networks." *Social Forces* 94, no. 1 (September 2015): 427–52. https://doi .org/10.1093/sf/sov041.

270 **assigned to a powerful supervisor:** Forrest Briscoe and Katherine C. Kellogg, "The Initial Assignment Effect: Local Employer Practices and Positive Career Outcomes for Work-Family Program Users." *American Sociological Review* 76, no. 2 (2011): 291–319. https://doi.org/10.1177 /0003122411401250.

270 **formal and informal mentors:** Ibarra, Carter, and Silva, "Why Men Still Get More Promotions Than Women."

270 **"frequency of interaction":** B. R. J. O'Donnell, "When Mentorship Goes Off Track." *The Atlantic,* July 28, 2017. https://www.theatlantic.com /business/archive/2017/07/mentorship-fails-psychology/535125/.

270 **One in five men:** Hewlett et al., "The Sponsor Effect: Breaking Through the Last Glass Ceiling."

271 **"name next to your performance":** Ibid.

271 **predictors of promotions and salaries:** Thomas W. H. Ng et al., "Predictors of Objective and Subjective Career Success: A Meta-Analysis." *Personnel Psychology* 58, no. 2 (June 2005): 367–408. https://doi.org /10.1111/j.1744-6570.2005.00515.x.

271 **"I've delivered":** Sylvia Ann Hewlett, "Make Yourself Sponsor-Worthy." *Harvard Business Review,* February 6, 2014. https://hbr.org/2014/02/make -yourself-sponsor-worthy.

272 **differentiate yourself from peers:** Ibid.

273 **"You are human":** Indra Nooyi, "Priyanka Chopra and Indra Nooyi on Breaking Barriers and Engaging Billions." Forbes Live, July 3, 2018. Video, 51:01. https://www.youtube.com/watch?v=dQzvkvMl9tE.

10. Everyone's Connected

275 **"Six degrees of separation":** John Guare, *Six Degrees of Separation: A Play.* New York: Penguin Random House, 1990, 81.

275 **attributed to a clever experiment:** Stanley Milgram, "The Small World Problem." *Psychology Today* 1 (May 1967): 61–67.

275 **a shortcut to:** Brian Uzzi, "Keys to Understanding Your Social Capital." *Journal of Microfinance/ESR Review* 10, no. 2 (2008): 3.

275 **"The Small-World Problem":** Jeffrey Travers and Stanley Milgram, "An Experimental Study of the Small World Problem." *Sociometry* 32, no. 4 (December 1969): 425–43.

277 **roughly six steps:** Peter Sheridan Dodds, Roby Muhamad, and Duncan J. Watts, "An Experimental Study of Search in Global Social Networks." *Science* 301, no. 5634 (August 8, 2003): 827–29. https://doi.org/10.1126 /science.1081058.

277 **small world:** Duncan J. Watts, *Six Degrees: The Science of a Connected Age*. New York: W. W. Norton, 2003.

277 **"capable of spanning critical divides":** Duncan J. Watts, *Everything Is Obvious: Once You Know the Answer*. New York: Crown Business, 2011.

278 **relying on mathematical models:** Duncan J. Watts and Steven H. Strogatz, "Collective Dynamics of 'Small-World' Networks." *Nature* 393 (June 1998): 440–42.

279 **a few shortcuts:** David Burkus, *Friend of a Friend: Understanding the Hidden Networks That Can Transform Your Life and Your Career*. New York: Houghton Mifflin Harcourt, 2018.

Acknowledgments

My future son was the size of a blueberry when I met Stephen and the team at Dutton. Since then, Julian made his way into this world, the book came to be, our family went on the "big trip," and my mom left this world. I had no idea so much life could happen during the span of a book's creation.

My husband, Nick, was as instrumental during each of these moments as he was in Julian's conception. This book is truly a joint endeavor. Nick created the network assessment, spent countless hours talking through ideas, helped with research, was a co-conspirator in conducting the study for the chapter Work/Life, read and edited each draft, went through the hell of fact-checking the book line by line, reassured me that it was worth the effort to get these ideas into the world during moments when I wasn't so sure, and provided endless emotional and moral support. But more than all that, he left an all-consuming career in New York for our family. In doing so, he created the space for me to write this book. There are few people who give as selflessly to their families as Nick does. Though he may not recall, during our wedding vows we pledged to "seek to understand ourselves and each other" and to "help our partner discover what is important to them and live their life based on those values." His promise to me is borne out in this book. His love and the way he lives his life reminds me on a daily basis of how I want to live mine. I am blessed to have him as a partner.

Getting to work with my agent and broker extraordinaire, Margo Beth Fleming, has been one of the greatest gifts of writing this book. From the very beginning, our relationship felt fated. One of those magical creations of social chemistry. At every stage of this process, from learning how to write to celebrating the completion of the manuscript over tea at the public library, Margo has gone far beyond what anyone could reasonably hope for in an agent. She made ironclad cases for pushing through on aspects of the book that I would have rather just glossed over, compassionately checked in on me after my mother died, and shared in one of the happiest moments of my life in the back of a taxicab. She is one of those rare friends who are able to be with you for the full range of the emotional spectrum. She is a brilliant and caring champion, and she was able to see more in this book than I could. I will be forever grateful to her for helping me see what she saw and for helping make it a reality.

One of the joys of this process was discovering a love of writing. My editor Stephen Morrow's love of language, words, and ideas proved to be contagious. Stephen has been a thoughtful, patient, and kind teacher. During moments when I was struggling with the book, Stephen's enthusiasm, mentions of listening to Silk Road, and stories about talking to strangers on the subway helped keep me going. Stephen's deep understanding of the social world, curiosity, and magic with words are infused on every page of this book.

My lifelong mentor, teacher, and friend, Peter Bearman, somehow imparted part of his extraordinary ability to find what is interesting about the world. Without Peter's influence, both my life and work would be far less interesting.

This book is very much an act of brokering and translating. Countless colleagues, role models, and network scholars have devoted their careers to producing the research that this book is based on. Work by Ron Burt, Robin Dunbar, Tiziana Casciaro, Tian Zheng, Matthew Salganik, David Obsfeldt, Martin Kilduff, Adam Kleinbaum, Mark Granovetter, Nicholas Christakis, Ko Kuwabara, Nan Lin, Peter Marsden, Isabel Fernandez-Mateo, Mario Small, Sandy Pentland, Paul Ingram, Rueben Thomas, Elizabeth Currid-Halkett, Ray Reagans, Bill McEvily, Martin Gargiulo, Brian Uzzi, Peter Bearman, James Moody, Miller McPherson, Dan McFarland, Andrew Hargadon, Duncan Watts, Bob Sutton, Blaine Landis, Stefano Tasselli, David Krackhardt, Scott Feld, Noam Zerubavel, Rob Cross, Ned Bishop, Tanya Menon, Dan Levin, Jorge Walter, Keith Murnighan, and Herminia Ibarra is featured prominently in the book. I am especially grateful to the Teaching Social Networks PDW crew, particularly Adam Kleinbaum, Isabel Fernandez-Mateo, Bill McEvily, and Martin Gargiulo, who organized it. My thinking about networks and how to translate networks research into practice has been profoundly influenced by this group. Work by psychologists Adam Grant, Francesca Gino, Dacher Keltner, Mitch Prinstein,

Cameron Anderson, Cassie Mogilner, Jane Dutton, Elizabeth Dunn, Amy Edmonson, Christine Porath, Nancy Rothbard, Tracy Dumas, Katherine Phillips, and Sylvia Ann Hewlett helped bring the human element to this book.

I am fortunate to work in a group of sociologists and psychologists who are dedicated to cross-disciplinary thinking: Jim Baron, Rob Bartholomew, Tristan Botelho, Tori Brescoll, Heidi Brooks, Rodrigo Canales, Julia DeBenigno, Cydney Dupree, Ivana Katic, Balazs Kovacs, Michael Kraus, Amandine Ody-Brasier, Jeff Sonnenfeld, Olav Sorenson, and Amy Wrzesniewski. Their influence is reflected in the "purpleness" of this book. While writing this book, lengthy conversations with Jeff Sonnenfeld, Michael Kraus, and Heidi Brooks offered important insights. I continue to learn from Victor Vroom's pedagogical genius. Since I arrived at Yale, Olav Sorenson has helped me grow as a network scholar and teacher. He has been an invaluable mentor. Amy Wrzesniewski has been a guiding light and role model. Jim Baron has been a tireless and patient supporter. I am grateful for his constant effort to keep our group growing and purple. Rob Bartholomew is often the glue that holds us all together. He is the convener that everyone wants as part of their team. Beyond shaping my academic thinking, my colleagues have taught me what it takes to create a workplace where candor, laughter, and intellect are all valued.

Ingrid Nembhard, who jointly conducted the research using wearable sensors described in this book, is the collaborator every academic dreams of. The research on work/life balance wouldn't have been possible without the help of Jessica Halten and her team. Lulu Change provided helpful research assistance. Tanja

Ru masterfully created the illustrations for this book. Hannah Fenney was super helpful throughout the editorial process. Heather Kreidler was invaluable in fact-checking the book. Special thanks to Amanda Walker, Natalie Church, Leila Siddiqui, Stephanie Cooper, and the Dutton team for getting this book into the hands of readers.

Not a day goes by that I am not filled with gratitude for having Lisa Uihlein as my guide on this extraordinary adventure to the fourth dimension. She is my greatest teacher. She saved my life and taught me how to live and love. I will never forget being in the hospital room when Julie Price told me that I never have to be alone again. She has stayed true to her word and provided me with support through the highs, lows, and ordinary moments of the journey of this book. Kevin Dowd is a role model and master storyteller with an unbeatable message. Thanks for always checking in to make sure I'm doing okay and keeping it real. Natasha Mclain made me believe and provided countless laughs over the past two years. I've done my best to pass along some of the wisdom that Lisa, Julie, Kevin, and Natasha have shared with me in this book.

I've been blessed with an amazing group of friends who have taught me about love, service, and the joy of living: Andy, Anna, Annie, Bob, Charlie, Chris, Christine, Chuck, Dan, Dave, Deb, Dianne, Don, Doreen, Elise, George, Herb, Irie, Jane, Janis, Jen, Jenny, Johnny, Kate, Katherine, Kevin, Kim, Kristin, Lauren, Linda, Louie, Mags, Mark, May, Moira, Naomi, Neil, Padrick, Richard, Robin, Ruth, Sarah, Sudie, Teresa, Terry, Tim, Trish, Vinnie, and Wayne.

Andrea Miller, Camilla Bolland, and Jennifer Jennings have been there for me since the beginning. It has been a wonderful wild ride. Living on a cul-de-sac has its benefits, and my friendships with Michelle Lopez, Sasha Rudensky, and Eli Huge are one of the greatest testaments to the power of neighborhoods. This book started as a playdate conversation with Emma Seppala, who has lovingly supported me throughout this process.

Without Shauna McMahon, this book wouldn't have been possible. Knowing you are loving and caring for my little ones while I'm writing and working is a source of endless comfort. Our entire family is blessed to get to learn from and be with you each day. Not only do we think of you as family, you are also one of my dearest friends.

My dad's endless curiosity and exuberance are reflected in this book. I am grateful for his unconditional support and inspiring me to always keep exploring. He and Cheryl McCue are my lifelines. They are who I reach out to in my moments of joy, fear, and sorrow and the only people I feel comfortable asking if I am crazy. Thanks for the continued reassurance that I am not and we can get through anything together. My brother, Andrew, has one of the biggest hearts of anyone I know. His love for me, my mom, and our family has made this past year a little more bearable. There are many moments I wouldn't have gotten through without him. I am also grateful to Roger and Janis Caplan, Zoe, Henry, and Hank Weed, Gaye and David McDonald, and Liz, Danny, Lindsey, and DJ King for showing me what family means.

My children have shown me the otherwise unfathomable dimensions of love: Sydney has more compassion than I knew was possible for an eleven-year-old. Watching her overcome her fears to pursue her passions has inspired me to try to do the same. One can also never be reminded enough that there isn't an occasion that breaking out into song or dance can't make better. Grace's sense of adventure, courage, and wonder make our world a more magical place. And Julian is simply pure joy. Not a day goes by when my heart doesn't feel stretched and softened from the love and light they've brought into my life.

Family is our first and deepest connection. Until I lost my mom, I did not fully appreciate the depth of this bond. For as long as I can remember, my mom always had a book within arm's reach. I hope that the lessons she imparted to me upon her death—find joy in the little things, protect the ones you love, and love with all your heart—will live on through this book.

Index

Index

Bonanno, Joseph, 88
Bonifas, Robin, 86
Boothby, Erica, 22
Bossard, James, 51
Bourdain, Anthony, 100–101,
    117, 133
Bowlby, John, 45–46
Boyd, Peter, 95–96
Bradford, David, 25–26
Briscoe, Forrest, 270
brokers
    approaches of, 102–105, 123–126,
        170–172, 184, 280
    atypical career paths of, 109–110
    benefits of, 6–7, 13, 164, 182–184
    bosses as, 183
    characteristics of, 7, 8, 30, 110–114,
        120–130
    diversity and, 91
    drawbacks of, 6–7, 126–130
    edge effect and, 108–109
    examples of, 100–102, 130–131
    logic of brokering, 102
    network size of, 40
    network structure of, 5–7
    politics and, 117–123, 124
    power paradox of, 114–117
    reputation of, 130–131
    social signature of, 67–68
    tortured brokers, 126–130
    triadic closure and, 103–104,
        108, 115
    types of, 105–107, 126–130, 182–183
    work/life balance of, 13, 245, 246,
        260–264, 272
    See also mixing network styles
Brooks, Alison Wood, 198–199
Bryan, John, 2
burnout, 153–154, 157–158, 164,
    259–260
Burt, Ronald, 73, 78–79, 106–107,
    124–125, 126–128, 170, 174–175

Cacioppo, John, 11–12
Canapari, Craig, 121
Caplan, Nicholas, 247
Caputo, Giovanni, 197–198
Carnegie, Dale, 158, 198
Casciaro, Tiziana, 16–17, 122–123
Castells, Pere, 102
Castro, Oriol, 102
Catron, Mandy Len, 97
cellular models, 163–164, 171–174
Chekhov, Anton, 73
Chiew, Anne, 184
Christakis, Nicholas, 5, 140–141
Chu, Johan, 3
Clinton, Bill, 77, 118
cliques, 84–88, 90, 99, 120–121, 280
close friends
    network size and, 38, 45
    reciprocity and, 42–43
    tie strength and, 40–43, 44–45
    (see also strong ties)
closeness. See intimacy
closure, 78–81, 92, 103–105, 108, 115, 236
Cohen, Allan, 25–26
Coleman, James S., 4–5
collaborative brokerage, 105–107
Communist Party, 164
concentric circles (Dunbar circles), 40
conveners
    attachment style of, 49
    benefits of, 7, 13, 164, 184, 280
    characteristics of, 8, 73, 92–98,
        127–128, 152–153, 181–182
    cliques, 84–88, 90, 99
    closure and, 78–81, 92, 104–105
    drawbacks of, 7
    examples of, 69–72
    gossip and, 78–81
    network size and, 40
    network structure and, 5–7, 28–29,
        81–84
    network structure of, 280

About the Author

Marissa King is professor of Organizational Behavior at the Yale School of Management, where she developed and teaches a popular course on networks. Over the past fifteen years, King has studied how people's social networks evolve, what they look like, and why that's significant. Her research has been featured in outlets such as *The New York Times*, *The Wall Street Journal*, *The Washington Post*, *U.S. News & World Report*, *Bloomberg Businessweek*, *The Atlantic*, National Public Radio, and other outlets.